XML For Dummies

D0509472

Reading the XML Specification

The World Wide Web Consortium's XML Specification (which you can read at `www.w3.org/TR/1998/REC-xml-19980210`) uses Extended Backus-Naur Form (EBNF) grammar. The grammar uses this notation (variables are in *italics*):

Comment	`/*comment*/`
Symbol may appear 0 or more times	`*`
Symbol must appear 1 or more times	`+`
Either one symbol or the other may be chosen	`|`
All others enclosed must be excluded	`[^excludeditem]`
Character is a literal	`"character"`
Hexadecimal number	`#xnumber`
White space	`S`
Range	`[rangebegin-rangeend]`
Regular expression	`(regular expression sequence)`
Validity constraint	`[VC:rule]`
Well-formedness constraint	`[WFC:rule]`

DTDs in a Nutshell

The following information pertains to Document Type Definitions (DTDs):

- ✔ A DTD is a set of rules defining what tags can appear in a given XML document and how they must nest within each other.

- ✔ You use the DTD to declare *entities,* which are reusable chunks of text that can appear many times but only have to be transmitted once to the viewing application.

- ✔ DTDs are not necessary in every instance of an XML document; an author can use an application-specific tag set or refer to some well-known external DTD.

- ✔ A DTD specifies the set of required and optional elements (and their attributes) for documents to conform to that type.

- ✔ A document's DTD specifies the names of the tags and the relationship among elements in that document.

IDG
BOOKS
WORLDWIDE

Copyright © 1998 IDG Books Worldwide, Inc.
All rights reserved.

Cheat Sheet $2.95 value. Item 0360-1.

For more information about IDG Books,
call 1-800-762-2974.

...For Dummies: #1 Computer Book Series for Beginners

XML For Dummies®

Cheat Sheet

XML Rules

Opening and closing parts of a tag set must always contain the same name in the same case: `<tag>` ... `</tag>` or `<TAG>` ... `</TAG>`, but not `<tag>` ... `</TAG>`.

Tags without content (called *empty elements*) must be written in an abbreviated form: The tag for a break is therefore `<BR/>`.

If you include an opening tag for an element type, you may not omit its closing tag: either `<tag>` ... `</tag>` or `<tag/>` is valid.

All tags must be nested correctly: `<tag><element>` ... `</element></tag>`, but not `<tag><element>` ... `</tag></element>`.

All attribute values must be enclosed in single or double quotation marks: `<elementType id ="value">` or `<elementType id ='value'>`.

Common Reserved Characters

XML uses certain reserved characters that cannot appear directly in an XML document's content, unless as part of a CDATA section. You may use such characters by using character references in your content as follows:

Character	Reference
<	<
>	>
&	&
'	'
"	"

The First (and Last) Word on Valid versus Well-Formed

A *valid* document must conform to the rules in its Document Type Definition (DTD), which states a set of rules that define what tags can appear in the document and how those tags may nest within one another. A *well-formed* document must have these characteristics:

- ✔ All beginning and ending tags match up.
- ✔ Empty tags follow the special XML syntax.
- ✔ All attribute values are contained within single or double quotation marks.
- ✔ All entities are declared.

...For Dummies: #1 Computer Book Series for Beginners

XML

FOR

DUMMIES®

by Ed Tittel, Norbert Mikula, and Ramesh Chandak

Foreword by Dan Connolly
World Wide Web Consortium Architecture Domain Lead

IDG Books Worldwide, Inc.
An International Data Group Company

Foster City, CA ♦ Chicago, IL ♦ Indianapolis, IN ♦ New York, NY ♦ Southlake, TX

XML For Dummies®

Published by
IDG Books Worldwide, Inc.
An International Data Group Company
919 E. Hillsdale Blvd.
Suite 400
Foster City, CA 94404
www.idgbooks.com (IDG Books Worldwide Web site)
www.dummies.com (Dummies Press Web site)

Library of Congress Catalog Card No.: 98-84966

ISBN: 0-7645-0360-X

Printed in the United States of America

10 9 8 7 6 5 4 3 2 1

1O/SQ/QU/ZY/IN

Distributed in the United States by IDG Books Worldwide, Inc.

Distributed by Macmillan Canada for Canada; by Transworld Publishers Limited in the United Kingdom; by IDG Norge Books for Norway; by IDG Sweden Books for Sweden; by Woodslane Pty. Ltd. for Australia; by Woodslane Enterprises Ltd. for New Zealand; by Longman Singapore Publishers Ltd. for Singapore, Malaysia, Thailand, and Indonesia; by Simron Pty. Ltd. for South Africa; by Toppan Company Ltd. for Japan; by Distribuidora Cuspide for Argentina; by Livraria Cultura for Brazil; by Ediciencia S.A. for Ecuador; by Addison-Wesley Publishing Company for Korea; by Ediciones ZETA S.C.R. Ltda. for Peru; by WS Computer Publishing Corporation, Inc., for the Philippines; by Unalis Corporation for Taiwan; by Contemporanea de Ediciones for Venezuela; by Computer Book & Magazine Store for Puerto Rico; by Express Computer Distributors for the Caribbean and West Indies. Authorized Sales Agent: Anthony Rudkin Associates for the Middle East and North Africa.

For general information on IDG Books Worldwide's books in the U.S., please call our Consumer Customer Service department at 800-762-2974. For reseller information, including discounts and premium sales, please call our Reseller Customer Service department at 800-434-3422.

For information on where to purchase IDG Books Worldwide's books outside the U.S., please contact our International Sales department at 650-655-3200 or fax 650-655-3295.

For information on foreign language translations, please contact our Foreign & Subsidiary Rights department at 650-655-3021 or fax 650-655-3281.

For sales inquiries and special prices for bulk quantities, please contact our Sales department at 650-655-3200 or write to the address above.

For information on using IDG Books Worldwide's books in the classroom or for ordering examination copies, please contact our Educational Sales department at 800-434-2086 or fax 817-251-8174.

For press review copies, author interviews, or other publicity information, please contact our Public Relations department at 650-655-3000 or fax 650-655-3299.

For authorization to photocopy items for corporate, personal, or educational use, please contact Copyright Clearance Center, 222 Rosewood Drive, Danvers, MA 01923, or fax 978-750-4470.

is a trademark under exclusive license to IDG Books Worldwide, Inc., from International Data Group, Inc.

About the Authors

Ed Tittel is the co-author of numerous books about networking and the Web, including *The CGI Bible* and *The Hip Pocket Guide to HTML* (the first book also features Mark Gaither, Mike Erwin, and Sebastian Hassinger; the second book features James Michael Stewart and Natanya Pitts). These days, Ed aims his efforts at Internet programming-related topics, both as a writer and as a member of the NetWorld + Interop program committee. He has also become quite active in MCSE certification-related activities.

Ed has been a regular contributor to the trade press since 1987 and has written more than 300 articles for a variety of publications, including *Computerworld, InfoWorld, Windows NT Magazine, IIS Solutions,* and *NetGuide.* He's also works for several online 'zines, including *SunWorld Online* and *C|Net Interactive.*

These days, Ed is working at home once again, tending the staff and the projects at his company, LANWrights, Inc. But his real job is perfecting his "universal tonic" — homemade chicken stock. When Ed isn't on the road or pounding the keyboard, he's either out playing pool, burning calories, or using that stock in his kitchen to create culinary compositions for friends and family.

Contact Ed at `etittel@lanw.com` or visit his Web site at `www.lanw.com`.

Norbert Mikula is a graduate of the Department of Applied Computer Science at the University of Klagenfurt in Austria and has been doing research and application development in the area of Internet and Internet-related technology since 1993. His early focus was on information delivery via the Web, which also involved the design of a number of Web servers in Europe.

In 1995, Norbert focused on intranet design following the approach of seamless integration of Web services into existing workflow processes. During 1996 and 1997, Norbert worked on his diploma thesis titled "Online Electronic Databooks." The core of this work was document publishing via the Web using SGML for markup, DSSSL as a formatting specification, and Java as the programming language of choice.

Currently, Norbert is Senior Online Information Architect, representing DataChannel in Bellevue, Washington. His focus is on publishing and document/metadata delivery systems. Norbert has been a speaker at a number of conferences and shows throughout the U.S. and Europe. Norbert is DataChannel's alternate representative to the W3C-XML Working Group and an active member of the W3C-XML Special Interest Group, as well as the XML Developers Group. He is DataChannel's primary representative to the W3C-RDF-Schema Working Group and the W3C-XSL Working Group, and attentive listener on the W3C-DOM Interest Group. He is also the author of DXP (DataChannel's XML Parser), the world's first full-featured XML parser written in Java.

Contact Norbert at norbert@datachannel.com.

Ramesh Chandak is a graduate with a Fellowship in Advanced Engineering Study from MIT (Cambridge, MA) and has a total of eight years of work experience in the IT industry. Ramesh has worked extensively with Internet, Microsoft, Sybase, Powersoft, and Java technologies. In addition, Ramesh has authored 11 books, served as technical editor on 13 books, and published more than 25 technical articles for several leading publishers on client/server, databases, multimedia, and Internet technologies.

Contact Ramesh at rksoftware@worldnet.att.net.

Authors' Acknowledgments

Our biggest thanks go to our readers, who we hope will embrace XML with the same fervor with which HTML was originally adopted. We encourage any and all feedback because that's what helps us to improve our work! We have way too many folks to thank, so we'd like to begin by thanking everybody who helped us whom we don't mention by name. Actually, we couldn't have done it without you, even if we don't name you here! Thanks for your help, information, and encouragement. Please keep your e-mail coming!

Ed Tittel

I must share my thanks with many different constituencies. I'll begin with friends and family — thanks to Mom, Dad, Kat, Mike, Helen, and new addition Colin, plus Tressa Riley and family, Yvonne Neeley, and the Tivoli team. Second, a talented crew of technical people helped me over a variety of humps, large and small. I would like to specifically mention Norbert Mikula, John Tigue, and John Sweitzer. Third, there's a whole crowd of other folks whose information has helped me over the years, especially the W3C's XML Working Group — most notably, Dan Connolly, Jon Bosak, Liam Quin, and Robin Cover. Finally, I'd also like to thank my co-authors for their inspired efforts, not just Norbert and Ramesh, but also Natanya Pitts; without her efforts, we couldn't have completed this project.

Norbert Mikula

I would like to thank my parents, Emil and Annemarie, and grandparents, especially Gerlinde and Hans, for their continuous support throughout my early years. Without them, I would have never been able to graduate. They always believed in me and gave support. A part of them will always be with me.

A number of people are key to one's development as a human and as a technologist. I would like to specifically mention my friends Robert, Michael, Ernst, and Gerald. In my professional life, I owe gratuity to Professor H. C. Mayr, Alfred Elkerbout, Gavin Nicol, Jon Bosak, Tim Bray, Marion Elledge, Tim Gelinas, and Dave Pool.

My wife, Irina, deserves a special mention here. Her love, understanding, encouragement, and support helped me through all those many important steps of my career over the last few years. Irina gives me all the strength I need to survive in this fast-paced industry. Thanks to Ed Tittel for letting me be a part of this exciting endeavor. Having to correct my poor English must have been a very challenging task; thus, special thanks to the editorial team who had to go through this.

Ramesh Chandak

Thanks, Mr. and Mrs. Ramkishorji Kabra and family, Mr. and Mrs. Gopaldasji Soni and family, for your love and encouragement throughout my career. Thanks, Purshottam, an exceptional talent, for your thoughtful insights, tips, and inspired efforts in helping me over a variety of humps, large and small. Thanks, Tapati Baisya (Babli), for your friendship. Thank you, Ed Tittel, Dawn Rader, David Johnson, and Mary Burmeister, a talented crew of people at LANWrights, Inc., for the opportunity to be part of this book. And last, but not the least, thanks, Kavita! You are the most wonderful person in my life. You are a tremendous supporter of my writing even though it steals time away from you.

Collectively

Together, we want to thank the editorial staff at IDG Books, especially Mike Kelly and Ellen Camm, our acquisitions editors; Robert Wallace, who remains our favorite IDG project editor; Diane Steele, who let us keep this "strange torpedo" moving even when we momentarily wandered off the beaten track; and all the other editorial and production folks, including Gwenette Gaddis, Donna Love, Darren Meiss, and Tom Missler.

Please feel free to contact any of us, care of Dummies Press, IDG Books Worldwide, 919 East Hillsdale Blvd, Suite 400, Foster City, CA 94404. Ed's e-mail address is `etittel@lanw.com`; Norbert's e-mail address is `norbert@datachannel.com`; Ramesh's e-mail address is `rksoftware@worldnet.att.net`.

ABOUT IDG BOOKS WORLDWIDE

Welcome to the world of IDG Books Worldwide.

IDG Books Worldwide, Inc., is a subsidiary of International Data Group, the world's largest publisher of computer-related information and the leading global provider of information services on information technology. IDG was founded more than 25 years ago and now employs more than 8,500 people worldwide. IDG publishes more than 275 computer publications in over 75 countries (see listing below). More than 60 million people read one or more IDG publications each month.

Launched in 1990, IDG Books Worldwide is today the #1 publisher of best-selling computer books in the United States. We are proud to have received eight awards from the Computer Press Association in recognition of editorial excellence and three from *Computer Currents'* First Annual Readers' Choice Awards. Our best-selling *...For Dummies®* series has more than 30 million copies in print with translations in 30 languages. IDG Books Worldwide, through a joint venture with IDG's Hi-Tech Beijing, became the first U.S. publisher to publish a computer book in the People's Republic of China. In record time, IDG Books Worldwide has become the first choice for millions of readers around the world who want to learn how to better manage their businesses.

Our mission is simple: Every one of our books is designed to bring extra value and skill-building instructions to the reader. Our books are written by experts who understand and care about our readers. The knowledge base of our editorial staff comes from years of experience in publishing, education, and journalism — experience we use to produce books for the '90s. In short, we care about books, so we attract the best people. We devote special attention to details such as audience, interior design, use of icons, and illustrations. And because we use an efficient process of authoring, editing, and desktop publishing our books electronically, we can spend more time ensuring superior content and spend less time on the technicalities of making books.

You can count on our commitment to deliver high-quality books at competitive prices on topics you want to read about. At IDG Books Worldwide, we continue in the IDG tradition of delivering quality for more than 25 years. You'll find no better book on a subject than one from IDG Books Worldwide.

John Kilcullen
CEO
IDG Books Worldwide, Inc.

Steven Berkowitz
President and Publisher
IDG Books Worldwide, Inc.

**Eighth Annual
Computer Press
Awards ⮞1992**

**Ninth Annual
Computer Press
Awards ⮞1993**

**Tenth Annual
Computer Press
Awards ⮞1994**

**Eleventh Annual
Computer Press
Awards ⮞1995**

Publisher's Acknowledgments

We're proud of this book; please register your comments through our IDG Books Worldwide Online Registration Form located at http://my2cents.dummies.com.

Some of the people who helped bring this book to market include the following:

Acquisitions, Development, and Editorial

Project Editor: Robert Wallace

Acquisitions Editors: Mike Kelly, Ellen Camm

Media Development Manager: Joyce Pepple

Permissions Editor: Heather Heath Dismore

Copy Editors: Gwenette Gaddis, Stephanie Koutek

Technical Editor: Liam Quin

Editorial Manager: Colleen Rainsberger

Editorial Assistant: Donna Love, Darren Meiss

Production

Associate Project Coordinator: Tom Missler

Layout and Graphics: Cameron Booker, Lou Boudreau, J. Tyler Connor, Maridee V. Ennis, Angela F. Hunckler, Drew R. Moore, Brent Savage, Deirdre Smith, Janet Seib

Proofreaders: Christine Berman, Michelle Croninger, Henry Lazarek, Janet M. Withers

Indexer: Liz Cunningham

Special Help

Joell Smith, Associate Technical Editor; Mark Kory

General and Administrative

IDG Books Worldwide, Inc.: John Kilcullen, CEO; Steven Berkowitz, President and Publisher

IDG Books Technology Publishing: Brenda McLaughlin, Senior Vice President and Group Publisher

Dummies Technology Press and Dummies Editorial: Diane Graves Steele, Vice President and Associate Publisher; Mary Bednarek, Director of Acquisitions and Product Development; Kristin A. Cocks, Editorial Director

Dummies Trade Press: Kathleen A. Welton, Vice President and Publisher; Kevin Thornton, Acquisitions Manager

IDG Books Production for Dummies Press: Beth Jenkins Roberts, Production Director; Cindy L. Phipps, Manager of Project Coordination, Production Proofreading, and Indexing; Kathie S. Schutte, Supervisor of Page Layout; Shelley Lea, Supervisor of Graphics and Design; Debbie J. Gates, Production Systems Specialist; Robert Springer, Supervisor of Proofreading; Debbie Stailey, Special Projects Coordinator; Tony Augsburger, Supervisor of Reprints and Bluelines; Leslie Popplewell, Media Archive Coordinator

Dummies Packaging and Book Design: Patti Crane, Packaging Specialist; Kavish + Kavish, Cover Design

◆

The publisher would like to give special thanks to Patrick J. McGovern, without whom this book would not have been possible.

◆

Contents at a Glance

Cartoons at a Glance

By Rich Tennant

page 159

page 309

page 73

page 9

Fax: 978-546-7747 • E-mail: the5wave@tiac.net

Table of Contents

Foreword

· ·

*O*ne day, I finally got Tim Berners-Lee to tell me why he invented the Web. First, the Web, this universal information space, stimulates and empowers each person who gets access to it. Sharing information is fun! Second, it facilitates understanding that is so critical to working in groups — groups of all sizes, from a family to an enterprise to a nation. Finally, the machines in this information space can eliminate the tedium of working with information — printing it out, copying it, finding it — and free people to use their creative energy. Tim's gut feeling was that as the computers take on more of the work, our ability to solve problems will be revolutionized. And he was right. The Web is the driving force in this digital age.

The Web is based on a simple model: global hypertext. Start with the sort of everyday documents that people are used to and add one killer feature: links that take you to documents and information located anywhere in the world.

The early success of HTML — before tables, fonts, and scripting — shows that links are more critical than all the powerful desktop publishing features. Of course, those desktop publishing features eventually came with the revisions of HTML. HTML was designed for use with stylesheets, but they didn't hit the scene until HTML was at Version 4.0. By then, the art of page design using stupid HTML tricks and images had become quite mature, and stylesheets faced stiff competition. But have no fear: Stylesheets are here to stay. They're indispensable for good information management.

And that's the name of the game: *information management*. Expect to hear it more often than the buzzword "money management" pretty soon. The electronic commerce revolution is simply a result of businesses exploiting the increase in efficiency of using the Web over traditional media such as paper and the telephone. Stylesheets are an example of this increase in efficiency: They preserve your investment in design — work that you can't *afford* to throw away and re-create time after time. Reusing work is more than just a good idea: It's a survival tactic in today's business environment.

Of course, you have to be linked to the community and you can't afford not to use stylesheets, but more than that: unless you're doing the most mundane tasks, you probably can't afford to force-fit your information into HTML and sift it back out again all the time.

Enter XML. XML is the evolutionary successor to HTML, in a "less is more" sort of way. If you're thinking that XML is all the stuff from HTML plus a few more bells and whistles, think again. It's the same pointy brackets, tags, and attributes, but when we talk about tag names, the slate is wiped clean. Using XML is like taking the training wheels off the HTML bicycle. That can be a little scary — until you get the hang of it. Then it sets you free! And getting the hang of it (and eventually becoming free) is where this book comes into the picture.

XML isn't really new technology — it's based on SGML and similar systems that date back to the 1960s. These systems have always been very powerful, but they have also been costly. So they were only worth the trouble for projects such as aircraft manuals. But as the world goes digital, almost everybody is taking on information management tasks nearly the size of an aircraft manual.

And XML is simpler — and cheaper to use — than SGML, because it benefits from all this experience: The parts of SGML that didn't prove critical just aren't in XML at all!

XML is just the right tool for modern information management. It's been in the shop for years and years in one form or another, but now it's hitting the Web scene in force. I hope you come to use this tool like a pro.

Dan Connolly
World Wide Web Consortium Architecture Domain Lead

Introduction

Welcome to the latest frontier of World Wide Web technology. In this book, we introduce you to the mysteries of the eXtensible Markup Language (XML), which promises to build tremendous additions to an already-formidable foundation built on the HyperText Markup Language (HTML) that has made the Web possible.

If you've tried to build complex Web pages that integrate multiple sources of data, require active and dynamic behaviors, and need lots of programming and tweaking to accommodate your special needs, XML may be able to come to the rescue. If you know HTML, you'll probably find it less of a stretch to add XML to your arsenal than you may believe. (No kidding!)

We take a straightforward approach to telling you about XML and what it can do for your online publishing efforts. We try to keep the amount of technobabble to a minimum and stick with plain English as much as possible. Besides plain talk about hypertext, XML, and the many special-purpose dialects that XML supports for chemists, mathematicians, push publishers, and many other online constituencies, we include lots of sample programs and instructions to help you use XML on your Web site.

We also include a peachy CD with this book that contains all the XML examples in usable form and a number of other interesting widgets for your own documents. We include numerous XML authoring tools, parsers, development kits, and other goodies, some of which you may find to be a source of inspiration and material for your own uses!

About This Book

Think of this book as a friendly, approachable guide to XML and to using this technology to extend your presence on the World Wide Web. Although XML is a bit more challenging to figure out than HTML, this book is organized to make it easy to grapple with the fundamentals and then to use them to good effect. We also document voluminous additional sources of information, training, and consulting, both online and off-line. Some topics that you find in this book include the following:

> ✔ An overview of XML's capabilities, terminology, and technologies
>
> ✔ A comparison of XML with its junior partner HTML and its senior partner SGML
>
> ✔ An overview of the newly minted XML standard
>
> ✔ Information on designing, building, and using XML's extensible characteristics
>
> ✔ Reviews of a slew of XML "dialects" — which are special-purpose markup definitions that support chemical and mathematical notation, push publishers, resource delivery, dynamic interfaces, multimedia, and other domains that require more functionality than plain-vanilla HTML can deliver

Although you may think that using XML requires years of training and advanced technical wizardry, we don't think that's true. If you can tell somebody how to drive across town, you can certainly use XML to build documents that do what you want them to. The purpose of this book isn't to turn you into a true-blue geek, complete with pocket protector; it's to show you what design and technical elements you need so that you under-stand what XML is and how it works, and to give you the know-how and confidence to use it to good effect!

How to Use This Book

Pick up this book to find out what XML is about and how you can use it to create custom markup to meet your particular information-handling needs online. You can also discover what's required to design and build effective documents to bring your important ideas and information to the entire Web, if that's what you want to do, or to your intranet, if your information is "for internal consumption only."

All XML code appears in monospaced type like this:

```
<Greeting>Hello, world!</Greeting> ...
```

When you type in XML tags or other related information, be sure to copy the information exactly as you see it between the angle brackets (< and >) because that's part of the magic that makes XML work. Other than that, we tell you how to marshal and manage the content that makes your pages special, and we tell you exactly what you need to do to mix the elements of XML with your own work.

Due to the margins in this book, some long lines of XML markup or designa-tions for World Wide Web sites (called URLs, for Uniform Resource Locators) may wrap to the next line. On your computer, though, these wrapped lines will appear as a single line of XML or as a single URL, so don't insert a hard return when you see one of these wrapped lines. Each instance of wrapped code is noted as follows:

```
www.infomagic.austin.com/nexus/plexus/lexus/praxis/
              this_is_a_deliberately_long.html
```

Throughout this book, we've been forced (due to paper-based limitations) to wrap code lines along multiple lines. Remember, though, that even though a line of code appears on two lines, make sure that you key it in only one line when you create the code for your own use. Don't insert a hard return!

XML is completely sensitive to how tag text is entered: It requires that you always use uppercase, lowercase, or both, exactly as they appear in the book (or more important, as they're defined in the Document Type Definition — DTD — that governs any well-formed or valid XML document). To make your own work look like ours as much as possible, enter all tag text exactly as it appears in this book.

Assumptions May Be Unwarranted, But...

Someone once said that making assumptions makes a fool out of the person who makes them and the person who is subject to those assumptions. Even so, we're going to make a few assumptions about you, our gentle reader:

- ✔ You can turn your computer on and off.
- ✔ You know how to use a mouse and a keyboard.
- ✔ You're already familiar with HTML and the Web, you understand the difference between a Web browser and a Web server, and you know what a plug-in is and why plug-ins are needed for so much Web-related work.
- ✔ You want to build your own XML documents for fun or profit or because it's part of your job.

In addition, we assume that you have a working connection to the Internet, and a modern Web browser — one that can support XML directly. (As we write this, Internet Explorer 4.0 is the only browser in wide distribution with this capability, but Netscape Navigator promises to become fully XML-compliant before the end of 1998.) Don't worry, though; if you don't have such a browser, part of what you'll find in these pages (and on the CD-ROM) is a collection of pointers that will help you obtain the tools that you need to work directly with XML on your own computer. You don't need to be a master logician or a programming wizard or have a Ph.D. in computer science to work with XML; all you need is the time required to learn its ins and outs and the determination to master its intricacies and capabilities.

If you can write a sentence and you know the difference between a heading and a paragraph, you will be able to build and publish your own XML documents on the World Wide Web. If you have an imagination and the ability to communicate what's important to you, and if you understand the special requirements in your content that makes XML more than just a "cool technology," you've already mastered the key ingredients necessary to build useful, attractive XML documents. The rest is details, and we help you with those!

How This Book Is Organized

This book contains five major parts. Each part contains two or more chapters, and each chapter contains several modular sections. Anytime you need help or information, pick up the book and start anywhere you like, or use the Table of Contents and Index to locate specific topics or key words.

Here is a breakdown of the five parts and what you'll find in each one:

Part I: Why XML Is "eXtreMely cooL"

This part sets the stage and includes an overview of and introduction to XML. It begins with an overview of XML's special capabilities and discusses the design goals and motivations that led to its creation and specification. We also discuss the special relationship between XML and HTML and explain why you can convert HTML to XML, but why it's probably not a good idea to try, nor may it even be possible, to convert XML to HTML. We also explain the even more special relationship between XML and SGML (the Standard Generalized Markup Language), which represents a truly mathematical subset-superset relationship. We conclude Part I of the book with an overview of the contents and notation that appear in the recently published XML Standard definition (also called the XML Specification). Use the last chapter in the part to help you read, interpret, and understand the specification's contents. As the blueprint for what XML is, how it works, and how XML processors (the software that reads, evaluates, and displays XML documents) function, this XML standard is the foundation on which XML itself rests, not to mention the rest of our book!

Part II: Extending Documents and Their Markup

XML mixes ordinary text with special strings of characters, called markup, that instruct XML processors how to display XML-based documents. In this part of the book, you find out about how XML documents must be structured and about the difference between a well-formed XML document and a valid XML document. We also tell you what's involved in defining custom XML markup and how to use what you've defined to extend and enhance how content can be presented within an XML document that uses custom markup. Then, we tackle XML's more complex notions of hyperlinking, which include bidirectional and multilink capabilities that extend and improve on the simple one-way, one-connection hyperlinks found in HTML.

From there, we tackle the notions of creating document stylesheets for XML documents, both in terms of current capabilities and in terms of a powerful, but not yet complete, XML Style Language (a.k.a. XSL). We conclude Part II with a discussion of character encodings and character entities, so that you can create powerful shortcuts for repetitive text elements in your XML documents and can break out of the narrow character sets to which HTML is normally constrained. If you need to include all kinds of exotic symbols or even languages such as Chinese, Korean, Japanese, and so forth in your documents, XML makes it much easier for you to do so than HTML!

Part III: XML Language and Application

Part III takes all the elements covered in Parts I and II and puts them together to help show you what others have done with XML to create special-purpose XML markup languages that we call "XML dialects." One way of looking at Part III is as a laundry list of several of the many important dialects that have already been — or are currently being — defined using XML. These include the Chemical Markup Language (CML), the Channel Definition Format (CDF) language, the Resource Description Framework (RDF), the HTTP Distribution and Replication Protocol (DRP), the Mathematical Markup Language (MathML), the Web Interface Definition Language (WIDL), the Synchronized Multimedia Interface Language (SMIL), and finally, the Open Software Description (OSD).

But aside from assembling as formidable a collection of acronyms and their underlying technologies as you're likely to find anywhere, this is more than just a laundry list — it's a tour-de-force demonstration of how XML can be used to create compact, powerful markup languages that can meet just about any kind of document-handling or information-delivery needs. Thus, these XML dialects also act as examples of what's possible within XML, as well as providing a toolkit that may be of significant interest to readers in its own right.

Part IV: The Part of Tens

In the concluding part of the book, we sum up and distill the very essence of what you've read. In this part, you have a chance to review the important but often covert role that SGML plays with XML, to observe some of the best and brightest uses of XML, to check out some of the most outstanding XML resources online, and to ponder answers to some of the most common questions about XML. Finally, you may end your XML odyssey by reading about some of the most compelling XML tools and software that you can then investigate further online or from the CD-ROM.

The CD-ROM

The materials on the CD-ROM are organized into separate modules that reflect the layout of the book itself. The CD is designed to help you match up the code and examples that appear within the pages of the book to their electronic counterparts on the CD itself. We think you'll want to take advantage of our work and let our fingers do the walking, so to speak, so you can find on the CD numerous examples and elements that may plug very nicely into your own XML documents ready for extraction and use.

We've also included two additional chapters — called Extra 23 and Extra 24 on the CD-ROM — that discuss many cool XML tools and a listing of great XML resources. Don't forget to take a look at those to start you on your way to XML mastery.

The remainder of the CD is devoted to as comprehensive a collection of tools and programs for XML as we were able to collect for your delectation and use.

By the time you make it through all the materials in the book and all the stuff on the CD, you should be pretty well-equipped to build your own XML documents and perhaps even ready to roll them out on your own Web site!

Icons Used in This Book

 This icon signals technical details that are informative and interesting but not critical to writing XML. Skip these if you want (but please, come back and read them later).

 This icon flags useful information that makes XML markup, Web-page design, or other important stuff even less complicated that you feared it might be.

 This icon points out information that you shouldn't pass by — don't overlook these gentle reminders (the life you save could be your own).

Be cautious when you see this icon. It warns you of things you shouldn't do; the bomb is meant to emphasize that the consequences of ignoring these bits of wisdom can be severe.

When you see this spider web symbol, it flags the presence of Web-based resources that you can go out and investigate further. You can also find all these references on the "Jump Pages" on the CD-ROM that comes with this book!

When you see this disc-shaped symbol, it indicates a resource, tool, or pointer to resources that you can find on the CD-ROM that comes with the book. To keep up with the latest version of these references, please visit the related "XML For Dummies Update" site that you'll find on the authors' Web server at `www.lanw.com/XML4Dum/`!

Here, you find the results of our best efforts to keep the information in the book current and a list of errata to straighten out any of the mistakes, boo-boos, or gotchas that we weren't able to root out of its contents before it went to publication. We hope you find this a convincing demonstration that our hearts are in the right place, but please share your feedback with us about the book. We can't claim that we'll follow every suggestion or react to every comment, but you can be pretty certain that those suggestions that occur repeatedly or that add demonstrable value to the book, will find a place in the next edition!

Where to Go from Here

This is the part where you pick a direction and hit the road! *XML For Dummies* is a lot like a recipe for goulash; you'll want to begin by taking a taste of what the final dish should be like, proceed to assemble the ingredients necessary for your own "document stew," and then get to work on cooking up what you need for yourself (or your organization). A certain amount of study will be involved, along with lots of Web surfing and investigation of our software and materials, not to mention the galaxy of stuff that's available online. To the untutored eye, it may even look as if you're fooling around — but we know that you're about to embark on a voyage of discovery that could change the Web as you (and we) know it. Good luck on your journey, and don't forget to keep your eyes on the information highway along the way.

Enjoy!

Part I

Why XML Is "eXtreMely cooL"

The 5th Wave — By Rich Tennant

"Here at MIC, leaders in OEM, it's SOP to wish a happy retirement to a great MIS like Douglas U. Hodges, or, DUH as we came to know him."

In this part . . .

This first part of *XML For Dummies* is the jumping-off point for your introduction to the eXtensible Markup Language — also known as XML. In this part, we do the following:

- ✔ Provide an overview of XML's background and its capabilities

- ✔ Explain the basic elements of XML syntax, document types, and the implications of XML for the Web

- ✔ Discuss the relationships among XML, its sibling HTML, and their parent SGML

- ✔ Provide an overview of the contents and notation that appear in the recently published XML Standard definition

The last item is a doozy. Because the specification is too long and complex to review in-depth, our goal is to help you learn how to read, interpret, and understand the contents of this all-important document — which is the foundation on which XML itself rests, not to mention the foundation for this book!

Chapter 1

What Is XML and Why Should You Care?

XML, the eXtensible Markup Language, is new and hot. Have your ever wanted to extend HTML beyond its limitations or define your own markup language? Have you ever wanted to have a document format that you can use to exchange data via the Internet?

Well, XML may be the solution for many of your problems. Although XML hasn't existed for very long, it is already employed in many different software products in many different industries. Is getting started with XML hard? No! Just check out this chapter and you'll find out about some of XML's history, what you can use XML to do, how HTML and XML are similar and different, and what kinds of XML applications are available right now.

An Informal Introduction to the eXtensible Markup Language

To understand new technology, knowing a bit about its history and the people behind it is often very useful. So here's the not-too-long history of XML and some background information. Soon, many folks will know and talk about XML; reading more about this will certainly set you apart from others.

A little bit of background

The eXtensible Markup Language (XML) has been developed by a working group of the World Wide Web Consortium (W3C). This working group consists of researchers and experts from many different areas of computer science technology: experts in Internet and intranet technology, leaders in the publishing industry, and experts in constructing markup languages.

The goal of this working group (officially called the W3C XML Working Group) was to bring SGML to the Web. SGML (Standard Generalized Markup Language), which is introduced and compared to XML in Chapter 3 of this book, is a language for the specification of markup languages. SGML is the parent of the well-known HyperText Markup Language (HTML).

XML's design was conducted by looking at the strengths and weaknesses of SGML. The result is a standard for markup languages that contains all the power of SGML but without all the complex and rarely used features.

The first working draft for XML was published in November 1996. XML was first shown to the public when SGML, the standard for document publishing that provides the foundation for XML, celebrated its 10th anniversary.

XML has already become a tremendous success. Since its early days, XML got a lot of attention from analysts, reporters, and the developer community. XML is either employed or is being introduced in many different scenarios.

XML suits different applications

If you look at today's Internet industry and at the many different research projects that are taking place, you realize that knowing the core applications of XML is sometimes difficult. In fact, case studies of XML never fail to bring up new and exciting possibilities and implementations in which XML can add value to an existing solution or where XML solves problems that nobody has dared to tackle so far.

Nevertheless, XML is very important in two classes of applications. Most applications of XML fall into one of the following categories: documents or data exchange and database connectivity, each of which is covered in the following sections.

XML for documents

More and more document authors are creating documents using XML, which is the intended use of the language. Using XML to create documents is very similar to creating HTML documents. The only difference is that XML provides a richer set of elements and is more extensible to various publishing media.

The XML Files and other XML phenomena

The folks who formed the W3C consortium for XML development now have all their speeches and technical information in hypertext format. Thus, you can go to their Web site and peruse what you need to know about structure, and you can do that when you need to know it — that is, while you're slaving over that hot XML markup you're creating!

Visit the site at www.w3.org/TR/WD-xml-lang.html#sec2.1 for more information.

We think the people who helped create XML must have been up on the mountain with Moses, because their "Ten Commandments" for XML became our goals as we constructed this book. Now you can see how we interpret

these goals and find out how you can put them into action.

Not only have the XML gods declared their collective wills, but they also started a regular e-zine online *(The XML Files)* where you can go to read the latest weekly gossip about XML and how it's developing. The figure in this sidebar shows what the home page looks like.

This e-zine will keep you abreast of all the latest goodies that are added to XML. Now isn't that one of the main reasons we're on the Web in the first place — so books like this can be related to online issues such as those *The XML Files* presents?

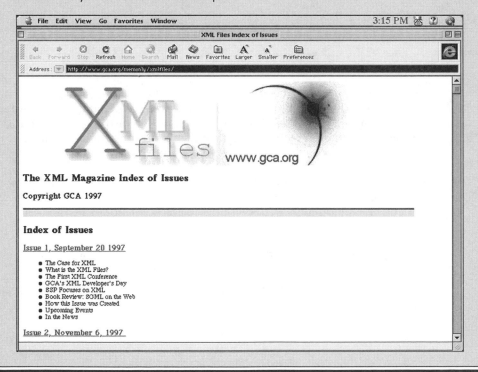

XML for data exchange

Say you want to exchange database information across the Internet. Imagine using a browser to send back to the server information about a questionnaire filled out by the user. This process and many others require a document format that is *extensible* — in other words, one that can be tailored toward a specific use and that is an open, nonproprietary solution. See Figure 1-1 for an illustration of this concept.

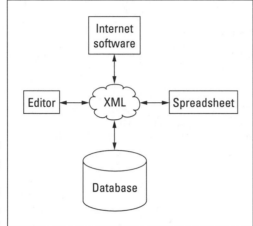

Figure 1-1:
Data
exchange
using XML.

XML is the solution for this kind of problem. XML is already being used and will become more and more important for exchange of data over the Internet in the future. The time of import/export filters for thousands of different interchange formats is gone. In many cases, XML can provide a single platform for interchange of data between applications.

Finding an interchange format that can be used for transfer of data between databases of different vendors and different operating systems was always difficult. That interchange is one of the major applications of XML.

If you know HTML, you know XML

If you are familiar with HTML, you are halfway to becoming an XML expert. Take a look at the following piece of text:

```
<P>
If you know HTML, you already know XML. Thus, you can get
started with XML <EM>right away</EM>.
</P>
```

If you know HTML, you probably said, "Sure, that is a typical piece of an HTML document." And you are absolutely right. This excerpt is something that could have come from a Web page. However, we say, "This is a piece of an XML document." So, who is right?

The truth is, we are both right. Indeed XML documents don't look all that different from HTML documents. XML documents use a syntax that has all the same bits and pieces that you know from traditional HTML pages. An XML document consists of a set of tags, such as ⟨P⟩ or ⟨EM⟩ in HTML. XML also allows you to use attributes and attribute values. Thus, the following piece of text could be seen as a piece of XML as well as HTML.

```
<P>
Both the HTML and the XML specifications can be found at
the Web server of the <A HREF="http://www.w3.org/">World
Wide Web Consortium</A>
</P>
```

Check out Chapter 2 for an in-depth discussion of how HTML and XML are similar and how they differ.

Marking Up Is Hard to Do — Not!

You may wonder whether getting started using XML to author your documents is difficult. It is not. As a matter of fact, to start creating your own XML documents, you just need a plain old text editor. If you think about using XML more often, for a lot of pages, you should be thinking about getting one of the newly available XML editors.

Break out that text editor!

To get started using XML, you can certainly use a very simple ASCII-based plain text editor.

Most text editors have predefined settings for the extension (the letters that come after the dot in a filename) of a document when you save it for the first time. You probably want your XML files to have an extension other than .txt, for example. If you use generic XML, just use .xml as the extension. If you use an example for a particular use of XML — Channel Definition Format (CDF — see Chapter 11), for example — use an extension that is more appropriate for that application. For CDF, .cdf would certainly be a good choice.

You can also create XML documents by using one of the more sophisticated document-authoring programs such as Microsoft Word or Corel WordPerfect. Keep in mind, however, that such programs usually store data in some kind of binary format as the application's native file-save format. (For example, creating a Word file and saving it will default to the .doc format, which is Word's native binary file format.) That format is not suitable for XML — or for HTML, in fact. Make sure to save your document as a text file if you want to use it as an XML document.

You must insert the markup yourself when using simple editors. In other words, if you have a paragraph like

```
This is about XML editing.
```

you will need to add the required markup by hand, to get something like this:

```
<Para> This is about XML editing. </Para>
```

If you use and edit XML files only occasionally, this probably will do. However, if you are thinking seriously about making XML your major format for documents, you need a more sophisticated program.

XML editors: More power, more convenience

XML editors often look like a blend of traditional word processors and HTML editors. To a large extent, you may not even be aware that you are working with XML.

XML editors have two distinct features that are essential for doing a good job in creating XML documents:

- **Ease of markup:** XML editors can add markup to text as simple as you can make a text bold in today's word processors. All XML editors provide the ability to simply select text with your cursor and choose the markup that you want to apply via a menu.

- **Enforcing document rules:** For many applications, XML editors can help you to find out which element types can be used within a certain context. This enables you to produce better documents because the editor prevents you from making certain mistakes. For example, if you specify that a `ChapterTitle` is only valid at the start of a new chapter and not within an ordinary paragraph, then the editor can make sure that you don't insert a `ChapterTitle` at the wrong place.

XML's Syntax and Rules of the Road

The core syntax of XML is not hard to learn and, as mentioned, if you know HTML, you already know XML. Take a look at the XML basics.

Element types and attributes

You need to be familiar with some vocabulary terms that will make understanding many things about XML easier. The important issue is the distinction between *element type* and *tag*. Don't worry: This isn't hard.

```
<P>About element types and tags</P>
```

If you look at this piece of XML code, you can see the `<P>` *tag.* If you look at an XML document, the portions of code that are surrounded by the brackets are tags. If we talk about concrete examples, we're talking about tags. However, if we mean the general concept, we talk about *element types;* the *P* in this tag is an element type.

Now, we have good news and bad news for you. The good news is that now you know the distinction between elements and tags. The bad news is that most people don't make the distinction. But now you know better than the rest of us.

XML allows you to add explicit information to your text about the semantics, or the meaning, attached to a piece of text. A human wouldn't find it hard to figure out that what's inside the following bit of code is a name; a machine probably would find it difficult, without having the additional information that is presented via the tag.

```
<Name>Norbert H. Mikula</Name>
```

The following examples show cases in which both humans and machines would have a hard time distinguishing a paragraph from a header.

```
<P>Some text</P>
```

```
<Header>Element types and attributes</Header>
```

That's why we talk about *markup,* or marking the text, and that's why we call the individual instances of element types "tags" because, like the tags that you find in department stores, they provide additional information about the object to which they are attached.

Tags have a general form, beginning with the *opening tag*. The opening tag looks like this: `<NameOfTheTag>`. Between the opening tag and the end, you usually have some text; but the tag can also be empty, or the content can be a mixture of other text and tags. You close with the *closing tag,* which has the form `</NameOfTheTag>`.

The opening and closing part of a tag must always contain the same name, and because XML is case-sensitive, the case (whether uppercase or lower-case) of that name must always be the same.

Imagine that you have a tag by itself, without any content. For example, you may see the HTML element type for a *break*. It has no content. Such tags can be written as follows:

```
<BR/>
```

XML differs from HTML in that you are not allowed to omit the closing tag. For example, in HTML you sometimes see something like this:

```
<P>One para
<P>Another para
```

The preceding code block would be illegal in XML; in XML, you must always include the closing tag, as follows:

```
<P>One para</P>
<P>Another para</P>
```

Attributes and *attribute values* are also a form to convey additional meaning. For example, suppose that you have a paragraph and that you want to indicate whether the text is finished or is a draft. You could say:

```
<Para><Draft>I still need to work on this</Draft></Para>
```

But you would need to change and rewrite that piece from "Draft" to "Final" after the status changes, but XML has a better way.

Attributes have a name and a value. You find attributes in conjunction with tags. The typical form of an attribute is *Attribute-Name="Attribute-Value".* You may know attributes from HTML; you must remember to always use quotation marks around your attribute values. You can use either double quotation marks (" ") or single quotation marks (' ').

```
<Para Status="draft">I still need to work on this</Para>
```

Often, you'll be unclear as to whether something should be an attribute or an element type. Many of the cases will be decided based on experience and by thinking about the implications of each way. See Chapter 6 for more details on attributes and element types.

Hierarchy

Think about a book and how an XML document that describes a book would look. A book, for our purposes, consists of a table of contents followed by a set of chapters. Each chapter has a title and consists of a set of paragraphs mixed with sections and their titles. Now, try to render this concept in XML, without the text.

```
<Book>
 <TableOfContents> ... </TableOfContents>
 <Chapter>
 <ChapterTitle>XML and why bother</ChapterTitle>
 <Para> ... </Para>
 <Section>
 <Title>The syntax</Title>
 <Para> ... </Para>
 </Section>
 ...
 </Chapter>
</Book>
```

As you can see, by nesting tags, XML provides you with the ability to describe hierarchical structures as well as sequences. See Figure 1-2 for an illustration of this idea.

Special characters

Certain characters play an important role in XML. For example, the less-than sign (<) is always used in the context of tags. As you can imagine, using < in your text can causes readability problems for a human — and readability gets really nasty for a machine that needs to process the information. That's why four particular characters are not allowed in your XML text. Instead, you must use a replacement for them, a *character reference*. We describe character references in full in Chapter 9. Here's a list of the special characters and what you have to use instead of them.

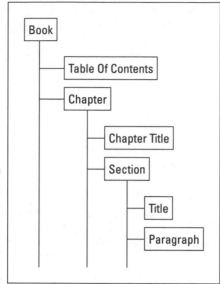

Figure 1-2:
A
"structured"
view of an
XML
document.

Write in your text . . .	Instead of . . .
&lt;	<
&gt;	>
&amp;	&
&apos;	'
&quot;	"

The Power of XML

XML is not limited to a fixed set of element types. Using XML, you can define your set of elements, or your own attributes, that you want to use within your document.

XML enables you to give more meaningful names to your markup. HTML's paragraph tag (<P>) is one of the most often used elements in today's Web documents. Maybe you use <P>, but you actually mean something that can be described differently than just *P* for paragraph.

More meaningful names in your documents

Imagine that you have HTML text like this:

```
<HTML>
<P>
This book is about the eXtensible Markup Language, its
foundations, the theory, and how to use it for your own
applications.
</P>
<P>
The authors are Ed Tittel, Norbert H. Mikula, and Ramesh
        Chandak
</P>
</HTML>
```

This is a normal HTML document. However, what if you want to express that you are talking about the cover of a book and want to make explicit that the last paragraph is about author information?

You can try this bit of code:

```
<Cover>
<Abstract>
This book is about the eXtensible Markup Language, its
foundations, the theory, and how to use it for your own
applications.
</Abstract>
<AuthorInfo>
<P>The authors are <Author>Ed Tittel</Author>,
<Author>Norbert H. Mikula</Author>, and <Author>Ramesh
        Chandak</Author>.
</P>
</AuthorInfo>
</Cover>
```

XML is all about allowing you to define and use your own elements and attributes — that's why XML is the "eXtensible" Markup Language.

XML defines new languages

You can define your own markup languages using XML. If you are not satisfied with HTML or if you need an element type that is completely different from one in HTML, make one up yourself. XML provides a syntax that you can use to describe exactly how your own markup language looks. Specifying what elements and attributes are allowed in your documents is called creating a *Document Type Definition* (DTD).

You don't have to go through this step. You can just start using your own elements right away. However, if you want other people to use your markup language, you need to explicitly say what elements and attributes are allowed and which elements can be used within other elements.

You will find out all the secrets about how to do this yourself later in this book. Now you may be asking "Geez, do I have to go through all this to get going with XML?" No. For many different applications and industries, the experts of their domain have already created specific markup languages that you can use. Here are some popular examples, some of which are described in detail throughout this book:

- ✔ **Channel Definition Format (CDF):** CDF has been developed to provide an open way to exchange information about channels on the Internet. If you are not sure what channels and CDF are, please read Chapter 11. If you have already used the channel features of programs such as Internet Explorer 4.0, read Chapter 11 to discover the details about how to use CDF for your own applications.

- ✔ **Mathematical Markup Language (MML):** Exchange of mathematical formulas has always been one of the biggest challenges for the World Wide Web. The Mathematical Markup Language defines the vocabulary to describe all the important things you need in mathematics. Even if you are not a mathematics expert, don't miss Chapter 14 for more about MML in this book.

- ✔ **Synchronized Multimedia Integration Language (SMIL):** Multimedia is becoming more and more important for the Internet. SMIL is a way of describing multimedia and is discussed in detail in Chapter 16.

- ✔ **Open Software Description (OSD):** Using markup for describing software is a concept that has been supported for some time. OSD, covered in detail in Chapter 16, is a technology that enables you to describe software and its components by using markup.

- ✔ **Chemical Markup Language (CML):** Specialized communities have already started to define their own markup languages. The Chemical Markup Language provides all the vocabulary for somebody who is eager to talk about molecules and atoms and so on. Figure 1-3 shows an illustration of CML, and Chapter 10 has more information about CML.

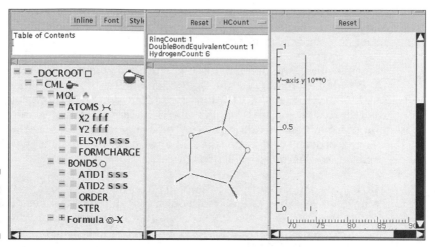

Figure 1-3:
XML for the
sciences.

The universe of XML-based markup languages is constantly expanding. The odds are high that you will find a specific markup language for your particular needs in the near future. If you don't find something that completely satisfies you, extend it — after all, XML is the _eXtensible_ Markup Language.

Web Pages Before — and After — XML

XML changes the way we publish information on the Internet. XML is not a replacement for HTML, but XML enables the Internet industry to invent a new set of powerful tools.

XML: One document, many different outputs

XML-based Web documents do not make any assumptions about how they are going to be used on the client side. In other words, HTML pages are designed for one particular purpose: the display of information inside your browser. Browsers easily process HTML documents, but software has a difficult time post-processing the information.

When we say post-processing, we mean to take the information that we have received and use it in some other process/software. For example, imagine that you receive a product order that was marked up in XML. An application that understands XML can use that data to automatically inform the production lines that they can start working on that product, and the application can also send the same data to a piece of software that automatically sends out orders for third-party parts that are needed for this product.

In many cases, XML documents will be used in conjunction with stylesheets to provide high-quality output on the screen. But the same data can also be used for sending the information to a speech-synthesis program that reads the text to a person with sight disabilities. Alternatively, you may also create output for a Braille reading device. The same document, in conjunction with a layout program and a stylesheet, may also be used for a high-quality printout, as illustrated in Figure 1-4.

The beauty of this concept is that you never need to change the actual XML data whenever you want to create output for different devices. You only need to use different pieces of software that know how to provide the output needed for a particular output format or piece of hardware.

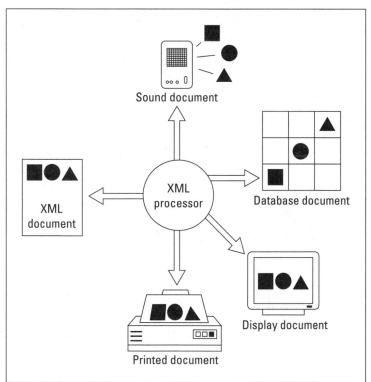

Figure 1-4:
XML for different outputs.

XML for data, HTML for display

In many cases, you will see a combination of XML and HTML. XML is all about preserving information. HTML is all about, or at least is accomplished at, displaying information within a browser. Why not combine the best of the two worlds?

The basic idea is to have the original data based on XML and all the rich markup and additional information about a document available. Then you can use the same document for many different purposes and you can use the "intelligence" in the data to build powerful applications. However, to display the data on the screen, the data will be translated to HTML, a concept that is illustrated in Figure 1-5.

This combination of XML to HTML can happen in one of two ways. The methods differ depending on the point in time at which the XML data is translated into HTML to be displayed inside the browser. In other words, XML stores the data, and HTML renders it in the browser.

- ✔ XML data is sent down to the client (your browser), and the browser uses a stylesheet — extra information that helps your browser know how to translate XML to HTML — to provide you with HTML data for your client.

- ✔ The XML data is kept at the server side and is converted to HTML on the fly before it is sent to a browser.

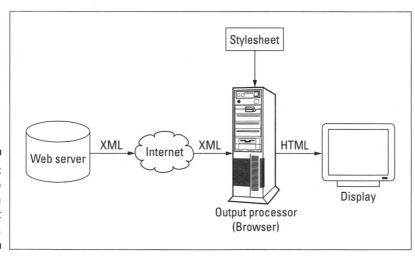

Figure 1-5:
XML to
HTML on
the client
side.

Better post-processing

HTML has always been criticized because the data in an HTML document is display-oriented — the data is hard to use for post-processing such as building indexes for searching. You can see the direct impact of this on your favorite search engine when you enter a query for a particular subject. Often, you get back either zero hits or about 100,000. We're not sure which situation is the better case, if either one is.

Because XML data preserves much contextual and semantical information, you'll find that building applications that do some "smarts" with electronic documents is much easier. Imagine XML documents that contain an `<author>` tag. Suddenly, you will be able to explicitly search the Web for all documents in which "Norbert H. Mikula" is the author. (Probably, you will pick your favorite author and not Norbert, but this is just an example anyway.)

XML will have a great impact on tools such as search engines because you will no longer have to rely on information that an HTML "title" or "H1" tag provides you with. Suddenly, you will be able to explicitly query for all documents that contain "XML" in their subject line.

Chapter 2

Kissin' Cousins: XML's Relationship to HTML

In This Chapter

▶ Understanding why HTML won't always do what you want it to

▶ Exploring the use of cascading stylesheets

▶ Figuring out what's wrong with HTML

▶ Making the switch from HTML to XML

XML and HTML both end in *ML,* so they appear to be related — and they are. Both are markup languages that use embedded codes to describe a document's text, and both are children of the much more complex SGML (Standard Generalized Markup Language, which we compare to XML in Chapter 3).

But we wouldn't go so far to say that if you know HTML, then XML is a snap to learn. Understanding how a markup language works is helpful in learning XML. But we suggest shelving some of your ideas about HTML — such as doing whatever it takes with the markup to make your page look right — if you're going to successfully work with XML.

We're well aware that you probably approach the topic of XML with at least a smattering of HTML knowledge, so it's important to expose the similarities — and important differences — between the two markup languages. Our goal in this chapter is to make sure that you have no misconceptions about XML being just another version of HTML. We compare HTML to XML and convert a functioning HTML document to a well-formed XML document.

The most important thing to discover in this chapter is that although XML and HTML are similar in parentage and construction, they are two different markup languages with different levels of generalization and purpose. You don't have to worry about converting all your HTML documents into valid XML, but rather you will want to decide which markup language is the best solution in any given situation.

Why HTML Won't Always Do What You Want

HTML was created as a document description language that allows users on disparate systems to share information. That information was expected to be text with a few graphics and hyperlinks thrown in — not databases of text, graphics, sound, video, and audio, as is the current state of the World Wide Web.

HTML is written in simple text and didn't originally support any non-text media. HTML isn't limited or broken; it is a viable solution for making information available to a wide variety of people in an electronic format. However, since its introduction to the world-at-large, HTML has been increasingly called on to provide solutions to problems it was never meant to solve. Among those things HTML wasn't built to do are

- Tightly control document display
- Be flexible enough to describe different and specific types of information
- Convey information in a variety of media formats
- Define complex linking relationships between documents
- Publish a single set of information in a variety of media

Web-page designers (like us, for example) sometimes catch themselves thinking, "But my heading has to be in 45.5pt Arial and centered in the second two-thirds of the page." Although this sentiment is a bit exaggerated, it's not far from the reality of what Web page designers expect their HTML to do and can't understand why it won't. HTML was not created as a page layout markup language but as a document description markup language. The whole idea behind HTML was for users to be enabled to describe a document's structure as well as the role each part of the document played, regardless of display.

Today's Web designers want to achieve the same formatting control over their Web documents as they have over print documents. They want what they see on their screens with their browsers to be exactly what any visitor to their sites will see. Two overarching problems interfere with a Web designer achieving this control:

- **HTML lacks control:** First and foremost, HTML doesn't include the mechanisms for maintaining this control. You can't specify the display size of a document or control the size of a browser window. These two variables are affected by the user's screen size and personal preferences. Although HTML 4 does include <FONT> tags to help you add font face, size, and color specifics to your documents, users can override your specifications in favor of their own.

✔ **Browsers vary in display:** Along with the different versions of the two most common browsers — Internet Explorer and Netscape Navigator/ Communicator — Mosaic, HotJava, and other graphical browsers make it impossible to know (unless you're on a homogenous intranet) exactly with which browser and on which platform your users are viewing your pages. And you can't realistically test every Web page on every available browser on every platform just to see what they see.

So far, two different attempts have been made to give designers the control they seem to be dying for: new tags and stylesheets.

Throwing new tags into the fray

No HTML-related solution exists to the need for tight control over Web pages. Tables, frames, and new formatting tags are some HTML-based solutions that have been implemented, usually by browser vendors first, to provide Web designers with increasing control over Web pages. This approach has a few problems.

✔ **HTML was never designed for the addition of formatting controls.** HTML is supposed to describe a document's structure regardless of its final display. The new tags don't describe structure at all; they simply provide formatting instructions.

✔ **Some tags originated as proprietary tags of a particular browser vendor.** This doesn't appear serious, but said tags weren't immediately made part of the official HTML specifications of the time. For example, even though the two most popular browsers (Microsoft Internet Explorer and Netscape Navigator) supported frames when HTML 3.2 was the current spec, frames only recently became a standard part of the HTML 4.0 recommendation. But versions 2.0 and earlier of these browsers don't support frames, so any HTML document that includes frames markup cannot be displayed by these older versions. See the problem?

New formatting tags were added to HTML by browser vendors in response to demands by some Web developers who wanted more control over their documents and who never fully understood the basic concepts behind HTML as a document structure definition language. Opinions on this subject vary, but we believe that these tags may have done more harm than good in the long run.

Cascading Style Sheets

The World Wide Web Consortium (W3C), which is the guiding body for the Web's development, realized that creating a plethora of new tags to account for every possible formatting need was unrealistic and inconsistent with the principles and concepts of HTML. HTML really needed a way to help a client (read *browser*) format a document without interfering with the description of its structure. This mechanism must also provide a way to specify how the same HTML file should be formatted based on the display mechanism — computer screen, overhead projector, braille printer — or the specific needs of a user. And this new wonder technology had to work with the existing HTML syntax and structures.

Enter *Cascading Style Sheets* (CSS), which enable you to define how certain HTML structural elements, such as paragraphs and headings, should be displayed without using additional HTML markup, but by using style rules instead. For example, the following shows some content from this chapter marked up with HTML, with a couple of headings thrown in for good measure (see Figure 2-1 for what this looks like when displayed in a basic Web browser):

```
<H1>Beyond the Call of Duty</H1>
<P> However, since its introduction to the world-at-large,
        HTML has been increasingly called on to provide
        solutions to problems it was never meant to
        solve. Among the things HTML wasn't built to do
        are: </P>
<UL>
<LI>tightly control document display
<LI>be flexible enough to describe different and specific
        types of information
<LI>convey information in a variety of media formats
<LI>define complex linking relationships between documents
<LI>publish a single set of information in a variety of
        media
</UL>
<H2>Onward Ho!</H2>
<P> Web-page designers (like us, for example) sometimes
        catch themselves thinking, "But my heading has
        to be in 45.5pt Arial and centered in the second
        two-thirds of the page." Although this sentiment
        is a bit exaggerated, it's not far from the
        reality of what Web page designers expect their
        HTML to do and can't understand why it won't.
        HTML was not created as a page layout markup
        language but as a document description markup
        language. The whole idea behind HTML was to be
        able to describe a document's structure as well
        as the role each part of the document played,
        regardless of display. </P>
```

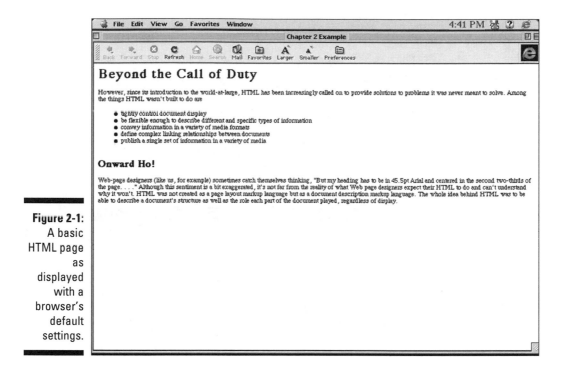

Figure 2-1:
A basic
HTML page
as
displayed
with a
browser's
default
settings.

As you know, a browser's default settings aren't always enough. Headings and margins add quite a bit to a page's final display. The next example links this sort of stylesheet, named `basic.css`, to our page and jazz it up a bit:

```
BODY {background: white}

H1 {margin-left: 5%;
    color: red;
    font-family: Arial;
    font-size: 20pt;
    }
H2 {margin-left: 7%;
    color: blue;
    font-family: Arial;
    font-size: 18pt;
    }
P {margin-left: 9%;
    font-family: "Comic Sans MS";
    font-size: 12pt;
    text-align: justify;
    }
```

(continued)

(continued)

```
UL {margin-left: 11%;
    font-family: "Comic Sans MS":
    font-size: 11pt;
    }
```

These style rules specify font size and face, as well as define a set of margins for each element. Figure 2-2 shows what the page looks like when the style rules do their thing.

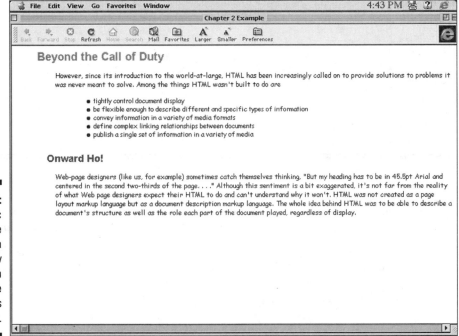

Figure 2-2:
A basic HTML page takes on a whole new look with a few simple style rules applied to it.

If we want to present this same information at a conference and the HTML page will be displayed on a screen displayed by an overhead projector instead of on a computer monitor, we must change the formatting to account for the new display circumstances.

Font size comes immediately to mind. The smallest size font you can use for on-screen display and expect anyone beyond the fourth row to be able to see your information is 24-point. We created this new set of style rules, called presentation.css, and applied the new set to the page in place of basic.css.

```
<STYLE>BODY {background: white}
H1 {margin-left: 5%;
   color: red;
   font-family: Arial;
   font-size: 44pt;
   }
H2 {margin-left: 7%;
   color: blue;
   font-family: Arial;
   font-size: 34pt;
   }
P {margin-left: 9%;
   font family: "Comic Sans MS";
   font-size: 24pt;
   text-align: justify;
   }
UL {margin-left: 11%;
   font-family: "Comic Sans MS";
   font-size: 24pt;
   }
</STYLE>
```

Figure 2-3 shows the display after these new style rules are applied. Notice that not all the text fits on the screen now, but it is big enough to be seen in the back of the room.

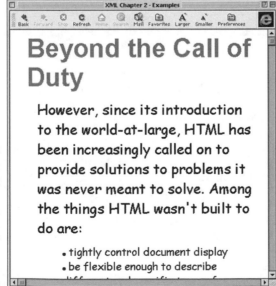

Figure 2-3: A new set of style rules changes the display of the same Web page.

But, because no new Web technology is perfect, Figure 2-4 shows what the styled page looks like when viewed by a browser that doesn't support CSS. Not the prettiest sight in the world, but at least the content and basic structure are intact. We can't say the same for HTML files formatted with complex tables or frames. Stylesheets were created to be backward-compatible and to allow style-challenged browsers to display page content, even if it isn't as pretty.

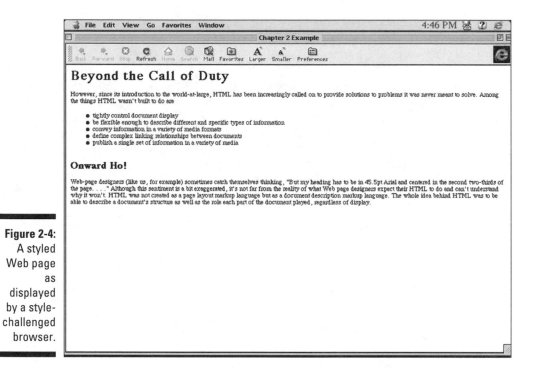

Figure 2-4:
A styled
Web page
as
displayed
by a style-
challenged
browser.

You can do so many more things to your pages with style rules that conventional HTML doesn't support. Margins are just the beginning. For a full rundown on all the stylesheet properties that you can apply to your HTML elements, visit the HTML Help site at `www.htmlhelp.com`.

Although the creation of new tags to meet every design issue has obvious flaws, the problem with CSS and other HTML-related stylesheets runs quite a bit deeper. In essence, the limitations of CSS lie in how they are tied directly to HTML and ultimately suffer from the same limitations that HTML does. Although you can create your own style rules, you have to choose from a collection of predefined properties and you must use HTML elements to invoke style rules. You can't create your own properties, and you certainly can't create your own HTML tags.

Although it's very true that stylesheets in general — and CSS specifically — have been the best thing to happen to HTML since Dan Connolly created the 2.0 specification, they can't extend HTML beyond HTML's inherent capabilities. That's why we need XML.

What's Wrong with HTML?

The short answer to the question "What's wrong with HTML?" is simple. Absolutely nothing at all.

What?! If there's nothing wrong with HTML, then why learn a new markup language like XML?

Well, nothing is *inherently* wrong with HTML, but it has limitations. HTML was created as a document structure description language but has been asked to do so much more. HTML doesn't fit every document in the world and isn't flexible enough to be extended to fit every document. So Web designers have been working to squeeze their documents into HTML markup, even if the language isn't a perfect fit with the document's needs.

XML meets those needs and provides solutions that HTML wasn't designed for. XML is a bit more complicated to learn but is so much more extensible than HTML. In other words, the ability to create your own tags and attributes, as well as alter those already defined in an existing DTD (Document Type Definition), makes it possible to extend XML to provide a customized solution to any information delivery need. With HTML, you use the tags in the DTD, and if they don't meet your needs, well, tough.

Making the Switch: HTML to XML

To illustrate the relationship between XML and HTML, we show you how to turn an HTML page from the LANWrights Web site into a well-formed XML document.

In this section, we toss around some terms that you may not be familiar with; you don't really need to understand them 100 percent for this exercise. Our goal is to show HTML as a document structure markup language, not as a page design markup language, and to demonstrate how XML builds on what you already know about HTML.

It's actually not as difficult as you may think to create a *well-formed* XML document out of an HTML document, especially if the original HTML document was written using correct HTML syntax. The characteristics of a well-formed XML document are the following:

- ✔ All tags have both a start-tag and an end-tag.
- ✔ All tags are nested correctly.
- ✔ All attribute values are in quotation marks.
- ✔ Empty elements are formatted correctly.

The first three requirements seem pretty straightforward, even though they aren't always necessary in HTML; XML dispenses with many HTML short-cuts and is very unforgiving of syntax errors and limitations. The final requirement differs from anything you've ever seen in HTML. Empty elements (such as hard rules and images) that insert something into the document rather than contain text require a specific format in XML.

So, now that you know the requirements of a well-formed XML document, let the switching begin. Our guinea-pig HTML page is the first portion of the current LANWrights "Coming Soon" page. It is shown in Figure 2-5 and uses the following HTML code:

```
<HTML>

<HEAD>
   <TITLE>LANWrights - Writing and Consulting - Coming
          Soon</TITLE>
   <LINK HREF="lanwstyle.css" TYPE=text/css REL=STYLESHEET>
</HEAD>

<BODY BGCOLOR="#FFFFFF" LINK="#800000" VLINK="#000080">

<CENTER>
<IMG SRC="graphics/comilogo.gif" WIDTH="466" HEIGHT="108"
ALT="Coming Soon @ LANWrights" BORDER="0">
</CENTER>

<P>The books below are still in development. When they are
          published they will
be transferred to the <A HREF="books.htm">Books in Print
          </A> page.

<P><B>Awaiting Publication</P></B>
```

```
<UL>
   <LI>Hip Pocket Guide to HTML 4.0<BR>
   by Ed Tittel, James Michael Stewart, and Natanya
           Pitts<BR>
   Expected Publication: December, 1997<BR>
   Publisher: IDG Books<BR>
   <BR>

   <LI>Networking Essentials Study Guide<BR>
   by Ed Tittel and David Johnson<BR>
   Expected Publication: February, 1998<BR>
   Publisher: Course Technology<BR>
   <BR>

   <LI>Windows NT Workstation Study Guide<BR>
   by Ed Tittel and Christa Anderson<BR>
   Expected Publication: March, 1998<BR>
   Publisher: Course Technology<BR>

</UL>

</BODY>
</HTML>
```

To turn this HTML page into a well-formed XML page, we make sure that it meets each requirement one-by-one.

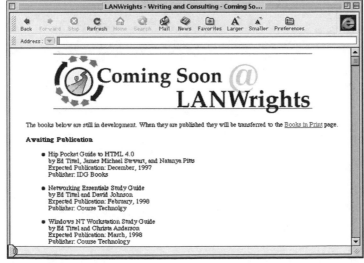

Figure 2-5:
The
LANWright's
Web page.

All elements have a start-tag and an end-tag

Several of the HTML tags act as text containers but don't require ending tags. <P> and <LI> are two common examples. Those tags work in non-pair containers because of a special SGML shortcut that allows the parser to assume that an ending tag would have occurred right before another start tag of the same element. So, in effect

```
<P>text text text
<P>text text text
```

is the same as

```
<P>text text text</P>
<P>text text text</P>
```

Going without an end code doesn't fly in XML. And so, in our sample document, we need to add an ending paragraph tag to this line of code:

```
<P>The books below are still in development. When they are
          published they will
be transferred to the <A HREF="books.htm">Books in Print
          </A> page.
```

We also must add ending list item tags to all three of these selections in the unordered list:

```
<LI>Hip Pocket Guide to HTML 4.0<BR>
by Ed Tittel, James Michael Stewart, and Natanya
          Pitts<BR>
Expected Publication: December, 1997<BR>
Publisher: IDG Books<BR>
<BR>

<LI>Networking Essentials Study Guide<BR>
by Ed Tittel and David Johnson<BR>
Expected Publication: February, 1998<BR>
Publisher: Course Technology<BR>
<BR>

<LI>Windows NT Workstation Study Guide<BR>
by Ed Tittel and Christa Anderson<BR>
Expected Publication: March, 1998<BR>
Publisher: Course Technology<BR>
```

Our corrected code looks like this:

```
<P>The books below are still in development. When they are
          published they will
be transferred to the <A HREF="books.htm">Books in Print
          </A> page.</P>
```

and

```
     <LI>Hip Pocket Guide to HTML 4.0<BR>
     by Ed Tittel, James Michael Stewart, and Natanya
          Pitts<BR>
     Expected Publication: December, 1997<BR>
     Publisher: IDG Books<BR>
     <BR>
     </LI>

     <LI>Networking Essentials Study Guide<BR>
     by Ed Tittel and David Johnson<BR>
     Expected Publication: February, 1998<BR>
     Publisher: Course Technology<BR>
     <BR>
     </LI>

     <LI>Windows NT Workstation Study Guide<BR>
     by Ed Tittel and Christa Anderson<BR>
     Expected Publication: March, 1998<BR>
     Publisher: Course Technology<BR>
     </LI>
```

And you thought this was going to be hard!

Tags are nested correctly

The rules of both XML and HTML syntax say that tags must be nested in a certain order. The rule is always to close first what you opened last. So, even though this HTML code

```
<I><B>test</I></B>
```

looks just fine in a browser, it's not correct technically. Instead it should be:

```
<I><B>test</B></I>
```

The bold tag is nested completely within the italics tag. XML requires that all tags be nested correctly, so we need to change this line from our sample page:

```
<P><B>Awaiting Publication</P></B>
```

to this correct syntax:

```
<P><B>Awaiting Publication</B></P>
```

Two down, two to go.

All attribute values are quoted

HTML requires that only certain attribute values, such as text strings and URLs, be quoted. Other values, such as image height and font size, produce the desired results regardless of the quoted state. In XML, all attribute values must be quoted. To bring our sample into compliance with this rule, we must change this link tag that works just fine in a Web page:

```
<LINK HREF="lanwstyle.css" TYPE=text/css REL=STYLESHEET>
```

to this correct XML syntax:

```
<LINK HREF="lanwstyle.css" TYPE="text/css"
      REL="STYLESHEET">
```

We're almost finished.

Empty elements are formatted correctly

The XML way of formatting empty elements may seem a bit strange, but remember that all other elements must have both a start-tag and an end-tag to be correct in XML. Changing the formatting of an empty element just a bit lets the parser know that the element is indeed empty and is not a broken container (in other words, a set of markup tags that have a start tag but no end tag). To create an empty element in XML, simply add a slash (/) right before the greater-than sign that closes the tag. An image tag that looks like this in HTML:

```
<IMG SRC="file.gif" ALT="image">
```

looks like this in XML:

```
<IMG SRC="file.gif" ALT="image" />
```

How easy is that?

If we want our sample document to be a well-formed XML document, we have quite a few empty tags that are formatted incorrectly. We need to add slashes to all our line break, image, and link tags. When we're finished fixing our empty tags (in addition to our other corrections), our well-formed XML document looks like this:

```
<HTML>

<HEAD>
   <TITLE>LANWrights - Writing and Consulting - Coming
          Soon</TITLE>
   <LINK HREF="lanwstyle.css" TYPE="text/css"
          REL="STYLESHEET" />
</HEAD>

<BODY BGCOLOR="#FFFFFF" LINK="#800000" VLINK="#000080">

<CENTER>
<IMG SRC="graphics/comilogo.gif" WIDTH="466" HEIGHT="108"
ALT="Coming Soon @ LANWrights" BORDER="0" />
</CENTER>

<P>The books below are still in development. When they are
          published they will
be transferred to the <A HREF="books.htm">Books in Print
          </A> page.</P>

<P><B>Awaiting Publication</B></P>
<UL>
   <LI>Hip Pocket Guide to HTML 4.0<BR />
   by Ed Tittel, James Michael Stewart, and Natanya Pitts
          <BR />
   Expected Publication: December, 1997<BR />
   Publisher: IDG Books<BR />
   <BR />
   </LI>
```

(continued)

(continued)

```
    <LI>Networking Essentials Study Guide<BR />
    by Ed Tittel and David Johnson<BR />
    Expected Publication: February, 1998<BR />
    Publisher: Course Technology<BR />
    <BR />
    </LI>

    <LI>Windows NT Workstation Study Guide<BR />
    by Ed Tittel and Christa Anderson<BR />
    Expected Publication: March, 1998<BR />
    Publisher: Course Technology<BR />
    </LI>

</UL>

</BODY>
</HTML>
```

Wow, wasn't that simple? And here you thought XML was going to be hard. Sure, you must remember some new rules, and things in XML are a bit more formal and less forgiving than in HTML, but XML and HTML are very similar in form and function.

Of course, a well-formed HTML document isn't necessarily a functioning HTML document. We assume in creating this sample XML document that an HTML DTD has been converted into a fully qualified XML DTD, and that's a pretty large assumption. For more on XML DTDs, the real guts of any XML document, visit Chapter 6.

An Addition to Your Arsenal

We won't even begin to suggest that XML will replace HTML or that you'll have to go through the arduous task of converting your HTML documents to XML (we bet that tools will be available to do that for you soon enough anyway). Rather, XML is a new tool with a familiar environment that you'll want to add to your Web development collection. XML and HTML are similar in many ways but do have their differences — rooted very much in their simplicity and extensibility levels — as you can see in the other chapters of this book.

This chapter gives you an HTML-relevant context in which to view XML; Chapter 3 traces XML's roots back to SGML. Don't be surprised if you discover that all of these "MLs" are part of one big and happy, if not always cohesive, family.

Chapter 3

Understanding XML's Relationship to SGML

● ●

In This Chapter

▶ Introducing SGML

▶ Examining the rules of SGML DTDs

▶ Dissecting the differences between SGML and XML

▶ Switching from SGML to XML

▶ Keeping things simple for conversion

● ●

*T*his chapter introduces you to Standard Generalized Markup Language (SGML), explains its basic concepts and building blocks, and describes some of the main features of SGML that have not been incorporated into XML (eXtensible Markup Language) standards. We conclude this chapter with a discussion of how to make the switch from SGML to XML.

If you have knowledge of SGML, this chapter helps you understand what you need to keep in mind when switching from SGML to XML. It should also help those planning to develop SGML/XML systems to design their DTDs (*Document Type Definitions*) so that their work can be used in both the XML and the SGML worlds.

Meet SGML

SGML is an international standard for the markup of electronic documents. It was defined by the ISO (International Standards Organization) who, in 1986, voted to publish it as a standard in the area of text processing. SGML's name during the standards process was ISO 8879. For kicks and grins, we decided to show you SGML's full name just this once: "ISO 8879: 1986 Information processing — Text and Office systems — Standard Generalized Markup Language (SGML)."

SGML was not just invented from scratch in 1986. The history of markup goes way back to the dinosaur age of computers. The origins of SGML date to the late 1960s. Charles F. Goldfarb and his colleagues at IBM were working on law information systems, and they invented GML (*Generalized Markup Language*) as a means for sharing documents between different systems involved in a publishing process. Thus, the concepts found in SGML are at least 30 years old.

A Gentle Introduction to SGML Principles and Practices

To understand the principles of SGML, you must first understand the history of typesetting systems and publishing (yes, this really is necessary). Once upon a time, when text was prepared for publishing, the plain text was interspersed with instructions for the layout machine. These instructions contained information about indentation, spacing, and other aspects of the visual appearance of the document. The syntax of the instructions had two important aspects, both of which caused problems:

- **Procedural information:** The markup used in documents was procedural in the sense that it didn't say anything about what an element was, only how it should be output by the rendering systems. In other words, instead of saying that the text following a "tag" is the title of a chapter, it said that the text following the tag has to be rendered in a 20-point font size with boldface applied. This approach caused all information about the semantics of a word or a phrase to be inaccessible to software.

- **Proprietary information:** Typesetting systems were very expensive, and each used its own proprietary way of describing a document's layout. Thus, a text setup created by one system could by no means be transferred to another. Due to this, interchange of documents and reuse of parts of a document were expensive and sometimes even impossible tasks. Whew!

The concepts and philosophy of SGML are based on two basic rules:

✔ **Separation of content and instructions:** Rendering instructions (information about the visual appearance of a document) have to be kept in a place outside of the original document. By using such an approach, rendering information appropriate for a specific situation can be added at any time using stylesheets (documents that described the layout/rendering of a document). See Figure 3-1 for a chart that shows how stylesheets, renderers, documents, and output relate to each other.

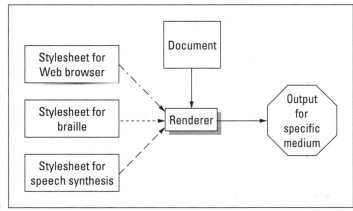

Figure 3-1:
Stylesheets provide flexibility in document output.

✔ **Capturing the meaning of the elements of a document:** SGML is based on the idea that you must "annotate" a document with text that describes the semantics of a part of the text. For example, if we write the title of a section, this knowledge can be preserved, as shown in the following code:

```
<Section>
<SectionTitle>
A Gentle Introduction to SGML Principles and Practices
</SectionTitle>
<Para>
To understand the principles of SGML ...
</Para>
</Section>
```

SGML uses DTDs to enforce these two basic rules. A *DTD,* or Document Type Definition, is a template for a document. For example, this book has a rigidly defined and adhered-to structure: The book consists of chapters, each chapter starts with an introduction, a number of sections that have their own headings follow the introduction, and each section contains paragraphs and/or subsections.

DTDs allow you to define a description of a class of documents. Suppose you have a DTD that defines the structure of a book in the ...*For Dummies* series. Every Dummies book must, therefore, conform to the structure as defined in the Dummies DTD. See Figure 3-2 for a visual representation of what we mean.

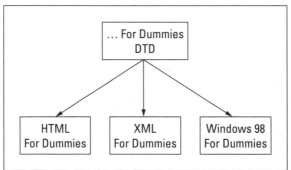

Figure 3-2:
DTDs are templates that describe a class of document.

Content models

SGML provides the means to express and define structures in a formal and concise way. These formal expressions are called *content models*. A content model defines what components a certain part of a document can contain. As mentioned in the preceding paragraph, a section of a document consists of a title, paragraphs, and optional subsections. These parts of a document that are explicitly defined as such are called *elements*. For example, Paragraph, Title, and Section are elements for a possible content model of a book. In other words, a content model for an element type is part of a DTD that describes a particular document element.

The formal definition of content models is very similar to the well-known regular expression used by programming languages, such as Perl. This example of a content model tells us that a section starts with a section title and is followed by a set of subsections and paragraphs:

```
<!ELEMENT Section (SectionTitle,(SubSection|Para)*)>
```

In SGML, DTDs are imperative, and the formal structure described in them must be obeyed. SGML documents either start with a reference to the definition of its DTDs or the DTD is at the beginning of it. An SGML system rejects a document if its structure does not conform to the rules as defined by its template — kind of like the IRS rejecting your tax form if you don't fill it out correctly.

DTDs and parsing

Very often, the markup of a document is added to the text by hand. Having large amounts of markup text can cause a severe bottleneck for text editing. SGML provides features that allow the necessary markup to be minimized.

Look at the following simple SGML document fragment:

```
<List>
<ListItem>
<Para>First part of a list</Para>
</ListItem>
<ListItem>
<Para>Second part of a list</Para>
</ListItem>
```

SGML reduces the amount of typing you have to do in your document. If we use some of the tag omission rules as defined in SGML, the fragment looks like this:

```
<List>
<ListItem>
First part of a list
<ListItem>
Second part of a list
</List>
```

You can still find the end of the paragraph and the end of the first list-item. In prose, you'd probably say that the end of the first list-item and the end of the paragraph are where the next list-item starts. SGML has formalized these rules to simplify document creation.

Tag omission, as described here, is very common in HTML, which is probably the best-known SGML application. Nevertheless, how do you know that a paragraph does not contain the next list-item? This is information an SGML system derives from the DTD. The DTD tells you which elements are allowed within a document and which are not.

SGML systems are able to derive the necessary information to create the full markup by looking at the DTD and by applying formalism explicitly defined by ISO 8879.

What SGML Can Do That XML Can't

XML and SGML differ considerably, both in document structure and suitability for a given task. SGML has strengths and limitations that XML doesn't share with its parent language, as the following subsections demonstrate.

Tag omission

Tag omission, as valuable as it can be when you have to edit your document by hand, has two potential problems:

- **Performance:** Having your SGML parser figure out where to insert such things as omitted closing element tags can become a costly and time-consuming task. This feature did not make it into the XML standard because the originators had this goal in mind: XML needs to be streamlined for high-performance processing.

- **Required DTD processing:** Tag omission requires the analysis of a DTD to create a fully tagged document. DTDs are an optional part of XML documents.

Inclusions and exclusions

Inclusions and exclusions enable you to add to a content model extra constraints that otherwise are hard to express.

- **Inclusions:** Think about an element type (or, less accurately, *tag*) for a comment. Most likely, you want the freedom to insert a comment anywhere in a document. Inserting information about the comment element type in each of the content models and at every possible place is too cumbersome a task. But by using *inclusions,* you can say: "In each place of this content model, the comment element type is a legal element." You augment such a content model by adding a comment element type as an inclusion, with a statement that says: At all places, starting with a section, a comment can be inserted.

  ```
  <!ELEMENT Section (SectionTitle,(SubSection|Para)*))
          +(Comment)>
  ```

- **Exclusions:** Exclusions allow you to say that, in this content model and in all content models that are children in this hierarchy, a certain element type is not allowed. In the following example, you first declare that a comment is allowed everywhere in your book document, and then you define what is allowed to be inside a comment: character data (PCDATA) or a part that you want to emphasize (EM):

```
<!ELEMENT Book (Title,Chapter*) +(Comment)>
<!ELEMENT Comment (#PCDATA|EM)* >
```

With this declaration, you can legally have a comment inside a comment (not a good idea). You cannot express this inside your content model; you can, however, restrict comment content by using exclusions. The following modification says that, although comments are allowed everywhere in your document as per your initial content model at the beginning, they are not allowed to occur within another comment:

```
<!ELEMENT Comment (#PCDATA|EM)* -(Comment)>
```

Short references

Short references (Shortrefs) are an XML feature of SGML that you use to specify a mapping from a character or string to some entity that contains replacement data for that character. Shortrefs are similar to a feature found in some word processors that expand a certain combination of characters to a full phrase. For example, you could define a mapping of the string "br-nhm" to the expanded version: "Best regards, Norbert H. Mikula."

Short references are also very interesting when you map, for example, a "carriage-return" into a "para" tag:

```
<abstract>
My first paragraph
My second paragraph
</abstract>
```

This could be automatically translated into:

```
<abstract>
<Para>
My first paragraph
</Para>
<Para>
My second paragraph
</Para>
</abstract>
```

Data tags

The data tags feature of SGML allows characters to have the semantics of both data and tags. You can use data tags with text written without any explicit markup, yet the parser recognizes the start and end tags. Given the appropriate definitions in a DTD, an SGML parser will still recognize this piece of SGML as a list of authors' names and affiliations:

```
<authors>
Ed Tittel, LANWrights, Inc.
Norbert Mikula, DataChannel
</authors>
```

Data tags and Shortrefs (covered earlier in this chapter) are somewhat the same, but the most important distinction is that data tags become a part of the actual text, whereas Shortrefs are pure markup.

Rank

The rank of an element represents its nesting level. You can view explicit information about an element's nesting level just by looking at the name of the tag (generic identifier):

```
<para1>This is a first level paragraph.
 <para2>This is the first second level paragraph</para2>
 <para2>This is the second second level paragraph</para2>
 <para2>This is the third second level paragraph</para2>
</para1>
```

SGML provides a more flexible scheme for expressing this information:

```
<para1>This is a first level paragraph.
 <para2>This is the first second level paragraph</para2>
 <para>This is the second second level paragraph</para>
 <para>This is the third second level paragraph</para>
</para1>
```

This second example is based on an explicit declaration in the DTD. It indicates the rank feature activated for the para element type. The second and third paragraphs of the second level don't include their nesting level as part of their name. An SGML system recognizes that those two paragraphs are at the same level as the first paragraph on the second level and assigns them their nesting level number automatically. If you need to rewrite that part and you want move the third paragraph on the second level to the first level, you do not need to change its name.

Link

The very complex topic of "link" is way out of the scope of this book. We discuss the link feature only to show that native SGML provides a way to separate content and formatting/processing instructions.

Imagine that you want to add some formatting instructions or a reference to a procedure in your tag. The result would look like this:

```
<para font="Times Roman" alignment="center">
Example for adding style information to an element.
</para>
```

This approach has a few major drawbacks. In the first place, you do not separate content and rendering information anymore. That problem, in itself, is already "bad style" for SGML. Also, you cannot support different styles for the same element.

One approach that SGML provides for that problem is to use the link feature. This feature lets you add formatting instructions — or other associations with that element — without ruining the content of the document. Using the link feature, you can specify the following using SGML:

```
<!LINK CenteredTimesPara
  para [ font="Times Roman" alignment="center" ]
>
```

SGML declarations

An SGML declaration contains certain instructions for an SGML parser. These instructions are independent of the DTD. An SGML declaration enables you to define a variety of different syntactical aspects of your document.

XML does not have such capabilities; however, an implicit SGML declaration describes certain aspects of an XML document when it is viewed as an SGML document. The following is only a partial list of the exciting things you can do with SGML declarations:

✔ **Document character set:** The document character set enables you to specify which character set is being used in your document. XML uses the ISO/IEC 10646 character set, which is similar to Unicode.

```
BASESET "ISO Registration Number 176//CHARSET
  ISO/IEC 10646-1:1993 UCS-4 with implementation
  level 3//ESC 2/5 2/15 4/6"
```

✓ **Quantity set:** In the quantity set, you can specify the upper limits of a set of quantity names. This example tells you that the length of names used for declaring element types can't be more than eight characters:

```
NAMELEN 8
```

✓ **Capacity set:** The capacity set helps you determine the storage requirements of an SGML document. Capacity defines how often an object of a certain category occurs in an SGML document — for example, the maximum number of elements being defined and information about the quantities of each. In this example of a capacity declaration, you can't declare more than 35,000 elements, and the length of an element name is defined in the quantity set (NAMELEN):

```
ELEMCAP 35000 NAMELEN
```

XML documents don't have limitations on the quantity or capacity of objects used in documents.

✓ **Delimiter set:** When you look at SGML documents, they usually use ⟨, /⟩, and ⟩ as delimiters to show the beginning and end of tags. However, in SGML, the SGML declaration can be used to assign different strings and characters that have the same semantics as the characters you're used to. (This feature is rarely used and is a source for potential confusion, but such assignments can solve very difficult problems in some situations.)

In XML, ⟨ and & are hardwired, and you know when you see these symbols that they denote markup. SGML has rules to determine whether ⟨ and & denote the start of a tag or entity reference, respectively. In XML, you can use these characters only to denote markup. To use these characters in text, you use character references, such as < for ⟨ and & for &.

Simplified comments

As with programming languages or word processors, comments are part of a document but aren't really a part of the document's content itself. In SGML, as well as in XML, comments start with the string ⟨!-- and end with -->. Furthermore, in SGML, comments can be interspersed in other markup with a starting and ending string --.

```
<!-- Content Model : Book          -->
<!-- A book consists of :          --
 -- a title, a set chapters        --
 -- we also include comments       -->
<!ELEMENT Book (Title,Chapter*) +(Comment) -- here we
          include comments -->
```

In XML, you can only open comments with `<!--` and close them with `-->`. You can't legally use the string `--` as interior comments. For XML, the example DTD chunk must be changed to this:

```
<!-- Content Model : Book             -->
<!-- A book consists of :             -->
<!-- a title, a set chapters          -->
<!-- we also include comments         -->
<!ELEMENT Book (Title,Chapter*)>
```

Attribute definitions

You use attributes to add information to an element. For example, say you want to add information about levels of confidentiality to a paragraph:

```
<Para confidentiality="Internal">
Secrets of project Texas at DataChannel
</Para>
```

The list of features of SGML that did not make it into XML is incomplete. This is just another example of how rich and complex full SGML can be. Please refer to in-depth SGML material to find out more about these features. Those mentioned in this chapter are those that you will most likely encounter when dealing with SGML documents.

In your DTD, you need to specify what the legal values for your attribute "confidentiality" are:

```
<!ATTRIBUTE Para confidentiality (Internal|Public)
           "Public">
```

This line tells you that two levels of confidentiality are available — "internal" and "public" — and public is the default.

In SGML, as well as XML, you can define, to a large extent, how legal values for attributes should look. In XML, you can choose from CDATA, ENTITY, ENTITIES, ID, IDREF, IDREFS, NMTOKEN, NMTOKENS, and NOTATION. SGML provides you with six additional attributes: NUTOKEN, NUTOKENS, NUMBER, NUMBERS, NAME, and NAMES.

By declaring attributes, you can also define what the default value for an attribute should be if it has not been specified. XML enables you to define explicitly what the default is (such as "Public" in the example on attributes), or you can choose one of these:

- ✔ REQUIRED: The attribute has to be specified, or it is an error.
- ✔ IMPLIED: The attribute is suggested.
- ✔ FIXED: Indicates that the attribute must have the value as specified after the "FIXED" keyword, or it is an error.

In SGML, you can also define the default to be CURRENT, which means that the default value is the last value that an attribute of this type had.

```
<Para Author="Norbert Mikula">
Written by Norbert
</Para>
<Para>
Also written by Norbert
</Para>
```

Assuming that we declared the attribute default as CURRENT in the DTD, then the second paragraph would also have Norbert Mikula as the author.

Making the Switch: SGML to XML

First of all, if you want to make the switch from SGML to XML, you must decide what type of switch you want to make. XML can be employed in many different ways. It can be used as a format for authoring systems or for information delivery across the World Wide Web.

Authoring

Often you find in publishing environments very sophisticated and complex authoring systems that have been developed using SGML. These systems represent a huge investment, and you probably do not want to simply forget about them.

Actually, we can think of no reason to switch from SGML authoring systems to XML-based authoring systems. SGML can be transformed to XML in a fairly straightforward way. Many well-established SGML authoring software already support export to XML format. Even if they don't, you can add a process to transform an SGML into XML for further processing.

Delivery

XML is designed for information exchange on the Internet, where XML can expose its full potential. A number of approaches have been developed that use SGML for sending documents from one place to another. However, these approaches have faced a number of problems.

- ✓ **Critical mass:** SGML systems, due to their power and complexity, have always been rather expensive, which makes it hard for an amateur to enter this arena. SGML use was often limited to experts, so it never became a widely used format for the average Internet user. XML is the result of stripping the complex features from SGML and providing the user with a powerful, easy-to-understand document format. For this reason, XML has become popular, and all major vendors in the SGML and Internet industries have included, or at least announced, XML support for their software products.

- ✓ **Speed:** SGML processing can be a time-consuming task. The somewhat complex syntactical rules of SGML and the reasoning a parser has to do when dealing with items such as tag-omission make building fast SGML processing tools difficult. On the Internet, processing speed is king. A document format should be designed so that a client can download and process that document quickly. XML was designed with such speediness in mind.

With or without DTD

You can translate SGML documents into XML in two ways. You can convert the document only, or you can convert the DTD as well, so that it conforms to an XML DTD (see Figure 3-3).

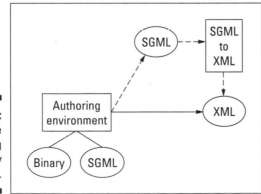

Figure 3-3:
The authoring and delivery process.

Translation without DTD

Translating without the DTD is the most straightforward way to convert an SGML document to XML. So-called SGML normalizers such as SPAM — SPAM is part of James Clark's SGML parser SP — essentially take an SGML document instance and a DTD and add markup that has been omitted by the author. The result is an SGML document that no longer uses the complex features of SGML. The final document is either very close to XML-ready or is an XML document. To take care of additional augmentation, the user may need to perform to the output of the SGML normalizer one more step via a post-processor (see Figure 3-4).

To find out more about SPAM, visit James Clark's site at `www.jclark.com/sp/spam.htm`.

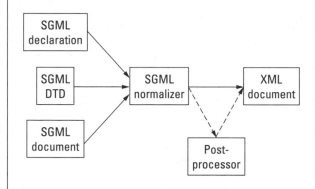

Figure 3-4: The SGML normalizer at work.

DTDs are used in XML, as well as in SGML, to make sure that a certain document adheres to structural requirements as defined by the designer of the document type. In many cases, just dropping a DTD and sending a document without it makes sense.

For example, say we have an XML document that was authored in an SGML environment. Assuming that the human editor didn't bypass it, the DTD for the SGML document makes sure that the document conforms to all rules prescribed for it. After the document leaves the publishing cycle — that is, after all the editors involved are finished working on the individual parts of it — the document can be translated to XML. Because we already made sure that the document conforms to its document type, we can send the text without its DTD and still be sure to have a valid document in which no important information is missing.

Translation with DTD

Translation with an SGML DTD is a more complicated task than translation without a DTD. Some SGML DTD constructs do not have a counterpart in XML DTDs. SGML DTDs are usually the result of a very thorough analysis of documents and their structure. Thus, if you really need to translate an SGML DTD to an XML DTD, the original SGML one serves as a valuable framework. Nevertheless, you still need to invest a lot of work into making all the parts and pieces of the DTD XML-compliant.

Important differences

Converting SGML documents to conforming XML documents isn't a straight-forward process. Keep the following items in mind when you want to engage in that process.

Case sensitivity

Names in XML are case-sensitive. SGML names, unless explicitly defined to be so, are not. This disparity means that these two declarations describe two different element types:

```
<!ELEMENT ChapterTitle (#PCDATA)*>
<!ELEMENT CHAPTERTitle (#PCDATA)*>
```

Restricted use of mixed content models

Mixed content models are content models in which you can mix element types and character data. The content of the following line of code is a simple example of mixed content models. It contains characters but also may contain other tags, such as <EM> for emphasis or <A> as an indicator of a hypertext reference:

```
<!ELEMENT Para (EM|#PCDATA|A)*>
```

This code is perfectly valid SGML, but it does not conform to an XML content model. In XML, the keyword for character data, PCDATA, must be at the beginning of the content model and cannot be nested somewhere within the content model. You must transform that line of code to:

```
<!ELEMENT Para (#PCDATA|EM|A)*>
```

& connectors

With SGML, you can use one operator in content models that you cannot use in XML: the "and" or & operator. The & operator enables you to say that something consists of a number of different elements, but you don't care about the order in which they appear within your document:

```
<!ELEMENT author (name & address & phone & fax)>
```

This SGML content model describes information about an author. The order of the different elements does not matter, as long as they are all present. The following are two different examples that conform to this description:

```
<author>
<name>Norbert H. Mikula</name>
<phone>(425) 462 1999</phone>
<fax>(425) </fax>
<address></address>
</author>
```

```
<author>
<name>Norbert H. Mikula</name>
<address></address>
<phone>(425) 462 1999</phone>
<fax>(425) </fax>
</author>
```

XML doesn't allow the use of & in content models. In XML, the same content model must be expressed this way:

```
<!ELEMENT author (name,address,phone,fax)>
```

You express the same information in this way, but the order is now relevant and the only valid piece of text in a document looks like this:

```
<author>
<name>Norbert H. Mikula</name>
<address></address>
<phone>(425) 462 1999</phone>
<fax>(425) </fax>
</author>
```

Named groups

Sometimes you want one content model to apply for more than one element type. Other times, you may want one set of attribute declarations to apply for more than one element. In SGML, you can use a named group to achieve that; for example:

```
<!ELEMENT (para|intro) (emphasis|anchor|footnote)>
<!ATTLIST (para|intro) id ID #REQUIRED>
```

In this example, both para and intro can use emphasis, anchor, and footnote inside them, and both need to have an id attribute defined.

XML doesn't allow named groups. Thus, the above statement must be rewritten like this:

```
<!ELEMENT para (emphasis|anchor|footnote)>
<!ATTLIST para id ID #REQUIRED>
```

```
<!ELEMENT intro (emphasis|anchor|footnote)>
<!ATTLIST intro id ID #REQUIRED>
```

Parameter entities can be used to achieve an effect that enables you to have your DTD be more maintainable than in this example.

Quotation marks

In one of the best known SGML applications, HTML, you often see markup sections that look like this:

```
<Para align=center>
```

No quotation marks appear around the values of attributes. SGML does not require them, but XML does. The quotation marks, in the form of " " or ' ', must surround attribute values:

```
<Para align="center">
```

XML prefix

In XML, all names beginning with the XML prefix are reserved and can't be used by other documents. To be more precise, because XML is case-sensitive, all combinations of the uppercase/lowercase "X"-"M"-"L" prefix are reserved.

For example, as we discuss in Chapter 6, XML provides a few special attributes such as:

```
xml:space or xml:lang
```

Other attributes and element names with special meaning may come to XML. In order to avoid conflicts and to make sure that only names "special" to XML can use the "XML" prefix, you are not allowed to use this "XML" prefix in situations other than those explicitly defined in the standard.

Web SGML Adaptations Annex

This optional extension to ISO 8879 — the official SGML spec — allows XML and SGML to have a cleaner relationship with each other than they would have otherwise. This extension to SGML allows you to use a set of features in SGML that are not in the original specification. Using these features, you can create documents that can be used in both the world of SGML and XML with less problems than otherwise.

Fully tagged documents

Web SGML (which is a "lite" version of SGML designed especially for the Web) introduces a new concept to the SGML community: *fully tagged*. A fully tagged document is described in XML terms as "well-formed." The most important novelty here is that fully tagged documents, even if they do not conform to a DTD, are valid instances of an SGML document. This makes every XML document, whether valid or only well-formed, a conforming SGML document (see Figure 3-5 for an illustration of that relationship).

White space

When you type text, you often insert white space characters, such as spaces, tabs, and empty lines, to make your document more readable:

```
<UL><LI><P><EM>"Readability is king,"</EM> he said.</P>
        </LI></UL>
```

This piece of an XML document would probably read much easier if presented in the following form:

```
<UL>
 <LI>
  <P><EM>"Readability is king,"</EM> he said.</P>
 </LI>
</UL>
```

Inserting this additional white space into your document results in many characters that aren't really part of the text; they exist only to improve the readability of the document.

SGML defines very sophisticated rules for a parser to figure out which white space is part of the text and which is not. If a parser recognizes white space that is not part of the content as such, it simply ignores it.

XML defines two types of behavior in terms of white space handling. One is the way traditional SGML would handle it; the second approach allows you to switch off this behavior. Thus, all white space would be considered part of the document and, hence, passed from a parser to the application.

The annex discussed in this section allows you to integrate the behavior of the latter case into SGML as well. One difference, however, is that with XML you can control this behavior on a per-element basis (see also the "xml:space" attribute). See the discussion on attributes in Chapter 6 for more information on this topic.

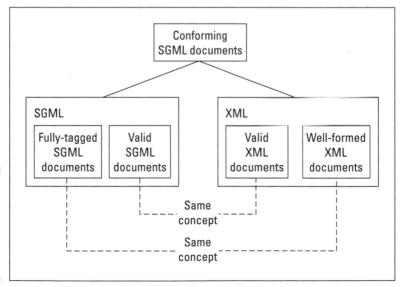

Figure 3-5:
Valid and well-formed in both SGML and XML.

Making SGML and XML Interoperate

The primary discussion in this chapter compares and contrasts SGML with XML. Each markup language is designed for a specific purpose, and each is very successful in its given purpose. If you work in SGML, your goal is to make sure that the two languages interoperate seamlessly.

If you plan to use XML for delivery and to use SGML for authoring and the rest of the prepublication process of a document, you probably want to design your DTDs and documents so that you can convert between the two standards without any problems.

Keeping things simple allows you to use all the software and knowledge of the two worlds and reduces your total cost of ownership tremendously because you won't have to worry about translation problems between the two file formats.

The bottom line is this: Don't use SGML features that have no equivalent in XML. If you start to use SGML/XML and you want to be in the SGML and the XML world at the same time, we suggest planning your system as if it were an XML system. SGML systems should have no problem dealing with the simpler XML. If you hit the ceiling with XML, you can add some of the SGML features as needed.

If you add SGML features, such as tag-omission, make sure that your documents can still be translated to XML in a straightforward and inexpensive way.

Chapter 4

A Blueprint for Extensibility: The XML Spec

● ●

In This Chapter

▶ Understanding the specification process

▶ Mapping the contents of the XML 1.0 specification

▶ Finding your way into Extended BNF grammar

▶ Expanding XML "production rules"

▶ Elaborating on specification examples

● ●

*T*he ultimate court of XML authority is based on its formal specification, as defined by the World Wide Web Consortium, also known as the W3C. As with most formal specifications, knowing how to interpret the contents of such dense and formidable documents requires a bit of education. In fact, it's pretty safe to say that what you bring with you to the document is at least as important as — if not more important than — the contents of the specification itself. In other words, if you don't understand what a specification is and the rules that govern its contents, it won't make any sense at all!

About the XML Specification!

Rather than repeating or rehashing the contents of the XML specification in this chapter, we're going to explain how you can tackle the original yourself, and we're also going to arm you with sufficient information so that you have some hope of figuring out the specification's sometimes seemingly impenetrable contents. If we can shed some light on how such documents work and how best to approach them, you may just figure this one out for yourself!

...ays remember that the specification is what establishes the rules for ...at is and is not legal for XML. To go straight to the source, consult the specification itself at the W3C's Web site:

```
www.w3.org/TR/1998/REC-xml-19980210
```

Even the name of the specification conveys information to those in the know — it begins with the string REC, which indicates that the specification is a "recommended" document. This means that it's more or less final, but one step shy of being an official standard. The string xml indicates the topic (which ought to be a no-brainer, given the focus of this book). And finally, the concluding string is an ISO date format that takes the form yyyymmdd, where yyyy is a four-digit year number, mm is a two-digit month number, and dd is a two-digit date. So the final part of the string translates to February 10, 1998, which happens to be the publication date for this particular specification. Any questions?

What's in the XML 1.0 Specification?

A quick peek at the specification document shows that it's broken into a number of sections, as follows:

✔ A header section that lists the version in multiple formats and points to the latest and previous versions. That section also names the document's editors and provides their e-mail addresses.

✔ A brief abstract that describes the specification. This abstract is short enough to be worth reproducing in its entirety, because it also provides the most succinct definition of XML imaginable:

> The Extensible Markup Language (XML) is a subset of SGML that is completely described in this document. Its goal is to enable generic SGML to be served, received, and processed on the Web in the way that is now possible with HTML. XML has been designed for ease of implementation and for interoperability with both SGML and HTML. *"Extensible Markup Language (XML) 1.0," W3C Recommendation February 10, 1998, pg. 1.*

✔ A status overview that describes the current status of the specification and points to the groups responsible for its contents, provides a list of errata, and provides other information about terminology that appears in the document.

✔ A detailed table of contents, followed by a list of appendixes.

✔ The body of the specification, which begins with an introduction, a statement of goals, and a list of specific, specialized terms with definitions, and then moves to define the complete syntax for creating and using XML documents.

> ✔ A collection of appendixes that include references and information about character classes, XML and SGML, expansion of entity and character references, deterministic content models, detection of character encodings, and the W3C's XML Working Group.

Reading the Specification

Although what we have to say next may seem trivial, in a way, it diminishes the serious thought and attention that must be expended when reading the XML document. This specification can be completely understood if you follow these four suggestions when approaching it:

> ✔ Pay close attention to Section 1.2 and all of Section 2, wherein the specialized terminology and reserved words unique to the specification are defined.

> ✔ Understand that the boxed text in the body defines all the "production rules" necessary to create well-formed or valid XML. By themselves, these rules completely define XML; the rest of the text in the document exists only to help mere humans understand what's going on and how these rules actually work.

> ✔ Follow all links religiously as you read. Because of the way that the formal grammar used in the XML specification works (it's called an *EBNF,* or Extended Backus-Naur Form, grammar), it's a good idea to read the specification on your computer. By doing so, you can follow links and expand the grammar as you read, and can save lots of manual page-flipping if you try to read a printed version. We cover this topic in more detail in the next section of this chapter, "Decoding the XML Production Rules."

> ✔ Expect to read this document at least twice (and follow all links religiously) to fully understand its implications and significance. The specification accumulates detail as it proceeds, which means that high-level constructs and concepts precede their underlying details.

In other words, roll up your sleeves and set aside the better part of a day to explore the specification. From another perspective, the body of the XML 1.0 specification consists of six numbered sections, as follows:

Section 1: Introduction. This section describes the intent and goals of the specification. It also introduces some specialized terminology that explains to readers and implementers how certain words or phrases must be interpreted, how a valid XML document must be formed, and how a correct XML processor (human or computer-based) must behave.

Section 2: Documents. This section describes the constituents that may appear in any well-formed or valid XML document, starting with the elements of a document itself and proceeding to lay the groundwork for how documents are expressed, what elements they may contain, what constitutes character data and markup, how to include comments in a document, and so forth.

Section 3: Logical Structures. This section explains the elements that can appear in an XML document in complete detail, with instructions on what constitutes markup tags and element type declarations. It also defines how element content may be expressed, including element names and types, attribute names, types, and values, how defaults are handled, and how an XML parser is to handle the data it finds in a document. This process is called *normalization* and represents the process of creating an internal representation of any XML document's contents.

Section 4: Physical Structures. This describes the storage units, called entities, that XML documents use to contain data, which may be either parsed (usually text, whether markup or content) or unparsed (usually not text, preserved for other uses). This part of the specification deals with how character and entity references must be interpreted and represented, addresses the notions of well-formedness and validity, and explains how character encodings may be named and handled. It also covers the details of how XML processors must behave when reading XML documents, which will probably be of interest only to those who must implement such processors.

Section 5: Conformance. This section describes the differences between XML processors that may or may not validate the documents that they process and how such processors may be used. As with Section 4, this section is likely to be of interest only to implementers of such processors.

Section 6: Notation. This section explains the formal grammar for XML used in the specification and what notation is used to represent the EBNF constructs within the production rules and their related constraints. We cover this in the next section of this chapter, "Decoding the XML Production Rules."

For most readers, Sections 1 through 3 and Section 6 will be the most important — unless you plan to build an XML processor. In that case, you want to familiarize yourself with this document in its entirety.

Decoding the XML Production Rules

Read through the specification and you see text boxes that define the rules by which XML behaves. These boxes include special kinds of statements called *production rules;* taken as a whole, the entire set of production rules that appear in this specification completely defines XML. Therefore, knowing how to read them is pretty important. To do that, you must understand how they're constructed and what the special symbols that appear within these boxes mean. This material is covered briefly in Section 6 of the specification; we try to cover it here in a more friendly fashion, and we include some examples also.

The Extended Backus-Naur Form (EBNF) was developed by computer scientists in the late 1960s as a way to rigorously express syntax rules for computer languages. Nicklaus Wirth, the developer of languages such as Pascal and Modula-2, helped to popularize this notation in books that defined these languages. Since then, EBNF has become a standard notation for stating the syntax of formal languages of all kinds. It works as well for XML, in fact, as it does for programming languages in general. But it is a specialized form of notation and takes a little getting used to!

The rules of production

An *EBNF grammar* consists of a series of production rules, where each such rule in the grammar defines one symbol, and takes the form:

```
symbol ::= expression
```

Symbols begin with an initial capital letter if the expression that appears to the right of the equivalence symbol (::=) represents a regular expression (see the Glossary for a discussion of this important term), or with a lower-case letter if the expression is not regular. Any literal strings on the right side of the equivalence symbol must be quoted wherever they appear.

Be aware that EBNF grammar is like a mathematical equation, in which the statement on the right side of the equal sign is equivalent to the statement on the left: $E=mc^2$. As in advanced math, EBNF notation puts the higher-level construct on the left side of the equivalence symbol and the sequence of lower-level constructs on the right side. As you read through an EBNF grammar, the process of understanding arises from realizing how increasingly complex productions can occur when higher-level constructs are replaced by sequences that may be created by expanding lower-level but equivalent structures.

The entire structure of XML, in fact, is expressed in production rule [1], which appears on page 5 of the specification:

```
[1] document ::= prolog element Misc*
```

This may be read to mean: "An XML document must include a prolog, followed by an element, followed by zero or more miscellaneous elements." Understanding the XML specification really involves understanding what constitutes a valid prolog, a valid element, and a valid miscellaneous element. As you read through the grammar, each of these constructs is defined by further rules that expand the definition for `prolog`, `element`, and `Misc`. Finally, by the time you're through with the spec, all the possibilities for expanding the most detailed of all legal right-side constructs have been exhausted.

The rules behind the (production) rules

To really understand EBNF, you need to understand its notation. Read this list of all the stuff you need to know:

- Comments can appear within a production rule, but must begin with `/*` and end with `*/`. Comments are included solely for human consumption and have no other significance to EBNF.

- When elements appear in a sequence, that sequence dictates the order in which they must appear, depending on what kinds of symbols are appended to those symbols.

- An asterisk (*) indicates that a symbol may appear zero or more times.

- A vertical slash between symbols means that only one may be chosen; sometimes such choices occur within parentheses or square brackets. In that case, only one item from within the container may be chosen. For example, production rule [5] defines a Name as follows:

```
Name ::= (Letter | '-' | ':') (NameChar)*
```

This may be decoded as "A Name may begin with a Letter, a literal hyphen, or a literal colon, followed by zero or more NameChars."

- Any sequence that occurs within parentheses is a regular expression. A regular expression is a sequence of elements that can be expressed concisely that permits a single pattern definition to match a wide variety of strings (for example, the pattern b*.exe matches beep.exe, bestofall.exe, and any other file that starts with a "b" and ends with ".exe").

- Characters or symbols that appear in plain square brackets define a *range,* or a scalar set of values, from which a value may be chosen, depending on how they appear. Thus, in rule [13], the string

```
| [a-zA-Z0-9]
```

means "or any character that falls in the range from lowercase *a* to lowercase *z,* uppercase *A* to uppercase *Z,* or the digits zero (0) through nine (9)."

✔ If the left square bracket is followed immediately by a caret symbol, the string means that all other characters or symbols enclosed by the square brackets must be excluded from the definition. Thus, the string

```
[^<&]*
```

that appears as the first right-hand term in production rule [14] means "The first character, or any number of repetitions that follow the first character, in CharData may neither be a less-than sign nor an ampersand."

✔ In a similar vein, specific characters or symbols may be excepted from an already-defined symbol definition to define another symbol. Thus, in production rule [15], the notation

```
((Char - '-')| ('-' (Char - '-')))*
```

means that no sequences of two hyphens may occur within the body of a comment. More explicitly, this rule may be decoded as "The contents of a comment may consist of one or more characters, as long as a single-character comment is not a hyphen and no sequences of two or more hyphens occur within those contents."

✔ Any characters surrounded by single or double quotation marks are literals, such as the hyphen and the colon shown in production rule [5].

✔ A plus sign indicates that one or more symbols must occur when following the production rule. Thus, production rule [7], which reads

```
Nmtoken ::= (NameChar)+
```

may be decoded as "A Nmtoken consists of one or more NameChars."

✔ The symbol S stands for white space, which is defined by one or more instances of a literal space character, a carriage return, a line feed, or a tab, as indicated in production rule [3]:

```
S ::= (#x20 | #x9 | #xD | #xA)+
```

Here the notation #x20 stands for "the hexadecimal number 20, equivalent to decimal 32." This format is used to express numeric character entities and is quite similar to the format used for HTML (except that it can distinguish between hexadecimal and decimal numbers).

✔ If a rule is followed by a string that begins with [VC: and ends with], this denotes a *validity constraint,* or a rule that must apply if the resulting XML production is to be valid. All XML must be well-formed, but it need not necessarily be valid.

✔ If a rule is followed by a string that begins with [WFC: and ends with], this denotes a *well-formedness constraint,* or a rule that must apply if the resulting XML production is to be well-formed. All XML must be well-formed, so such constraints define important required characteristics for XML productions.

Believe it or not, this relatively short list of notation encompasses a mere 15 types of markup and completely covers the syntax that informs EBNF. If you can deal with this collection of special rules and constructs, you can work your way through the XML specification!

Understanding XML Examples in the Spec

If you pay careful attention to the boxed text used for production rules, you see that two kinds of items are therein. Those that begin with numbers in square brackets on the left margin are production rules, but those that include no such beginning are actually examples of XML. They are supposed to illustrate a well-formed or valid utterance created by following the production rules discussed earlier in the section, "Decoding the XML Production Rules."

For example, Section 2.7 of the specification deals with an important carryover from SGML called CData, which defines a special kind of character data in XML documents. CData declarations permit all kinds of literal characters, including those that may otherwise be treated as markup when a document is parsed by an XML processor, to be inserted anywhere in a document.

Section 2.7 defines the following production rules for CDATA Sections within XML documents:

```
[18] CDSect ::= CDStart CData CDEnd
[19] CDStart ::= '<![CDATA['
[20] CData ::= (Char - (Char* ']]>' Char*))
[21] CDEnd ::= ']]>'
```

Another example of the specification reads:

```
<![CDATA[<greeting>Hello, world!</greeting>]]>
```

When you carefully read the preceding set of rules, this sequence makes perfect sense. By decoding the sequence, you find that all CData sections must begin with the string <![CDATA[and end with the string]]>. No data between those beginning (CDStart) and ending (CDEnd) strings can include the string]]> (because it denotes the end of a CData section).

What the example illustrates is that valid XML — as occurs in the content of the CDATA section in the example <greeting>Hello, world!</greeting> — is perfectly legal. As it happens, defining CDATA provides a dandy trick to permit markup to be quoted within XML documents (unlike HTML, which requires use of character entities to reproduce markup inside an HTML document under all circumstances). In other words, CDATA elements make it a lot easier for XML documents to describe XML markup than it is for HTML documents to describe HTML markup. For those who must document markup and how it works — like your humble authors — CDATA elements can be a real godsend!

Most of the other examples in the specification not only illustrate the rules they follow, or the constructs they discuss, but also provide insight into how XML can and should be used most effectively. That's why the examples are worth particular attention: Take time to think your way through not just what they say but also what they can mean for you when you start building your own XML documents.

Following the Rules for XML

Although the XML specification is not terribly long as such documents go (at 36 pages, it's actually pretty svelte for such a document, and is in fact 25 pages shorter than its December 8, 1997, predecessor), the specification is even more compact when you stop to consider that this entire extensible markup system is defined using a mere 83 production rules. By themselves, these rules would require less than eight pages to represent them in their entirety. But their discussion and exploration, and the definition of the terms they employ and the context in which they appear, is what requires the other 28 pages for the specification. (We say that discussion and exploration of the production rules also drive the nearly 400 pages in this book!)

Clearly, when you're talking about formal language specifications, a little bit can go a long, long way. In fact, because XML is extensible, it covers an infinitude of possible markup and related tags and attributes. But even this short discussion should arm you pretty well as you tackle the XML specification on your own. Should you still feel a little less than fully prepared, try reading more about EBNF at this Web page:

```
www.cs.upe.ac.za/staff/csabhv/slim/ebnf.htm
```

Otherwise, a good book on programming languages should help you figure out whatever details we did not cover to your complete satisfaction or edification. Look for one of these titles: Rachel Harris's *Abstract Data Types in Standard ML* [Metalanguage], Wiley, New York, 1993; Pratt, et al.'s, *Programming Languages: Design and Implementation,* Prentice Hall, Upper Saddle River, NJ, 1996; or Friedman, et al.'s, *Essentials of Programming Languages,* MIT Press, Boston, 1992.

Also, for more discussion of the XML specification itself, be sure to check out the XML resources that are mentioned in Chapters 20 and 22 of this book. Robin Cover's excellent XML site includes a great deal of useful commentary and discussion that you should find quite helpful when decoding the XML specification.

Part II

Extending Documents and Their Markup

The 5th Wave   By Rich Tennant

"UNFORTUNATELY, THE SYSTEM'S NOT VERY FAULT-TOLERANT."

In this part . . .

This part includes information on how XML documents must be structured, and about the difference between a well-formed XML document and a valid XML document. In addition, we provide some info on what's involved in defining custom XML markup, and then about using what you've defined to extend and enhance how content can be presented in an XML document that uses custom markup. This part is where you find out about the all-important Document Type Definition (also called the DTD) that defines any XML document's markup, structure, and capabilities.

In the second half of this part, we plunge into XML's complex hyperlinking capabilities and explore some historical models that led to such capabilities. We also take a look at what's involved in using document style-sheets for XML documents. Finally, we discuss the character encodings and character entities that permit you to create powerful shortcuts for repetitive text elements in your XML documents.

Chapter 5

Good XML Springs from Good Structure

*I*n this chapter, we explore the meanings of the terms *valid* and *well-formed*. Then, we show you some techniques used in good coding. In addition, knowing how complete XML gives a good, overall structure is always useful. This leads to the topic of what well-formed really means. Finally, you'll know you've got XML coding right.

Understanding Valid and Well-Formed

Two terms are often bantered around whenever XML is discussed by techy types: *valid* and *well-formed*.

People who know SGML are used to the concept of validation; in XML, validation means exactly the same thing it does in SGML.

A valid document must have a DTD — a grammar or set of rules that define what tags can appear in the document and how they must nest within each other (see Chapter 3). The DTD is also used to declare entities — reusable chunks of text that can appear many times but only have to be transmitted once (which speeds transmission). A document is valid when it conforms to the rules in the DTD. Although DTDs are not necessary in every instance with XML, they do lend an extra organizational structure for those who want to employ it.

Validity is useful because an XML-savvy editor can use the type declaration to help (and, in fact, require) users to create documents that are valid; such documents are much easier to use and to reuse than those that can contain any old set of tags in any old order.

The concept of a *well-formed* document is something that is relatively new in XML. A document that is well-formed is easy for a computer program to read and ready for network delivery. Specifically, well-formed documents have these characteristics:

- ✔ All the beginning tags and ending tags match up.
- ✔ Empty tags use special XML syntax (such as `<empty/>`).
- ✔ All the attribute values are nicely quoted (for example, `<a href="http://www.textuality.com/xml.html">`).
- ✔ All the *entities* (reusable chunks of data, much like macros) are declared.

*V*alid and *well-formed* are very important concepts to understand when working with XML documents. Just keep in mind that a valid XML document follows the tags and nesting rules set up in the document's DTD, whereas a well-formed XML document is properly structured for computer use.

Good Bodies Make for Good Reading

Have you ever picked up an instruction manual and wished you hadn't? You know the ones, filled with grammar errors, poor syntax, and just plain lousy sentence structure. You wonder why the author wrote it. The same value judgment can be made on XML code. If it does not contain some kind of internal structure (readable by human beings), then it may not be good-quality coding. One of the advantages of XML is that it can be readable like text. So, you should strive at every opportunity to make your documents readable by humans.

This section covers how you can create good coding in a step-by-step way.

The virtues of completeness

Figure 5-1 shows you, in flowchart fashion, how "complete" XML should be seen in relationship to structure and content. Note that the "presentation" is the goal of the coding process, and this requires that you keep the presentation in mind throughout your coding project.

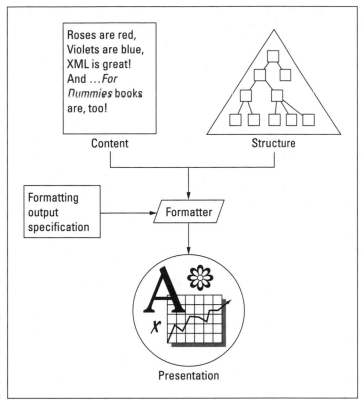

Figure 5-1:
The XML coding process.

SGML is an internationally standardized language for defining sets of tags. HTML represents just one of the element type tag sets that can be created using SGML. Now that the HTML 4.0 DTD has been completely specified, documents can be verified as HTML 4.0-compliant. Because SGML is a subset of XML, the rules of completeness in SGML can hold true for XML as well.

As with SGML documents, XML documents are composed of elements (storage units that contain text and/or binary data). Text is composed of character streams that form both the document's character data content and the document's metadata (externally defined documents) markup. Markup describes the document's storage layout and logical structure. XML also provides a markup mechanism to impose constraints on the storage layout and logical structure of documents, and it provides mechanisms that can be used for good coding.

In style and structure, XML documents resemble HTML documents; however, when Web servers with XML content prepare data for transmission, they typically must generate a context wrapper with each XML fragment, including pointers to an associated DTD and one or more stylesheets for formatting. Web clients that process XML must be able to unpack the content fragment, parse it in context according to the DTD (if needed), render it (if needed) in accordance with the specified stylesheet guidelines, and interpret the hypertext semantics (such as links) associated with each of the different document tags correctly.

Although it does help with document organization, a DTD is not required for an XML document; instead, an author can simply use an application-specific tag set. A DTD is still useful because it allows applications to validate the tag set for proper usage. A DTD specifies the set of required and optional elements (and their attributes) for documents to conform to that type. In addition, the DTD specifies the names of the tags and the relationship among elements in a document.

Well-formed XML implies more than it says

When an XML author creates well-formed attribute/value pairs and start/end tags, the overall project looks clean and logical to the eye. You should, therefore, understand how well-formed *implies* much more than it *says,* especially in regard to the use of attribute/value pairs and start/end tags in XML documents.

The following two examples of Personal Data Card (pCard) documents illustrate the power and simplicity of XML. In the first example, the DTD is given as part of the XML document; in the second example, the DTD is not given, but it exists in an externally defined document (metadata).

In this first example, we look at annotated attribute/value pairs. We write a simple XML document that contains only tags annotated with attribute/ value pairs, which means that the document has no content other than the tags. These tags can then be parsed and processed by software programs.

Our simple example is a document that maintains a list of people's personal electronic cards. In addition, we want each "pCard list tag" to contain five attributes: a person's first name, surname, company, e-mail address, and Web page address. We can specify default values for attributes to guarantee that every tag has the same number of attribute/value pairs (although some values may be null). The declaration of default attributes is lexically scoped (textually searched) by the pCard element (although in this case it has no effect, because none of the elements omits an attribute).

Here's the example with the DTD as part of the document:

```
<!DOCTYPE pCard "http://www.aasu.edu/~jdoe/schemas/pCard">

<pCard
 firstname = "Homer"
 lastname = "Simpson"
 company = "Macrosoft"
 email = "simpson@ms.com"
 homepage = "http://www.ms.com"
/>

<pCard
 firstname = "John"
 lastname = "Doe"
 company = "All American State University"
 email = "doe@mail.aasu.edu"
 homepage = "http://www.myhome.com/~jdoe/"
/>
</pCard>
```

Note how XML's formatting is human-readable as well as machine-readable. Empty lines immediately following a > or immediately preceding a < in the document are ignored by the parser, and white space inside tags is ignored (a situation that is not true for HTML).

In this second example, the DTD is not given but exists in an externally defined document. As a text-based format, XML is designed to store and transmit data. This can be done through arbitrary attribute/value pairs (as demonstrated in the first example), or it can be done by strategically embedding tags around content to give that content more meaning.

Consider the following XML coding:

```
<!doctype html>
<html version="-//W3C//DTD HTML Experimental 970324//EN">
<head>
<title> Jim's pCard List </title>
</head>
<body>

<h1> Jim's pCard List </h1>
```

(continued)

```
<pCard MONTH=1 YEAR=1998>
<FIRSTNAME> John </FIRSTNAME>
<LASTNAME> Doe </LASTNAME>
<COMPANY> All American State University </COMPANY>
<EMAIL> doe@mail.aasu.edu </EMAIL>
<HOMEPAGE> http://www.myhome.com/~jdoe/ </HOMEPAGE>
</pCard>

<pCard MONTH=2 YEAR=1998>
<FIRSTNAME> Homer </FIRSTNAME>
<LASTNAME> Simpson </LASTNAME>
<COMPANY> Macrosoft Corporation </COMPANY>
<EMAIL> simpson@ms.com </EMAIL>
</pCard>

<hr/>
<address><a href="mailto:doe@mail.aasu.edu">
John Doe</a></address>
<!-- Created: Tue Jan 03 01:23:42 MET DST 1998 -->
<!-- hhmts start -->
<!-- Last modified: Fri Jan 23 22:32:42 MET DST
<!-- hhmts end -->
</body>
</html>
```

Note that the DTD is not embedded in the document. We could specify it elsewhere if we needed to validate the tag set and content data structures, or we could omit the DTD.

By binding a meaning to the XML tag <pCard>, we understand what is contained in that element:

- ✔ The start tag
- ✔ The end tag
- ✔ The content between those tags

In this case, the pCard element has two attributes: MONTH and YEAR. These values correspond to the month and year the pCard entry was added. Now, the DTD may specify that the pCard element must contain the FIRSTNAME, LASTNAME, COMPANY, and EMAIL elements, and may contain a HOMEPAGE element as well. Additionally, the DTD may specify that any HOMEPAGE element that does appear in a valid electronic business card document must be nested within a pCard element.

After a document type's elements have been specified in a DTD, the stylesheets, scripts, and programs can be associated with any element in that document type — for example, a custom script, applied to a specific business card entry, that opens a separate fancy window that displays the card in a classy font, color, and arrangement, or a stylesheet associated with the business cards that displays all entries of people at Macrosoft with the Macrosoft logo.

The forms of metadata provided in the first example (attribute/value pairs) and the second example (start/end tags) demonstrate the different ways that document content can be marked up with metadata to enable searching for information in the document, generating information from the document, and filtering the content of the document. Metadata spans a wealth of information, from digital signatures and authentication seals, to prices and time stamps, to links that point to related information.

How to Tell When You've Got It Right

XML enables authors to specify their own document syntax, hypertext link semantics, and presentation style. After you create new tags and elements with the new attribute/value metadata, you can re-encode any systematic, structured document format using XML. If you're a perfectionist, then you'll do well with this step-by-step approach to coding XML.

Chapter 6
Building XML Markup

An XML *Document Type Definition* (or *DTD*) specifies the valid syntax, structure, and format for defining the XML markup elements. If you do not follow the DTD for your XML document, the XML parser and browser will complain about the XML documents that you create. A browser can't properly process and display an XML document that does not conform to the XML DTD that is applied to it. Therefore, gaining a good understanding of and familiarity with XML's DTD is very important.

Remember that XML is a language and the DTD defines the way you can use the language. XML is an object-oriented markup language. As with any other object-oriented language, you can also define or create objects with XML. In addition, you can define attributes for the objects and specify values for the attributes. An XML object is more commonly referred to as an XML *element*. You can represent an XML element by using an XML tag. You can also define attributes for the XML element and specify values for the XML element's attributes. For example, to define an element book, you can use the `<elementType>` ... `</elementType>` tag as shown in this code snippet:

```
<elementType id="automobiles">
   <string/>
</elementType>
```

The following code shows another example of defining an XML element with attributes and values for the attributes:

```
<elementType id="car">
 <attribute name="doors" default="four"/>
</elementType>
```

The preceding code defines an element with id car. The two attributes for the element are name and default. The value for the attribute name is doors. The value for the attribute default is four.

This chapter provides an overview of the XML DTD and shows how you can use the DTD to define schemas for your application's XML data. A *schema* is a pattern that represents the data's model defining the elements (or objects), their attributes (or properties), and the relationships between the different elements. One item that you should note here is that XML has an overarching DTD in which all extensions take part, and that each extension of XML can have a DTD that further defines that extension's data.

Note that the XML specification is evolving and so is the DTD. Although this chapter provides an overview of the XML DTD, the chapter does not cover each and every DTD. By gaining a basic understanding of the XML DTD, you can understand the more advanced definitions easily.

For XML DTD information, visit

```
www.microsoft.com/standards/xml/xmldata.htm
```

To make the information in this chapter more accessible to you, our gentle reader, we first explore exactly what a DTD and a schema are (and why you should care). The bottom line is that the method used to organize your data directly affects how the schema is organized. From there, we'll take a look at the XML tags that you can use to manage your information. Get ready, it's time to dig into the DTD.

What's So Special about an XML DTD?

XML is a special markup language, a language that you can use to represent structured data. XML has its own DTD. Similarly, XML applications such as Chemical Markup Language (CML), Mathematical Markup Language (MathML), and so on, have their own DTDs. (For more about CML, see Chapter 10; for more on MathML, see Chapter 14.)

To represent data in a structured format, you must first understand the markup language's DTD. The following is an example of an XML DTD:

```
<!ENTITY % typelinkattrs
 'id ID #IMPLIED
 type CDATA #IMPLIED'>
```

If the previous example of an XML DTD is about as clear as dishwater, take a look at Chapter 4. In that chapter, we include an explanation of how to read such examples from the XML specification.

An IMPLIED attribute means that you can choose not to specify the attribute and a value for the attribute for the given element, yet the XML parser will not complain. The other option is REQUIRED, which means that you must specify the attribute and a value for the attribute for the given element; otherwise, the XML parser will not like your values.

The preceding DTD specifies that you can define the attributes id and type for an element as shown in the following code:

```
<elementType id="products">
 <string/>
</elementType>

<elementType id="videocards">
 <element type="#products" occurs="ONEORMORE"/>
</elementType>
```

The first definition defines an element with an id of products. The element's contents can be of type string. The second definition defines another element with an id of videocards. In addition, the definition specifies that the element with an id of videocards is of type products. The differentiation to make here is between element type (two words) and the elementType (one word) string. Simply, the element type products is a subset of the first elementType videocards.

Another example of an XML DTD is

```
<!ENTITY % elementAttrs 'occurs
          (REQUIRED|OPTIONAL|ONEORMORE|ZEROORMORE)
          "REQUIRED" '>
```

The preceding DTD specifies that you can define an element with an attribute whose occurs value can be set to one of the four possible options: REQUIRED, OPTIONAL, ONEORMORE, and ZEROORMORE. The default value, as the DTD indicates, is REQUIRED. Note that the DTD indicates the default value within quotation marks.

The following is an example of defining a schema based on the preceding XML DTD:

```
<elementType id="Cities">
    <element type="#state" occurs="OPTIONAL"/>
    <element type="#company" occurs="ONEORMORE"/>
    <element type="#name" occurs="ONEORMORE"/>
</elementType>
```

The schema defines an element with an id of Cities. The element Cities includes three elements: state (occurs="OPTIONAL"), company (occurs="ONEORMORE"), and name (occurs="ONEORMORE"). What all this means is that a Cities element doesn't absolutely require a state element to be valid. A Cities element can also have one or more company elements and one or more name elements.

The following schema defines an element with an id of Cities and the element Cities includes three elements: state, company, and name. The occurs value for the element name is the default: REQUIRED. That is, every Cities element must include a name:

```
<elementType id="Cities">
    <element type="#state" occurs="OPTIONAL"/>
    <element type="#company" occurs="ONEORMORE"/>
    <element type="#name"/>
</elementType>
```

XML is all about representing structured data. To represent data, you must define a schema for the data and then add the data itself. A schema represents the data's model defining the elements (or objects), their attributes (or properties), and the relationships between the different elements. Just as you define a schema or model for your application's relational database management system (RDBMS) — such as Microsoft Access, Sybase SQL Server, Oracle, and so on — you can define a schema or model for your application's XML data. The actual data that you add must meet the model's definitions and rules; that way, you know how the parser and browser are expected to react.

If you do not have a relational model of your data, consider creating one. Basically, a relational model is a division of data into rows and columns, in which columns represent the attributes of object fields and the rows represent instances or records in database-speak. Figure 6-1 shows the relational model for the authors table. The table includes three fields: firstName, lastName, and ssn.

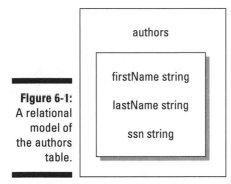

Figure 6-1:
A relational
model of
the authors
table.

To define an XML schema for the authors table, do the following:

1. **Represent each of the three fields within the authors table as an XML element by using the** `<elementType>` ... `</elementType>` **tag pair.**

   You represent these fields as shown in the following code:

   ```
   <elementType id="firstName">
       <string/>
   </elementType>
   <elementType id="lastName">
       <string/>
   </elementType>
   <elementType id="ssn">
       <string/>
   </elementType>
   ```

2. **Represent the authors table itself as another XML element.**

   Within the `authors` element's definition, include a reference to the three fields (or elements) `firstName`, `lastName`, and `ssn`, as shown in this code:

   ```
   <elementType id="authors">
       <element id="fn" type="#firstName"/>
       <element id="ln" type="#lastName"/>
       <element id="sn" type="#ssn"/>
   </elementType>
   ```

What's in a Definition?

To create a DTD, you must define a schema. A schema represents the data's model defining the elements (or objects), their attributes (or properties), and the relationships between the different elements. To define a schema, use the `<s:schema>` ... `</s:schema>` tag pair as shown:

```
<?XML version='1.0'?>
<s:schema id="demographics">
        <elementType id="firstName">
          <string/>
        </elementType>

        <elementType id="lastName">
          <string/>
        </elementType>

        <elementType id="ssn">
          <string/>
        </elementType>

        <elementType id="Person">
          <element id="fn" type="#firstName"/>
          <element id="ln" type="#lastName"/>
          <element id="sn" type="#ssn"/>
          <key id="k1">
            <keyPart href="#fn"/>
            <keyPart href="#ln"/>
            <keyPart href="#sn"/>
          </key>
          <attribute name="title" default="manager"/>
        </elementType>
</s:schema>
```

Here's a breakdown of the parts in this schema:

- ✔ The `<s:schema>` ... `</s:schema>` tag pair's id attribute specifies the schema's name, which is demographics.

- ✔ The declaration defines three elements: firstName, lastName, and ssn.

- ✔ In addition, the schema defines another element Person that includes the three elements (firstName, lastName, and ssn). Together, these three elements constitute the primary key for the element Person. (For more about primary keys, see the sections "Primary key" and "Multi-part primary keys," later in this chapter.)

- ✔ The schema also defines an attribute title for the element Person. The attribute's default value is manager.

Don't worry about trying to understand all the tags (such as `keyPart`) in the previous code block. What we want to focus on in this example is how schemas are formulated and how the parts — element, attribute, and value — work together to create a schema.

Add a Tag for Fun and Profit

After defining the schema for your application's data, you can create the XML file that includes the XML tags and data. In other words, you can create the XML tags and specify values for the tags and their attributes. The following XML is an example of the data you can create based on the schema defined in the preceding section:

```
<Person>
   <firstName>Jackie</firstName>
   <lastName>Chang</lastName>
   <ssn>555-00-1212</ssn>
</Person>
```

Creating XML tags from existing relational data models can be both fun and profitable. XML opens a whole new universe of options and services. For example, if you work with relational databases, you can offer services such as the following:

- ✔ Generate XML data files from existing relational data models; you can even create tools that generate such files
- ✔ Convert or upgrade existing Web sites to benefit from XML
- ✔ Use XSL stylesheets to display the XML data in the browser by using a given stylesheet (see Chapter 8 for more information on XSL stylesheets)
- ✔ Provide rich implementations of Web sites by using XML and XSL with HTML

Add Attributes to Augment Your Documents

The following example of XML data is one that you can create based on the schema defined in the section "What's in a Definition," earlier in this chapter. This example demonstrates the use of the Person element's title attribute. The following example overrides the default value (manager) for the title attribute:

```
<Person title="programmer">
  <firstName>Jackie</firstName>
  <lastName>Chang</lastName>
  <ssn>555-00-1212</ssn>
</Person>
```

By adding attributes to the XML elements, you can characterize the nature and behavior of the XML elements. Combine XML with XSL and you can augment your XML documents by using attributes. For example, you can specify an XSL rule to direct the browser to display the names of all the managers (the attribute is title and the value is "manager") in red. Similarly, you can specify another XSL rule to display the names of all the programmers (the attribute is title and the value is "programmer") in blue.

For more about how to use XSL and about displaying XML documents in an HTML browser, check out Chapter 8.

Making Formal Definitions Pay

This section presents an overview of the different XML tags, their attributes, and how you can use them to define the XML DTD and data for your application. A basic XML DTD consists of an element and the attributes for the element. In addition to using the default attributes for the XML elements, you can define your own attributes and set their values.

The <elementType> ... </elementType> tag pair

To define an element, use the <elementType> ... </elementType> tag pair. To assign an identifier to the element, use the tag's id attribute. The following is an example of declaring an element products by using the <elementType> ... </elementType> tag pair. The definition also specifies that the element products can contain only data of type string, and nothing else:

```
<elementType id="products">
 <string/>
</elementType>
```

The type *attribute*

After defining an element products, you can define additional elements that are of type products. A videocard, for example, is a type of product. To declare another element that is of type products, use the type attribute as shown in this snippet of code:

```
<elementType id="videocards">
 <element type="#products" occurs="ONEORMORE"/>
</elementType>
```

The occurs *attribute*

To specify the number of occurrences of an element within another element, use the element's occurs attribute. Specifying a value of ONEORMORE for the occurs attribute, for example, indicates that the element should occur at least once.

The following is an example of using the occurs attribute. The example uses the products and videocards elements. Note that the videocards element occurs twice (because of the attribute definition ONEORMORE) within the products element:

```
<elementType id="videocards">
 <element type="#products" occurs="ONEORMORE"/>
</elementType>

<products>
 <videocards>MegaUltra 3Dvideo 900</videocards>
 <videocards>VisualWonder MADEX8000</videocards>
</products>
```

The valid values for the occurs attribute are

- REQUIRED
- OPTIONAL
- ZEROORMORE
- ONEORMORE

The following XML markup is another example of using the occurs attribute. The element state is OPTIONAL, and you must have at least one occurrence (ONEORMORE) of the elements company and name:

```
<elementType id="Cities">
  <element type="#state" occurs="OPTIONAL"/>
  <element type="#company" occurs="ONEORMORE"/>
  <element type="#name" occurs="ONEORMORE"/>
</elementType>
```

The following XML markup is valid because the markup satisfies the preceding schema:

```
<Cities>
  <name>Jacksonville</name>
  <company>NationsBank of Florida</company>
  <company>Merrill Lynch</company>
  <state>Florida</state>
</Cities>
```

In addition, the following XML markup that does not include any element of type state is also valid because the schema indicates that the element state is OPTIONAL:

```
<Cities>
  <name>Jacksonville</name>
  <company>NationsBank of Florida</company>
  <company>Merrill Lynch</company>
</Cities>
```

However, the following XML markup is not valid because the markup does not include any element of type company and the schema for element of type Cities specifies that the element company must occur at least once:

```
<Cities>
  <name>Jacksonville</name>
  <state>Florida</state>
</Cities>
```

Defining your own attributes for the elements

In addition to the elements, you can define attributes for the elements. To do so, use the <attribute/> tag as shown in the following lines of code. You can specify a name and a default value for the attribute, as we demonstrate in this code block:

```
<elementType id="organ">
  <element type="#vendor"/>
  <element type="#dealer" occurs="ONEORMORE"/>
  <group groupOrder="OR">
  <element type="#model"/>
  <element type="#price"/>
  </group>
    <attribute name="pipes" default="40"/>
</elementType>

<organ>
 <vendor>Next Generation Calliopes, Inc.</vendor>
    <dealer>First Avenue House of Organs</dealer>
    <dealer>Regency Pipe Organ Company</dealer>
 <price>$15,000</price>
    <model>Circus Screamer 1000</model>
    <pipes>40</pipes>
</organ>
```

Within the schema definition just shown, the attribute tag defines an attribute `pipes` for the element `organ`. In addition, the schema defines the attribute's `default` value as 40. When defining the data that conforms to this schema definition, you can use the attribute `pipes` as shown. The value for this attribute is enclosed within the attribute's tag pairs. Within this example, the value is 40. You can, of course, use a different value depending on your application's requirements. The attribute `pipes` represents an example of defining and using your own attributes for your application's XML elements.

Open and closed content

By default, any XML schema that you define is considered open content unless otherwise specified. The following XML markup shows an example of defining a closed content schema by using the attribute `content="closed"`. A closed content schema cannot contain any elements other than the ones you define in the schema:

```
<elementType id="organ" content="CLOSED">
  <element type="#vendor"/>
  <element type="#dealer" occurs="ONEORMORE"/>
  <group groupOrder="AND" occurs="OPTIONAL">
  <element type="#model"/>
  <element type="#price"/>
  </group>
</elementType>
```

The following XML markup is invalid because the schema that we just defined does not include an element of type `pipes`:

```
<organ>
 <vendor>Monkey Mate Grinders, Inc.</vendor>
    <dealer>Organ Grinders R Us</dealer>
    <dealer>Roadside Musicians Showplace</dealer>
 <price>$1,500</price>
    <model>E-Z Wind Music Maker</model>
    <pipes>4</pipes>
</organ>
```

Grouping the elements

The following XML markup shows an example that uses the `<group>` ... `</group>` tag pair. By using this tag pair, you can specify whether a certain set of elements must occur together. The set of elements together is treated as a single element. For example, the following XML markup indicates that the elements `model` and `price` constitute a group and the elements `model` and `price` must occur together or not at all. In addition, the order in which they occur is also important. The element `model` must precede the element `price` because the *definition* includes the element `model` before the element `price`:

```
<elementType id="organ">
 <element type="#vendor"/>
 <element type="#dealer" occurs="ONEORMORE"/>
 <group occurs="OPTIONAL">
 <element type="#model"/>
 <element type="#price"/>
 </group>
</elementType>
```

The following XML markup is valid because the elements `model` and `price` are not listed at all. The schema we just defined indicates that the occurrence of the group is `OPTIONAL`:

```
<organ>
 <vendor>Classical Wind Machines</vendor>
    <dealer>House of Pulpit Thunder</dealer>
    <dealer>The Pipe Organ Showcase</dealer>
</organ>
```

The following XML markup is also valid because both the elements model and price exist and the element model precedes the element price:

```
<organ>
 <vendor>Classical Wind Machines</vendor>
    <dealer>House of Pulpit Thunder</dealer>
    <dealer>The Pipe Organ Showcase</dealer>
 <model>Sunday Squall 88 w/Wake 'em Up Overdrive</model>
 <price>$105,000</price>
</organ>
```

Grouping order of AND

To define the ordering of a group's elements, use the `<group>` ... `</group>` tag pair's groupOrder attribute. The valid values for the groupOrder attribute are AND and OR. To let the elements within a group appear in any order, use AND as the value of the groupOrder attribute:

```
<elementType id="organ">
 <element type="#vendor"/>
 <element type="#dealer" occurs="ONEORMORE"/>
 <group groupOrder="AND" occurs="OPTIONAL">
 <element type="#model"/>
 <element type="#price"/>
 </group>
</elementType>
```

The following XML markup shows that the element price precedes the element model. This is because the schema that we just defined uses AND as the value of the groupOrder attribute:

```
<organ>
 <vendor>August Wind Instruments</vendor>
    <dealer>Classical Brass, Inc.</dealer>
    <dealer>King's Pump Organ Dealership</dealer>
    <price>$85,000</price>
    <model>Eargeschplittin Loudenboomer</model>
</organ>
```

Grouping order of OR

If any of the group elements will do, use OR as the value of the groupOrder attribute, as shown here:

```
<elementType id="organ">
 <element type="#vendor"/>
 <element type="#dealer" occurs="ONEORMORE"/>
 <group groupOrder="OR">
 <element type="#model"/>
 <element type="#price"/>
 </group>
</elementType>
```

The following XML markup is valid because only one of the group's elements appears (the element `model`), which satisfies the schema that we just defined:

```
<organ>
 <vendor>The Calliope Source</vendor>
    <dealer>Sounds of the Riverboat on Main</dealer>
    <dealer>Circus Supplies and Tentage</dealer>
    <model>New Orleans Gambler Series A</model>
</organ>
```

The following XML markup is also valid because the markup specifies the other group element — `price`. This also satisfies the schema that we just defined:

```
<organ>
 <vendor>The Calliope Source</vendor>
    <dealer>Sounds of the Riverboat on Main</dealer>
    <dealer>Circus Supplies and Tentage</dealer>
 <price>$88,050</price>
</organ>
```

Specifying a default value

To specify a default value for an element, use the `<default>` ... `</default>` tag pair as shown in this code:

```
<elementType id="organ">
 <element type="#type"/>
 <element type="#pipes" occurs="OPTIONAL">
 <default>40</default>
 </element>
</elementType>
```

You can specify default values only for the elements with `occurs` values of `REQUIRED` and `OPTIONAL`. You cannot specify default values for elements with `occurs` values of `ZEROORMORE` or `ONEORMORE`.

The following XML markup is valid because you can specify a default value for an element (in this case, `pipes`) whose `occurs` value is `REQUIRED`:

```
<elementType id="organ">
 <element type="#type"/>
 <element type="#pipes" occurs="REQUIRED">
<default>10</default>
 </element>
</elementType>
```

The following XML markup is invalid because you cannot specify a default value for an element (in this case, `model`) whose `occurs` value is `ONEORMORE`:

```
<elementType id="organ">
 <element type="#price"/>
 <element type="#model " occurs="ONEORMORE">
<default>calliope</default>
 </element>
</elementType>
```

Specifying a fixed default value

To specify that the default value is the only allowed value, use the `<presence="FIXED">` tag with the `<default>` ... `</default>` tag pair as shown in the following code:

```
<elementType id="organ">
 <element type="#type"/>
 <element type="#pipes" occurs="OPTIONAL"
       presence="FIXED">
<default>40</default>
 </element>
</elementType>
```

Numeric values

To specify a valid range for the numeric values, use the `<min>` ... `</min>` and `<max>` ... `</max>` tags as shown in the following:

```
<elementType id="rating">
    <string/>
</elementType>

<elementType id="TVShow">
    <element hef="#rating">
        <min>0</min><max>9</max>
    </element>
</elementType>
```

The mathematical representation is 0 <= rating < 9. That is, the TV show's rating can be greater than or equal to the minimum value, but it must be less than the maximum value. Note that the rating cannot be equal to the maximum value.

Declaring datatypes

To declare an element's datatype, use the `<datatype/>` tag as shown. The `<datatype/>` tag declares the element `size` of `datatype` integer:

```
<elementType id="size">
    <datatype dt="int"/>
</elementType>
```

Primary key

If you have worked with databases, you know the meaning of a primary key. Simply put, a *primary key* is an element's unique identifier. For example, you can identify a house uniquely by its street number and street address. The two identifiers together constitute a primary key. As another example, you can uniquely identify a person by his or her first name, last name, and Social Security number. The three identifiers together constitute a primary key.

Similarly, you can define a primary key for an XML element. The following XML markup defines the elements `isbn` and `book`. The definition for the element `book` declares a primary key by using the `<key>` ... `</key>` tag pair. The primary key identifying the element `book` is the element `isbn`:

```
<elementType id="isbn">
    <string/>
</elementType>

<elementType id="book">
    <element id="p1" type="#isbn"/>
    <key id="k1">
        <keyPart href="#p1"/>
    </key>
</elementType>
```

Multipart primary keys

You can identify a house uniquely by its street number and street address. Each of the identifiers constitutes a key. The primary key identifying a house is multipart: street number and street address. Similarly, you can uniquely identify a person by his or her first name, last name, and Social Security number. The three identifiers constitute a *multipart primary key*.

The following XML markup defines the elements firstname, lastname, and ssn. The definition for the element person declares a multipart key by using the <key> ... </key> and <keyPart> ... </keyPart> tags:

```
<elementType id="firstName">
    <string/>
</elementType>

<elementType id="lastName">
    <string/>
</elementType>

<elementType id="ssn">
    <string/>
</elementType>

<elementType id="Person">
    <element id="fn" type="#firstName"/>
    <element id="ln" type="#lastName"/>
    <element id="sn" type="#ssn"/>
    <key id="k1">
        <keyPart href="#fn"/>
        <keyPart href="#ln"/>
        <keyPart href="#sn"/>
    </key>
</elementType>
```

Foreign key

If you have worked with databases, you know the meaning of a foreign key. Simply put, a *foreign key* is a reference to an element within the definition for another element.

The following XML markup shows an example of declaring the element book as a foreign key within the definition for the element author by using the `<foreignKey/>` tag. The author element's contents are a foreign key identifying a book by isbn:

```
<elementType id="isbn">
    <string/>
</elementType>

<elementType id="book">
    <element id="p1" type="#isbn"/>
    <key id="k1">
       <keyPart href="#p1"/>
    </key>
</elementType>

<elementType id="author">
    <string/>
    <foreignKey range="#book" key="#k1"/>
</elementType>
```

Multipart foreign keys

If more than one identifier constitutes a foreign key, you can declare the multipart foreign key by using the `<foreignKey>` ... `</foreignKey>` and `<foreignKeyPart>` ... `</foreignKeyPart>` tags as shown in the following code block. The author element's definition includes a foreign key reference to the element Person. The identifiers constituting the foreign key are the elements firstName and lastName in this example:

```
<elementType id="firstName">
   <string/>
</elementType>

<elementType id="lastName">
   <string/>
```

```
</elementType>

<elementType id="ssn">
    <string/>
</elementType>

<elementType id="Person">
    <element id="fn" type="#firstName"/>
    <element id="ln" type="#lastName"/>
    <element id="sn" type="#ssn"/>
    <key id="k1">
        <keyPart href="#fn"/>
        <keyPart href="#ln"/>
        <keyPart href="#sn"/>
    </key>
</elementType>

<elementType id="author">
    <element id="ap1" type="#firstName"/>
    <element id="ap2" type="#lastName"/>
    <foreignKey range="#Person" key="#k1">
        <foreignKeyPart href="#ap1"/>
        <foreignKeyPart href="#ap2"/>
    </foreignKey>
</elementType>
```

Hierarchy

The following XML markup shows an example of representing a hierarchy of elements. By representing a hierarchy of elements, you can define the relationships between the elements. A hierarchical representation implies inheritance of the attributes. That is, the child node in the hierarchy inherits the attributes of its parent. You can, of course, override the inherited value in the child node's definition. When you define your application's XML schema, evaluate the relationships between the schema's elements and determine if a hierarchical relationship exists between them. Figure 6-2 illustrates a hierarchical model of automobile data in a database. You can interpret Figure 6-2 as follows: The highest level element is automobiles. Cars and vans are of type automobiles. Two examples of type cars are listed: 4-dr sedans and 2-dr sedans. To represent such a hierarchy, use the <superType/> tag. The following XML markup represents the hierarchy shown in Figure 6-2:

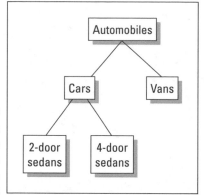

```
<elementType id="automobiles">
  <string/>
</elementType>

<elementType id="cars">
  <superType type="#automobiles"/>
</elementType>

<elementType id="vans">
  <superType type="#automobiles"/>
</elementType>

<elementType id="4-dr sedans">
  <superType type="#cars"/>
</elementType>

<elementType id="2-dr sedans">
  <superType type="#cars"/>
</elementType>
```

Aliases

Sometimes you may want to use the same element in different contexts. For such cases, you can define an alias for the element. An alias represents another name for the element. Also, if the element's original definition specifies a long name for the element, you may want to define an alias representing a shorter name for the element. To define an alias for an element, use the `<correlative/>` tag. The following XML markup defines an element `country` and then defines another element `nation` that is an alias for the element `country`:

```
<elementType id= "country">
    <string/>
</elementType>

<elementType id= "nation">
    <correlative type="#country"/>
    <string/>
</elementType>
```

```
<World>
    <nation>United States of America</nation>
</World>

<Person>
    <name>Henry Ford</name>
    <country>United States of America</country>
</Person>
```

Using elements from other schemas

Sometimes you may want to use elements and attributes that you define for
one schema within another schema. Why? Because this approach promotes
reusability. You can simply reuse the elements and attributes defined for one
schema within another schema, thereby not having to rewrite the elements
and attributes from scratch. Rewriting from scratch creates unnecessary
duplicate code and is obviously not the best approach. To use elements and
attributes from another schema, use the `<element/>` tag's `href` attribute as
shown. Specify the schema's URL along with the element's name (in this
example, the element is `dateofbirth`) as the value of the `href` attribute.
The `dateofbirth` element is shown only as an example. In a real world
application, you would reuse the elements you have already defined that
best fit your application requirements:

```
<?XML version='1.0'?>
<s:schema>
      <elementType id="firstName">
        <string/>
      </elementType>

      <elementType id="lastName">
        <string/>
      </elementType>
```

(continued)

(continued)

```
        <elementType id="ssn">
          <string/>
        </elementType>

        <elementType id="Person">
          <element id="fn" type="#firstName"/>
          <element id="ln" type="#lastName"/>
          <element id="sn" type="#ssn"/>
          <element href="http://employees.lst/dateofbirth"/>
        </elementType>
</s:schema>
```

Show Me the Examples

Before defining the XML data for your application, you must define a schema for the data. A schema defines the structure and relationship of the elements that constitute the data for your application.

This section discusses a couple of examples:

- ✔ The first section discusses an XML schema and shows how you can use the schema to define your application's XML data.
- ✔ The second section discusses the reverse approach. Given the XML data, this example shows how you can arrive at the XML schema for the data.

From the schema to the data

The following schema defines four core elements: name, isbn, price, and description. The schema also defines the element books that comprises the four core elements. Note that the occurrence of the element description within the element books is OPTIONAL. That is, a book may or may not have its description associated with it.

In addition, the schema defines a higher-level element publishers. The element publishers is a higher-level element because the element comprises another element, books. One or more occurrences of the element books must appear within the element publishers. That is, a publisher must have at least one book associated with it.

Schema

```
<?xml:namespace name="urn:uuid:BDC6E3F0-6DA3-11d1-A2A3-
          00AA00C14882/" as="s"/?>
<?xml:namespace href="http://www.ecom.org/schemas/ecom/"
          as="ecom" ?>
<s:schema>
          <elementType id="name">
        <string/>
    </elementType>

    <elementType id="isbn">
        <string/>
    </elementType>

    <elementType id="price">
        <string/>
    </elementType>

    <elementType id="description">
        <string/>
    </elementType>

    <elementType id="books">
        <element type="#name"/>
         <element type="#isbn"/>
         <element type="#price"/>
         <element type="#description" occurs="OPTIONAL"/>
    </elementType>

    <elementType id="publishers">
        <element type="#books" occurs="ONEORMORE"/>
    </elementType>
</s:schema>
```

Data

Based on the schema that we just defined, the following XML markup is valid because the markup satisfies the schema's DTD:

✔ The element books has one or more occurrences within the element publishers.

✔ The data does not include a description for the book *WebTV For Dummies,* but it includes descriptions for the other two books. This is okay because the element description, as we just defined within the schema, is OPTIONAL.

✔ The content of all the four core elements (name, isbn, price, and description) is of type string.

```
<?XML VERSION='1.0'?>
<publishers>
    <books>
        <name>Figure Skating For Dummies</name>
 <isbn>0-7645-5084-5</isbn>
        <price>$19.99</price>
        <description>Figure Skating For Dummies gives you
            the inside scoop about ways to improve and
            enhance your performance.</description>
    </books>
    <books>
        <name>Dating For Dummies</name>
 <isbn>0-7645-5072-1</isbn>
        <price>$19.99</price>
        <description>With Dating For Dummies, you have
            everything you need to make the dating game work
            for you.</description>
    </books>
    <books>
        <name>WebTV For Dummies</name>
        <isbn>0-7645-0150-X</isbn>
        <price>$19.99</price>
    </books>
</publishers>
```

From the data to the schema

This example discusses an approach that's actually the reverse of the example in the previous section. Given the XML data, the example shows how you can arrive at the XML schema for the data. The methodology by which you examine the data to determine a schema for it is actually quite simple. First, build the tree of nodes. Identify the parent node for this tree. Subsequently, identify the child nodes. Then, identify the attributes for each node. From the values of these attributes, determine the data type for each attribute. After you have all this information, you are ready to define the schema.

Data

In this example, the highest level element is Products. Two other elements — VideoCards and DigitalCameras — fall within the element Products. Each of these elements has one or more occurrences within the element Products. The data does not include a description for any of the products because the core element description is OPTIONAL for the elements VideoCards and DigitalCameras. The content of the elements name and price is of type string. The core elements, therefore, are name, price, and description.

```
<?XML VERSION='1.0'?>
<Products>
     <VideoCards>
          <name>CoolVideo</name>
          <price>$189.95</price>
     </VideoCards>
     <VideoCards>
          <name>Cool 3D</name>
          <price>$149.95</price>
     </VideoCards>
     <DigitalCameras>
          <name>MaxView 8000</name>
          <price>$199</price>
     </DigitalCameras>
     <DigitalCameras>
          <name>DigitalView 2000</name>
          <price>$699</price>
     </DigitalCameras>
</Products>
```

Schema

The following schema defines three core elements: name, price, and description. The schema also defines a couple of additional elements
VideoCards and DigitalCameras that comprise the three core elements.

XML is case-sensitive. If you define an element VideoCards with capitals *V*
and *C,* you must use the element's name as it is in the XML data that you define.

Note that the occurrence of the element description within the elements
VideoCards and DigitalCameras is OPTIONAL. In addition, the schema
defines a higher-level element Products. The element Products comprises
both the elements: VideoCards and DigitalCameras. The occurrence of
the elements VideoCards and DigitalCameras within the element Products is ONEORMORE. In other words, you must have one or more occurrences
of both the elements VideoCards and DigitalCameras in the element
Products.

```
<?xml:namespace name="urn:uuid:BDC6E3F0-6DA3-11d1-A2A3-
          00AA00C14882/" as="s"/?>
<?xml:namespace href="http://www.ecom.org/schemas/ecom/"
          as="ecom" ?>
<s:schema>
     <elementType id="name">
          <string/>
     </elementType>
```

(continued)

(continued)

```
        <elementType id="price">
            <string/>
        </elementType>

        <elementType id="description">
            <string/>
        </elementType>

        <elementType id="VideoCards">
            <element type="#name"/>
            <element type="#price"/>
            <element type="#description" occurs="OPTIONAL"/>
        </elementType>

        <elementType id="DigitalCameras">
            <element type="#name"/>
            <element type="#price"/>
            <element type="#description" occurs="OPTIONAL"/>
        </elementType>

        <elementType id="Products">
            <element type="#VideoCards" occurs="ONEORMORE"/>
            <element type="#DigitalCameras"
                occurs="ONEORMORE"/>
        </elementType>
</s:schema>
```

Make your code reusable

The best approach to designing and representing data by using the XML markup elements is to use a relational data model as the basis. If you already have a relational model of your data, you can use the model as the basis for creating the XML schema. If you do not have a relational model of your data, consider creating one.

When creating a schema for your application's XML data, try defining the elements as self-contained objects or units as much as possible. Save the schema separate from the data — in a separate file with the extension .dtd. Keeping the schema separate from the data gives you the opportunity to reuse the schema across several of your other XML applications.

If you are familiar with object-oriented programming, you can think of an XML element as an object and the XML element's attributes as the object's attributes. As a result, the basic principles and benefits of designing reusable code also apply in creating XML DTDs and schemas.

Chapter 7

Meet XML's Multiway Hyperlinks

● ●

In This Chapter

▶ Linking with XML

▶ Comparing pointers to references

▶ Linking bidirectionally

▶ Creating multiway links

● ●

*T*he great thing about the Internet in general, and the Web specifically, is hyperlinking. Hyperlinking allows resources stored on one server to reference resources — not necessarily of the same type — stored on servers across the street or across the world.

SGML, the parent of all markup languages, doesn't support a markup-specific linking mechanism. As far as the rest of the world knows, hyperlinking is specific to HTML. For HTML's sibling XML to be a viable Internet technology, it had to have its own linking mechanism, be compatible with existing HTML linking mechanisms, and also support the extensibility and robustness inherent to XML.

Enter the eXtensible Linking Language (XLL). In Chapter 4, we show you how the initial part of XML specification fully describes the syntax of the language. In this chapter, we show you a second part of the specification that is concerned with linking capabilities of XML documents — capabilities resembling the hypertext features of HTML.

Uncertain proposals in an uncertain world

Although XML is officially a standard, many things about its related technologies — such as stylesheets and linking — are still very much in the development stages. Although links will be an integral part of future implementations of XML, exactly how linking should be implemented in XML is still very much in the discussion stages.

All linking mechanisms and specifics we discuss in this chapter are part of a constantly changing proposal that is still under development. In many cases, we point you to Web sites instead of repeating what they say on the printed page because the sites, and their subject, are guaranteed to change several times throughout the production of this book and for many months afterward.

If you didn't know already, the Web is almost always the most up-to-date resource you can turn to after you've used our book to understand the basics. As long as you keep in mind that everything we discuss here (as well as everything about the Web) is never set in stone, you'll be prepared for anything.

Linking in XML

Start at the very beginning (a very good place to start) with a look at XML's basic linking mechanisms. Before we jump right in, prepare yourself for a linking experience like none you've had before. This ain't your mama's HTML link.

A simple link that you can use to connect an XML document to another Internet resource — not necessarily another XML document — probably has been assigned one of several parameters, including

- One or more strings that describe the role the link plays in the document and that double as a label for the link
- Instructions that tell the user agent what to do with the link, such as
  - Replace the current document
  - Open the link in a new window
  - Insert the contents of the link into the current document
- Specifics on whether the user has to click the link to activate it or whether the link is automatically activated when it's detected by the processing application

In addition, proposed mechanisms will include extended support for "regular" Internet addresses (URLs). Not only will an XML document be able to link to another Internet resource, but also it will be able to point to specific parts of the resource or search the resource. Although HTML can do this by including question marks in URLs for searching or embedding `<A NAME=>` tags within an HTML document to link to a specific point in the document, XML links will be able to do so without either of these special mechanisms.

How will XML do these wondrous things? Listen closely, grasshopper: XML will be able to describe the linked resource in detail, saying things such as "include everything from the fourth paragraph of the third chapter to the end of the fifth chapter" or "only the third sidebar." XML needs to know something about the linked resource's DTD so that it can process the elements, but if HTML is treated as a subset of XML, this means that this specified linking is possible from XML document to XML document or from XML document to HTML document.

To save bandwidth and processing time, the developer can dictate that the linked document or fragment is extracted and stored on the linked document's server (in a cache to be deleted after use). As an alternative, the linked document may be downloaded to the linking document's server and dissected as necessary by the parsing application.

To make things even better (or more confusing), XML links don't necessarily have to be stored in-line but can be stored externally to the document. This means that the links do not have to be included in either of the documents linked together by the link. Links can be stored as a group in one document and activated all at once by the user. Imagine an XML document that really comprises fragments from several other documents, all included in the document at one time when the user loads the document or clicks a link. In addition, you can create collections of interlinked documents and link the collections together.

Comparing Pointers to References

Take a close look at exactly how XML links work. To point or refer to locations in the current document or some other Internet document — not necessarily XML or even SGML-based documents — use these two elements:

- Pointer (`<xptr>`): Links to another location in the current document or one in an external document
- Reference (`<xref>`): Links to another location in the current document or one in an external document; this type of link uses an extended pointer notation that can be modified by additional text or comments

Both pointers and references have these functionality-extending attributes:

- ✔ doc: Identifies the document that contains the reference
- ✔ from: Identifies the beginning of the section of a resource to be linked
- ✔ to: Identifies the end of the section of a resource to be linked

Both the from and to attributes use the TEI extended linking notation. This special notation is described in the Extended Pointers section at the Textuality Web site: www.textuality.com/sgml-erb/WD-xml-link.html. (Note that this is a working draft and will change like a chameleon in no time. If that happens, search for "Extended Pointers" and you should be able to find it.)

If you're familiar with HTML, you probably notice that a target attribute isn't listed in the preceding attributes section. Instead, the elements use the to and from attributes to link all or a part of the resource specified by the doc attribute. For more detailed information, look for the "Simple Links" and "Extended Pointers" sections of the Textuality Web site mentioned at the preceding Web icon.

The from and to attributes use keywords drawn from a predefined list like the one located at the URL that follows. We'd like to include the whole list here, but it will have probably changed at least twice before the book goes to press. For a complete and updated list, check the "Extended Pointers" section on the Textuality Web site at www.textuality.com/sgml-erb/WD-xml-link.html. Pay close attention to the pointer and reference examples given on the site. They, too, will change as the linking proposal does.

For the technically minded (or just plain masochistic) who enjoy reading technical specifications, the pointer and resource elements are formally defined in the XML specification at www.w3.org/TR/1998/REC-xml-19980210. The following is the official section of the specification for describing extended pointers:

```
<!-- 14.2.1: Extended pointers -->
  <!ELEMENT xref  (%paraContent) >
  <!ATTLIST xref %a.global;
%a.xPointer; >


  <!ELEMENT xptr  EMPTY >
  <!ATTLIST xptr %a.global;
%a.xPointer; >
<!-- This fragment is used in sec. 14 -->
```

If you have trouble reading these formal definitions, don't panic! Just check out our discussion in Chapter 4, in which we explain how to read the XML specification. Besides, specification interpretation is a skill worth listing on a résumé!

Rules of the code road

The values of the attributes for the `<xptr>` and `<xref>` elements must be specified in a certain way. If the pointer or reference element doesn't have any attributes at all, it is linked to the *root*. The root is the same as the document element — the top-level element that contains the remainder of the XML document — of the document in which the pointer or reference appears. Using a Web page as an example, the `<HTML>` element is the root. When a user clicks on a link with no attributes, the browser brings up whatever content has been predefined as the default automatically, sort of like a default area in an image map.

Any resource listed as a value for the `doc` attribute must be declared in the document's Document Type Definition (DTD) as an external entity. When a resource is named as the value of the `doc` attribute, the entire resource is linked. Information about what specific portion of the resource should be linked to are given in the values of the `from` and `to` attributes. Here are a few notes about those attributes:

- ✔ If the `from` and `to` attributes are not included, the entire resource is linked to by default.

- ✔ If both the `from` and `to` elements are included, the specified fragment of the resource begins at the point the `from` attribute marks and stops at the end of the string listed in the `to` attribute. Wow, the link begins at `from` and ends at `to` — how hard is that?

- ✔ If the `to` point is before the `from` point, the link is broken. (Okay, so that seems obvious, but we just had to say it.)

- ✔ If only the `from` value is included, the `to` value automatically defaults to the exact same value as the `from` value.

- ✔ Finally, a pointer or reference with a `to` value but without a `from` value is broken.

Linking Up the Web in New Ways

Hyperlinks make the Web go; the `<A HREF="whatever">` idiom has become universal with Web gurus. However, XML extends hyperlinks in a couple of useful directions.

Pick one of these things: Multiple-choice links

Borrowing part of an example from Michael Sperberg-McQueen's post to the W3C (located at lists.w3.org/Archives/Public/w3c-sgml-wg/ 1997May/0493.html), and charging it up a bit, we use the following code to walk you through including a different kind of link in a Web page. The example is taken from a description of a chess tournament:

```
<P>Faced with a tight situation, Karpov found a
<X>
<L ROLE="EG" TITLE="Russian translation"
        SHOW="NEW" HREF="/cgi-bin/xlate?term="checkmate"
        />
<L ROLE="ToMove" TITLE="Jump to move in game record"
        SHOW="REPLACE" HREF="game.html#Move127" />
<L ROLE="PIC" TITLE="Illustration" SHOW="EMBED"
        HREF="pix.xml#DESCENDENT(1,FIG,CAPTION,CHECKMATE)"
        />
<L ROLE="CourseNotes" TITLE="Course Notes"
        HREF="notes.xml#ID
        (def-Checkmate)..DITTO,NEXT(3,P)" />
    checkmate</X>.</P>
```

In a browser, this code would look something like:

Faced with a tight situation, Karpov found a *checkmate*.

When users click on "checkmate," though, they don't get the usual Web behavior of charging off after that link. Instead, they see a menu with four entries:

- **Russian translation:** Choosing the Russian translation runs an ordinary CGI script. The attribute SHOW="NEW" means that rather than replacing the current page, the results of the script would show up in a new window (as if you'd said TARGET=_NEW in an HTML page).

- **Jump to move in game record:** This option, which is a link into an HTML page, would behave exactly as the Web does today.

- **Illustration:** This very interesting option is a link to an XML file. The text after the # in the URL says that the link is to the first FIG element that has the attribute "CAPTION, CHECKMATE". Also, because of the attribute SHOW="EMBED", rather than replace the current page with the page or text that the link refers to, that target material would be inserted in the display at the location of the link.

- **Course Notes:** This option links to a "span" of text in an XML file — specifically, the first three paragraphs following a tag that has the attribute ID="def-Checkmate".

In our humble opinion, these straightforward extensions of the Web's current linking facilities add a lot of richness and cost very little. In the preceding example, one link leads to four more links, each of which contains unique and useful resources.

Going both ways: Bidirectional links

The most important thing to remember about bidirectional links is that they always exist in reverse position, which means that bidirectional links allow the processing system to deduce the inverse relationship between two links. Okay, now in English: Usually, we create links with one direction in mind, but the reader may be just as interested in the reverse link. See?

If future XML linking proposals can include a way to create bidirectional links to protected databases — without endangering the security of the database — the database's content is automatically enhanced because the information from the other end of the link is effectively added to the database. Bidirectional links may also be useful in the wild world of data-management. When a document is moved or deleted, bidirectional links will make finding dangling links much easier.

Every which way but loose: Multiway links

XML-LINK, an extension of the XML language, is one of the most exciting aspects of XML. Even though it isn't part of the XML specification technically, the developers expect that most XML applications will make use of it. XML-LINK allows one part of a document to point to another part and, in doing so, builds a robust data structure. Because it's similar to the pointer mechanisms in C or Java, XML-LINK is well suited for working within complex systems.

Even though you may not know it, you've been working with a subset of XML-LINK when you use the anchor and image tags in HTML. When you click on the contents of an anchor, the contents of the linked resource usually either replace your display with the content or open up a new window to display the content. The only way to have one document's link open the resource on the same screen is to use FRAME, and frames have their own problems. With XML-LINK, you can have some or all of the linked resource replace the current content, open into a new window, or be included with the current document directly, without frames. Combine stylesheet positioning with XML links, and frames will be a thing of the past.

Because the XML-LINK specification is so powerful, it can scale to support many thousands of links or work with a small collection. The ultimate implementation of XML linking will be dependent upon the development of a group of generic, multipurpose applications for both developers and end users. With the popularity of XML growing in leaps and bounds, expect many of these applications to be developed in the near future.

Simple XML links are already implemented in JUMBO, the package created to work with the Chemical Markup Language (CML) vocabulary of XML. For more info on JUMBO and CML, take a peek at Chapter 10.

The simple XML link (`<XML-LINK="SIMPLE">`) has two configurable options, as detailed in the following:

- ✔ `ACTUATE=(user|auto)`

    - **USER:** Specifies that the user should initiate the activation of the link (usually clicking text or an embedded image or button)

    - **AUTO:** Specifies that the link should be automatically activated as soon as the user agent comes in contact with it

- ✔ `SHOW=(new|replace|embed)`

    - **NEW:** Causes the linked resource to be opened into a new window or object; equivalent to the attribute `TARGET=_blank` for the anchor tag in HTML

    - **REPLACE:** Causes the linked resource to be opened into the same window as the referring document, replacing it; equivalent to an anchor tag without a `TARGET` attribute in HTML

    - **EMBED:** Causes the linked resource to be embedded into the referring document — without replacing it, but effectively becoming a part of it; no equivalent for this action in HTML

The settings for these two options are combined into six attributes for the simple link element:

- ✔ **USER REPLACE:** The link is activated by the user, and the contents of the link replace the contents of the referring document.

- ✔ **USER NEW:** The link is activated by the user, and the contents of the link are opened in a new window.

- ✔ **USER EMBED:** The link is activated by the user, and the contents of the link are inserted into the referring document in the same place as the link.

- ✔ **AUTO REPLACE:** The link is automatically activated by the user agent, and the contents of the link replace the contents of the referring document.

✔ `AUTO NEW`: The link is automatically activated by the user agent, and the contents of the link are opened in a new window.

✔ `AUTO EMBED`: The link is automatically activated by the user agent, and the contents of the link are inserted into the referring document in the same place as the link (like HTML's `image` tag).

You can use software such as Panorama Publisher to expand the linking attributes into new areas. For example, you can develop documents with a variety of multiway links to all sorts of applications — both online and off-line — and you are in charge all the way!

An SGML document includes the XML document instance and the DTD that was used to create it. Panorama is flexible because it can understand any DTD. For example, the technical manual that is shipped with Panorama uses the industry standard DOCBOOK DTD, whereas the Acoustic Sound Generator (see Figure 7-1) sample uses the CALS DTD, but they could have published a document based on any valid DTD, including

✔ Air industry standard DTD (ATA)

✔ HTML DTD

✔ Railroad Industry Standard DTD (EPCES)

✔ Your own tailor-made DTD

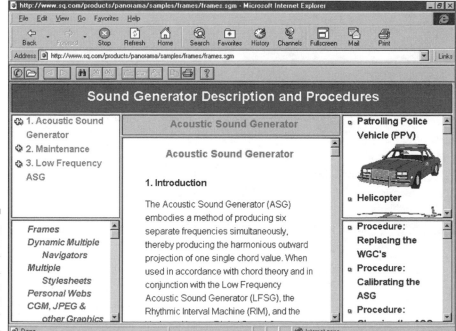

Figure 7-1:
A Panorama
Publisher
creation —
Acoustic
Sound
Generator

For more information on Panorama and other XML authoring tools, check out the Extras section on the CD-ROM. Extra 25 includes descriptions of some of the best tools available, including hyperlinks to more Web-based information and demo downloads. In addition, we've included demo versions of many of these packages right on the CD-ROM, to save you the download time.

Taking Linking to a Whole New Level

Obviously, although the XLL specification and XML linking in general are still in the development stage, a great deal of thought has gone into how the mechanisms should work, what limits of HTML they should replace, how they should work with existing Web linking mechanisms, and how extensible they should be. As with all things about Web XML, linking will change a great deal in the coming months, but its very brief history ensures that its future will be so bright that we'll all have to wear shades.

Chapter 8

Extending Your Sense
of XML Style

●●●

●●●

*T*his chapter presents an overview of the Extensible Style Language (XSL) and how you can use XSL to render formatted output. Throughout this chapter, we detail the features and advantages of using XSL and the tools that you can use to create, edit, and view your XSL files. If you understand the XSL tags and their attributes, you can be programming in XSL in no time.

In this chapter, we also cover XML Styler, an XSL editor from ArborText. And we take you step-by-step through the creation of an XML document with an XSL stylesheet.

Starting with Something Stable: CSS1 and CSS2

A CSS (Cascading Style Sheet) defines the specification for an HTML document's presentation and appearance. For example, you can direct the browser to display a paragraph in green by using CSS. You can direct the browser to display the page's title in a certain font by using CSS. In essence, you can use CSS to define the document's presentation style.

Similarly, XSL (Extensible Style Language) defines the specification for an XML document's presentation and appearance. Both CSS and XSL provide a platform-independent method for specifying the document's presentation style. Presently, two specifications for CSS exist: CSS1 and CSS2. Because CSS2 builds on CSS1, all valid CSS1 stylesheets are valid CSS2 stylesheets.

The W3C (www.w3.org) has already endorsed the CSS1 specification. The CSS2 specification is in the working draft stage. For more information on the CSS1 specification, visit the W3C site.

In the fall of 1997, Microsoft (www.microsoft.com), ArborText (www.arbortext.com), and Inso Corporation (www.inso.com) proposed the XSL specification to the W3C for their approval on making XSL the standard style language for XML documents. XSL is based on DSSSL (Document Style Semantics and Specification Language). In fact, DSSSL is a superset to XSL. DSSSL is a document style language used primarily with SGML (Standard Generalized Markup Language) files.

Examining the XML Style Language (XSL)

You can define two types of rules within an XSL stylesheet: construction rules and style rules.

- ✔ Defining a *style rule* includes specifying a pattern and an action that the rule applies when the specified pattern is found. In other words, you can tell XML that every time a certain instance occurs, a specified action should be taken.

- ✔ Defining a *construction rule* involves specifying a pattern and constructing an element (for example, constructing a division by using the `<DIV> ... </DIV>` tags) when the specified pattern is found.

The following code provides an example of an XSL style rule. As the code shows, an XSL rule defines the presentation and appearance of an XML document's target elements:

```
<xsl>
 <style-rule>
 <target-element type="products"/>
 <apply font-weight="italic"/>
 </style-rule>
</xsl>
```

The definition is enclosed within a pair of <xsl> ... </xsl> tags. Just as you enclose the CSS style definitions for an HTML document within a pair of <STYLE> ... </STYLE> tags, you enclose the XSL construction and style rules within a pair of <xsl> ... </xsl> tags. The XSL style rule shown here indicates that the target element (that is, the element to which the style rule will be applied) is of type products. The rule also indicates applying the font style of italic to the target element.

XML is a case-sensitive language. All XSL tags are lowercase.

Each style rule includes a pattern and the action to be applied to the pattern. The pattern in the preceding code is <target-element type="products"/> and the action is <apply font-weight="italic"/>. This code produces an italic font for all products element types.

The next code block is an example of an XSL construction rule. The rule applies to target elements of type automobiles. The rule constructs a division (using the <DIV> ... </DIV> tags) with the given characteristics (font size of 14 points and the serif font family) for each element of type automobiles. The <DIV> tag indicates divisions in a document and can be used to group block elements together. Because the <DIV> ... </DIV> tag includes the <children/> tag, the rule also applies to all the child elements of type automobiles:

```
<xsl>
 <rule>
 <target-element type="automobiles"/>
 <DIV font-size="14pt"; font-family="serif">
 <children/>
 </DIV>
 </rule>
</xsl>
```

The pattern in this code is <target-element type="automobiles"/> and the element constructed is <DIV font-size="14pt"; font-family="serif"><children/></DIV>. The outcome of this code would produce 14 point serif for all automobiles element types and all child elements of automobiles.

Putting Things Right: Positioning Objects

Using an element's position attribute, you can qualify the patterns within the style rules, in that you can specify the element's position with respect to its siblings. The valid values for position are

✔ `first-of-type`: The element must be the first sibling of its type.

✔ `last-of-type`: The element must be the last sibling of its type.

✔ `first-of-any`: The element must be the first sibling of any type.

✔ `last-of-any`: The element must be the last sibling of any type.

The following code shows an example of using the position attribute. The style rule shown applies the specified action (`font-weight="italic"`) to the first target element of `type products`. In other words, the first instance of element type `products` will be rendered in italics.

```
<xsl>
 <style-rule>
 <target-element type="products" position="first-of-type"/>
 <apply font-weight="italic"/>
 </style-rule>
</xsl>
```

The following code shows another example of using the `position` attribute. The style rule shown applies the specified action (`font-weight="bold"`) to the last target element of `type telephones`:

```
<xsl>
 <style-rule>
 <target-element type="telephones" position="last-of-type"/
      >
 <apply font-weight="bold"/>
 </style-rule>
</xsl>
```

Similarly, you can use the position attribute to apply style rules to the first target element of any type (`position="first-of-any"`) and the last target element of any type (`position="last-of-any"`).

Cooking Up Coherent Styles

Using XSL styles, you can define named styles and inline styles. You can define scripts and macros in your XSL stylesheets. You can also import one XSL stylesheet into another.

Keep in mind, however, that the XSL specification is evolving. To keep abreast of the latest and greatest on the XSL specification, visit the site at `www.microsoft.com/standards/xsl/xslspec.htm`.

Named styles

By using named styles, you can assign a name to the style. After you assign a name to the style, you can apply the style to as many elements as you want. Naming a style is similar to declaring a function and then using the function at as many places in your application as you need to.

The following code shows how you can create a named style by using the `<define-style/>` tag to define a style object. You can use a named style in both style rules and construction rules; this code produces a font style in italics:

```
<define-style name="font-style"; font-weight="italic"/>
```

The following code shows an example of using the named style in a style rule:

```
<style-rule>
 <target-element type="products"/>
 <font-style quadding="center"/>
</style-rule>
```

This code produces a style rule that states that all `products` element types are centered.

The following code shows an example of using the named style in a construction rule:

```
<rule>
 <element type="chapter">
 <target-element type="heading"/>
 </element>
 <paragraph use="title-style">
 <children/>
 </paragraph>
</rule>
```

This code produces a construction rule that applies the named style `title-style` to all the `chapter` element types. The `chapter` element types include the `heading` element types.

Inline styles

Sometimes, you don't really need to create a complete XSL file because you need to style only one or two of the elements in the XML document. In such cases, you can use *inline styles*. You use an inline style to declare a style for an element in the XML document itself. The following code shows an example of defining an inline style. To define an inline style, use the XSL `namespace` followed by two colons. Then, specify the property whose value you want to set, followed by the value itself, as shown in the following line of code:

```
<PARA xsl::background-color="orange">
```

This code produces a paragraph style with a background color of orange.

The next piece of code shows another method that you can use to define an inline style. Define a construction rule and specify a value for the rule's ID. To associate the rule with an element, use the rule's ID, as shown in the following bit of code (the ellipsis — three dots — shows that more code can go in that spot):

```
<rule>
 <target-element id="myrule"/>
        <SPAN font-weight="bold" color="white">
        <children/>
        </SPAN>
</rule>
...
<PARA id="myrule">
```

This code produces a construction rule that states that all `myrule` element types are white and use a bold font style.

Scripts

You can write scripts by using the `<define-script>` ... `</define-script>` tag and then use the script in a construction or style rule. Within the script, you can define both functions and variables. The following code shows an example of an XSL script:

```
<define-script>
 var incrMargin = "30";
 function newMargin(currMargin){
 return (incrMargin + currMargin);}
</define-script>
<rule>
 <target-element type="heading"/>
 <DIV margin-right=newMargin(10)>
        <children/>
 </DIV>
</rule>
```

This code defines a script and produces a construction rule. The script defines the function `newMargin()`, and that function returns the sum of the current margin and the variable `incrMargin`'s value. The construction rule states that all `heading` elements use a right margin, the value of which is the `newMargin()` function's return value.

Macros

You can group HTML and CSS objects together by defining a macro and then reuse the macro across multiple rules. To define a macro, use the `<define-macro>` ... `</define-macro>` tag. After defining the macro, you can use the macro as a tag in the XSL rule.

The following code shows an example of aggregating the objects `<DIV>` ... `</DIV>`, `<paragraph>` ... `</paragraph>`, and `<contents>` ... `</contents>` into a single macro welcome-message and then using the macro for target elements of `type welcome`:

```
<define-macro name="welcome-message">
 <DIV>
 <paragraph>
 Welcome to CyberTetris!
 <contents/>
 </paragraph>
 </DIV>
</define-macro>
<rule>
 <target-element type="welcome"/>
 <welcome-message font-weight="bold">
 <children/>
 </welcome-message>
</rule>
```

This code defines a macro (`welcome-message`) and produces a construction rule. The macro defines a paragraph text. The construction rule states that all `welcome` element types call the `welcome-message` macro and apply a font style of bold.

Importing stylesheets

You can nest XSL stylesheets by importing one XSL stylesheet into another XSL stylesheet using the `<import/>` tag:

```
<import href="mystyle.xsl">
```

This code imports the XSL stylesheet, `mystyle.xsl`.

XSL Tools and Resources

In this section, we examine a few of the available XSL tools (Microsoft XSL command-line utility, XML Styler, and DocProc). You can use the Microsoft XSL command-line utility to generate HTML files from XML data files and XSL stylesheets. ArborText's XML Styler includes a graphical user interface that you can use to edit and manipulate your application's XSL stylesheets. DocProc is an XSL processor.

Microsoft XSL command-line utility

You can download Microsoft's XSL command-line utility by following these steps:

1. **Point your browser at** www.microsoft.com/xml/.

   A framed page appears.

2. **Click the <u>XSL Stylesheets</u> link in the leftmost (navigation) frame.**

   Information about XSL appears in the rightmost (information) frame.

3. **Scroll down a bit in the information frame and click the <u>MS XSL Processor</u> link.**

   Another page appears in the information frame.

4. **Scroll down a bit in the information frame and click the <u>Microsoft XSL Command-line Utility</u> link.**

   Yet another page appears in the information frame. This latest page contains information about the command-line utility.

5. **Read the text and follow the directions to download the processor and the samples.**

You can use a browser such as Navigator or Internet Explorer to view the HTML files that the MSXSL utility generates. Both of these browsers include the Java Virtual Machine (JVM), so you don't need to install the JVM separately.

Using the Microsoft XSL command-line utility, you can generate HTML files from XML data files and XSL stylesheets. You can then view the HTML files in your browser. To try out this utility, just follow these steps:

1. **Install the MS XSL command-line utility and samples in a directory (\XSL, for example).**

   Now you want to switch to the DOS prompt in Windows 95.

2. **In Windows 95, choose Start⇨Run.**

   The Open dialog box appears.

3. **Type** command **in the text field of the dialog box and click OK.**

    Windows 95 starts a DOS session, and you see the traditional command prompt (something like C:\Windows).

4. **Switch to the directory in which you stored the utility.**

    We stored ours in \XSL. Now you can use the utility.

5. **See how the utility works by typing the following at the command prompt and pressing Enter:**

```
msxsl -i sample.xml -s sample.xsl -o view1.html
```

    The `-i` parameter specifies the input file (`sample.xml`), the `-s` parameter specifies the XSL file (`sample.xsl`), and the `-o` parameter specifies the output file (`view1.html`). To view the HTML file, open `view1.html` in Internet Explorer.

You can also try a different stylesheet (for example, `alternate.xsl`) and view the results in Internet Explorer. The download includes the file `alternate.xsl`.

The HTML files generated by the command-line utility work when viewed by both Internet Explorer 4 and Netscape Navigator 4. This is not the case with the HTML files that use the Microsoft XSL ActiveX control. The HTML files that use the Microsoft XSL ActiveX control work only with Internet Explorer 4. Netscape Navigator does not include built-in support for ActiveX controls. (See the section "XSL gets active!," later in this chapter, for more about that control.)

ArborText XML Styler

XML Styler by ArborText provides a graphical user interface (GUI) to create, edit, and manipulate your XML stylesheets. XML Styler makes it easy for you to create XSL stylesheets because you do not need to remember the syntax of the different XSL commands for creating patterns, actions, and so on.

XML Styler is written in standard Java. Presently, XML Styler is available for the Windows 95 and Windows NT platforms only. You can download XML Styler Version 0.9 from the ArborText Web site at `www.arbortext.com`.

Although XML Styler is written in standard Java, the product is currently "bound" into a WIN32 executable that uses the Microsoft Java Virtual Machine (JVM). Therefore, to run the current version of XML Styler, you must have Internet Explorer 4.x installed on your system. ArborText plans to release an "unbound" version of XML Styler, which you can run with the Sun JVM (or others).

To view the result of applying the XSL stylesheet that you create with XML Styler, you must install the Microsoft XML ActiveX control to run with Internet Explorer 4.*x*. You can then apply the XSL stylesheet to an XML document and see the results in Internet Explorer 4.*x*. Presently, Internet Explorer 4.*x* is the only browser that supports XSL.

Docproc

Sean Russell (from the University of Oregon Department of Physics) wrote Docproc, an XSL processor, using Java. Docproc supports all three types of objects: HTML, CSS, and DSSSL objects. You can download Docproc, including the source code, from `jersey.uoregon.edu/ser/software/docproc_1/`.

XSL gets active!

Presently, the Microsoft XSL ActiveX control tool is available for use with XSL. Using the Microsoft XSL ActiveX control, you can view XML data that uses the XSL stylesheets in Internet Explorer. As a result, you do not need a separate browser to view the results of applying the XSL stylesheets to XML documents.

You can find out a whole lot about the ActiveX control by following these steps:

1. **Point your browser at** `www.microsoft.com/xml/`.

   A framed page appears.

2. **Click the <u>XSL Stylesheets</u> link in the leftmost (navigation) frame.**

   Information about XSL appears in the rightmost (information) frame.

3. **Scroll down a bit in the information frame and click the <u>MS XSL Processor</u> link.**

   Another page appears in the information frame.

4. **Scroll down a bit in the information frame and click the <u>Microsoft XSL ActiveX Control</u> link.**

   You have arrived at your final destination: A page about the ActiveX control appears in the information frame.

An ActiveX control is a reusable object based on the Microsoft ActiveX technology. ActiveX is not a programming language. It is a set of technologies that includes ActiveX controls, Active Server Pages, Active documents, ActiveX scripting, and so on.

For more information on ActiveX technology, visit the Microsoft Web site at www.microsoft.com/activex.

If you use Internet Explorer and you want to better understand how the Microsoft XSL ActiveX control works, look at a simple XSL ActiveX control demo. Point your browser to www.microsoft.com/xml/xsl/XMLViewerDemo/XMLViewer.htm. If this is the first time you are visiting the site, Internet Explorer downloads, installs, and registers the XSL ActiveX control automatically. Isn't this wonderful? The browser is taking care of installing and registering the necessary components on your system! Note that the XSL ActiveX control works only with Internet Explorer 4. Internet Explorer displays the page, as shown in Figure 8-1.

As you can see, the browser displays the XML data in a very basic format. Notice the different XSL stylesheets that are available on the browser's left side view. To apply a particular stylesheet and view the results in Internet Explorer, point your mouse to the XSL Stylesheets column and click the name of the stylesheet that you want to attach. For example, if you click bids-table.xsl, the browser displays the results of the raw XML code shown in Figure 8-1 in a tabular format, as shown in Figure 8-2.

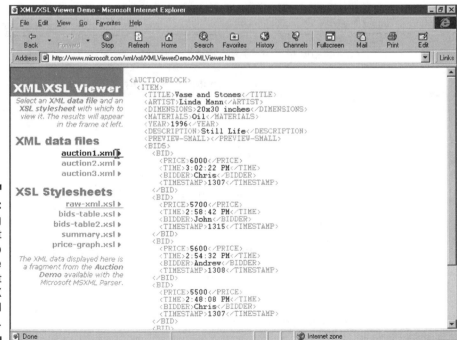

Figure 8-1: Using Internet Explorer to view the Microsoft XSL ActiveX control demo.

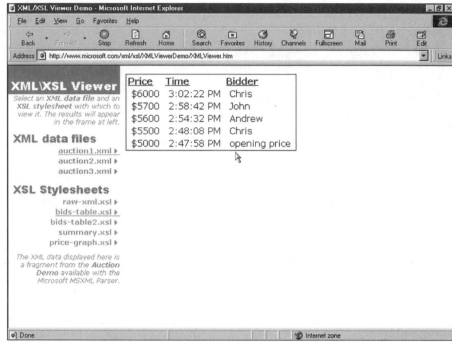

Figure 8-2:
Applying
the `bids-table.xsl`
stylesheet.

As the demo shows, the XSL ActiveX control lets you view the results of applying an XSL stylesheet to an XML data file in Internet Explorer. You need these components and files: XSL ActiveX control, XML data file, XSL stylesheet, and Internet Explorer. That's it!

The XSL ActiveX control demo does not work in Netscape Navigator because Netscape Navigator does not support ActiveX technology.

Creating XSL Stylesheets

You can create XSL stylesheets in two ways. You can use your favorite text editor (Notepad or WordPad, for example) to create the stylesheets. This is obviously the hard way because you must type every line of code manually, making the probability of introducing errors higher. In addition, you must also format and indent the code manually. Internet Explorer 4 includes an XML parser written in C++ and optimized for performance. However, this XML parser is non-validating. That is, the parser cannot identify errors in the code. Microsoft distributes the source code for a validating XML parser (`www.microsoft.com/xml`), written in Java, that developers can use to incorporate into their applications.

Use a GUI editor, such as XML Styler by ArborText, for an easier way to create XSL stylesheets. XML Styler takes the headache away from remembering each and every command, its syntax and structure, and so on. Simply point and click your way to creating the stylesheets.

XML Styler is a new product — Version 0.9. We can certainly expect enhancements and modifications to this tool as both XML and XSL gain popularity and the vendor works on improving the tool. In addition, we can expect new tools from other vendors.

The following sections explain both methods of creating XSL stylesheets. To view the results in Internet Explorer, make sure that the Microsoft XSL ActiveX control is installed and registered on your system. Note that the XSL ActiveX control works only with Internet Explorer 4. This control does not work with Netscape Navigator 4 because Navigator does not support ActiveX controls. (See the section "XSL gets active!," earlier in this chapter, to find out how to install the ActiveX control.)

The following steps outline how XML, XSL, and HTML work together:

1. **Create the XML document containing the data.**
2. **Create the XSL stylesheet containing the style and construction rules.**
3. **Create the HTML document that uses the XML data and XSL rules.**
4. **Load your browser, point it to the HTML file, and view the XML document as styled by the XSL stylesheet.**

The following subsections explain these steps in further detail.

All the files you create in the next few subsections must reside within the same directory in order for them to work.

Creating a stylesheet by hand

Follow these steps to create and view XML data in Internet Explorer using XSL stylesheets:

1. **Create the XML document.**

   You can create the XML document by using an XML editor or by using your favorite text editor (such as Windows Notepad). The following shows the code for a sample XML document file, which you should name `products.xml`:

```
<?XML VERSION='1.0'?>
<Products>
    <Communications>
        <name>email 97</name>
        <price>$37.95</price>
        <description>email 97 is the electronic mail
            management system for you!</description>
    </Communications>
    <WebDesign>
        <name>Emblaze WebCharger</name>
        <price>$89.95</price>
        <description>Improve the appearance and perfor-
            mance of your Web site with WebCharger.</de-
            scription>
    </WebDesign>
    <Graphics>
        <name>QuarkXPress 4</name>
        <price>$689.95</price>
        <description>QuarkXPress 4 gives you the tools to
            express your ideas with innovation and imagina-
            tion.</description>
    </Graphics>
</Products>
```

Note that, in the above code, the products.xml document includes the
following hierarchy of tags. These tags are case-sensitive. The style
rules that you create in the next step depend on these tags. For example, a style rule for the Products tag does not work for the PROD-
UCTS tag.

```
Products
    Communications
        name; price; description
    WebDesign
        name; price; description
    Graphics
        name; price; description
```

2. Save the XML document and create the XSL stylesheet.

You can create the XSL stylesheet by using an XML editor or by using
your favorite text editor (such as Windows Notepad). The following
shows the code for a sample XSL stylesheet file, which you should
name products.xsl:

```
<xsl>
 <rule>
   <root/>
   <HTML>
```

```
        <BODY font-family="Arial, helvetica, sans-serif"
           font-size="12pt" background-color="#EEEEEE">
          <children/>
        </BODY>
     </HTML>
  </rule>
  <rule>
     <target-element type="Communications"/>
     <DIV background-color="orange" color="white"
        padding="4px">
          <select-elements>
             <target-element type="name"/>
          </select-elements>
          :
          <select-elements>
             <target-element type="price"/>
          </select-elements>
        </DIV>
     <DIV margin-left="15px" margin-bottom="1em" font-
        size="11pt">
          <select-elements>
             <target-element type="description"/>
          </select-elements>
        </DIV>
  </rule>
  <rule>
     <target-element type="WebDesign"/>
     <DIV background-color="red" color="white"
        padding="4px">
          <select-elements>
             <target-element type="name"/>
          </select-elements>
          :
          <select-elements>
             <target-element type="price"/>
          </select-elements>
     </DIV>
     <DIV margin-left="15px" margin-bottom="1em" font-
        size="11pt">
          <select-elements>
             <target-element type="description"/>
          </select-elements>
     </DIV>
  </rule>
  <rule>
```

(continued)

(continued)

```
    <target-element type="Graphics"/>
    <DIV background-color="blue" color="white"
        padding="4px">
        <select-elements>
            <target-element type="name"/>
        </select-elements>
        :
        <select-elements>
            <target-element type="price"/>
        </select-elements>
    </DIV>
    <DIV margin-left="15px" margin-bottom="1em" font-
        size="11pt">
        <select-elements>
            <target-element type="description"/>
        </select-elements>
    </DIV>
</rule>
<rule>
    <target-element type="name"/>
    <SPAN font-weight="bold" color="white">
        <children/>
    </SPAN>
</rule>
<rule>
    <target-element type="price"/>
    <children/>
</rule>
<rule>
    <target-element type="description"/>
    <SPAN font-style="italic">
        <children/>
    </SPAN>
</rule>
</xsl>
```

Within the stylesheet, you define a construction rule for the root HTML
level — that is, the HTML document's body. In addition, you define construction rules for the target elements Communications, WebDesign, and
Graphics.

For each of these target elements, you define a background color by using
the <DIV> ... </DIV> tag. To display the product's name and price within
the target element's background color, you use the <SELECT-ELEMENTS> tag.
To display the product's description below the product's name and price,

you use the `<DIV>` ... `</DIV>` tags. The properties you set for the two divisions or sections of the page are different. For the first division (the page's first section), you set the background color, foreground color, and padding properties. For the second division, you set the division's left and bottom margin and specify the font size.

In addition, you define construction rules for the `name`, `price`, and `description` tags. In the `name` tag's construction rule, you use the `<SPAN>` tag to display the data in a structured format (foreground color of white and font weight of bold). In addition, you include the `<children/>` tag so that the rule applies to all of the `name` tag's children, if any. Similarly, you define construction rules for the `price` and `description` tags.

You have one more step before you can view the contents of your XML document as styled by the XSL stylesheet. You need to create an HTML document that you can use to view the information in the XML document. To create the document, see the subsection "Creating the HTML document," later in this chapter.

Creating a stylesheet in XML Styler

You can use the ArborText XML Styler to create stylesheets. In fact, you can open in XML Styler a stylesheet like the one created in the preceding subsection, "Creating a stylesheet by hand." XML Styler recognizes the construction rules that you define and presents them in the Construction Rules tab, as shown in Figure 8-3. The XML Styler displays five additional tabs: Style Rules, Named Styles, Macros, Scripts, and ID/Class Names.

XML Styler is still in its infancy stage. As a result, it is not a robust product yet. Presently, the tool does not include everything that you may be looking for from an XSL editor.

As an example of using XML Styler, try creating a construction rule for the `Communications` tag. As the following steps show, you want to set the background color, foreground color, and padding properties for the page's section that displays information about the communications products.

Before you follow the next set of steps, you need to create the XML document as detailed in the preceding subsection, "Creating a stylesheet by hand." The steps in this section require that the document `products.xml` exists.

To create a construction rule for `Communications` using XML Styler, follow these steps:

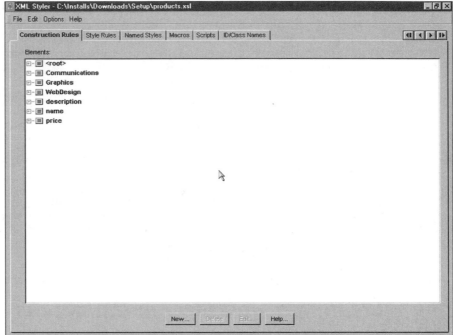

Figure 8-3:
XML Styler
displaying
the
construction
rules
defined
within the
`products.`
`xsl` file.

1. **Open XML Styler.**

   The application prompts you to create a new stylesheet (default) or to open an existing stylesheet. To proceed with the default choice, click OK. XML Styler displays the New Style Sheet – Collect Tags dialog box.

2. **In the New Style Sheet dialog box, choose Collect Tags.**

3. **Choose the second option (Yes, Collect Tag Names from an Existing Document), specify the path for the XML document (`products.xml`), and click Next.**

   XML Styler displays the New Style Sheet – Default Font dialog box. The dialog box prompts you to specify the default choices for font size, font weight, and font family.

4. **Accept the default choices and click OK.**

   XML Styler reads the tags from the XML document and displays them in the XML Styler – untitled.xsl window.

5. **To add a new rule to a tag, click on the tag once to highlight it (for example, Communications) and click New.**

   XML Styler displays the Describe New Element – Element Name window, as shown in Figure 8-4.

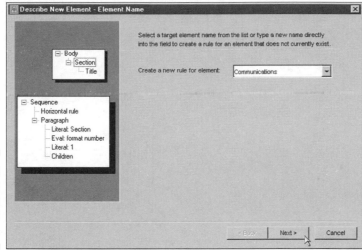

Figure 8-4:
Describing
the new
element in
XML Styler.

6. **Accept the default option (Communications) and click Next.**

   XML Styler displays the Describe New Element – Flow Object Used window.

7. **Specify the HTML or CSS object that you want to use in the rule (in this case, DIV), and then click Finish.**

   XML Styler returns you to the XML Styler – untitled.xsl window.

8. **To edit the rule for the Communications tag, double-click Communications, and then double-click By Itself.**

   XML Styler displays the Edit Rule window.

9. **Click DIV in the Edit Rule window's right pane.**

10. **In the Font tab, choose white from the Color drop-down list box, and choose blue in the Background Color drop-down list box, as shown in Figure 8-5.**

As you can see, the tool does not provide a way to add another property (for example, padding) and a value for the property (4px) because the tool is still in its first release. As ArborText works on improving the tool and its features, we can expect a better and efficient version of the tool in the future.

Presently, the best way to create XML stylesheets is by first using XML Styler and then using Notepad or WordPad to include the additional properties and their values, if need be.

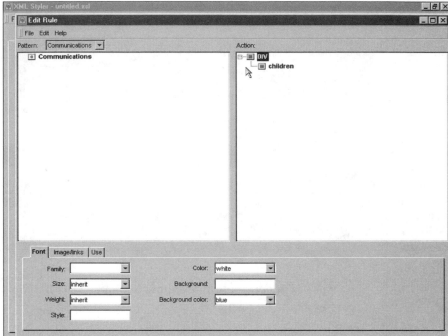

Figure 8-5:
Specifying
the
attributes
for the
<DIV> tag.

11. Save the stylesheet as products.xsl.

12. Create the HTML file products.htm.

As stated in the final step, you need to create an HTML document that you can use to view the information in the XML document. To create the document, see the subsection "Creating the HTML document," next in this chapter.

Creating the HTML document

You can view an XML document, as styled by an XSL stylesheet, through an HTML document and a browser. If you create the XML document products.xml and the stylesheet products.xsl by either method outlined earlier in this chapter (in the sections "Creating a stylesheet by hand" and "Creating a stylesheet in XML Styler"), then you can use the HTML code in this section to create products.htm (or products.html, if you use a Macintosh). Create the HTML file by using your favorite HTML editor, such as Microsoft FrontPage 98 or Sausage Software's Hot Dog, or type the HTML code in Windows Notepad or your favorite text editor.

You may decide to build the HTML file using any of a number of programs available on the market today. We can't include steps that cover every possible HTML editor, but we can describe what elements must appear in the HTML document and how they need to relate with each other.

As you read the paragraphs describing how the HTML code works, be sure to refer to the code block for all the details.

Within the HTML file, you need to include a reference to the Microsoft XSL ActiveX control by using the <OBJECT/> tag. The control's ID parameter specifies the control's name, the classid parameter specifies a unique hexadecimal identifier for the control, and the codebase parameter specifies the URL that the browser downloads from, and then installs and registers the control if it is not already registered on your system.

In addition, you should include the parameters documentURL and styleURL. The documentURL parameter specifies the XML document (products.xml) and the styleURL parameter specifies the XSL document (products.xsl), as shown in the following code. Without this information, the Microsoft XSL ActiveX control does not know what XML document to display in the browser or how to display it.

Using the <DIV> ... </DIV> tag, you can define a division in the Web page and assign the ID of xslTarget to the division. This is the division, or rather section, of the page where the browser displays the XML data. In addition, you can write a script for the window's onload event. In the script, you declare a variable xslHTML and assign the value of the XSLControl. htmlText property to the variable. Then, you assign the variable to the xslTarget section's innerHTML property, as shown in the following code. In effect, you are assigning the ActiveX control's htmlText property to the division's innerHTML property so that the browser displays the XML data in the specified division. Check out the following code for the details:

```
<HTML>
<HEAD>
<TITLE>Product Catalog</TITLE>
</HEAD>
<SCRIPT FOR="window" EVENT="onload">
var xslHTML = XSLControl.htmlText;
document.all.item("xslTarget").innerHTML = xslHTML;
</SCRIPT>
<BODY>
<OBJECT ID="XSLControl"
CLASSID="CLSID:2BD0D2F2-52EC-11D1-8C69-0E16BC000000"
CODEBASE="http://www.microsoft.com/xsl/xsl/msxsl.cab"
```

(continued)

(continued)

```
STYLE="display:none">
<PARAM NAME="documentURL" VALUE="products.xml">
<PARAM NAME="styleURL" VALUE="products.xsl">
</OBJECT>
<DIV id="xslTarget"></DIV>
</BODY>
</HTML>
```

To view the results, open the HTML file in Internet Explorer (see Figure 8-6).

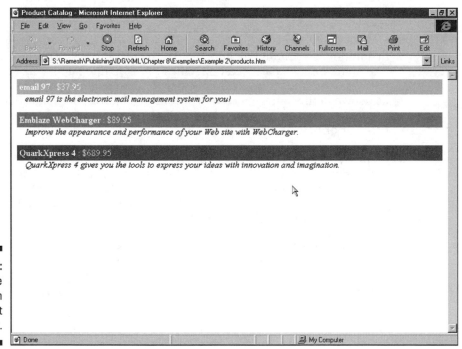

Figure 8-6:
Viewing the
XML data in
Internet
Explorer.

When Will XSL Be Ready for Prime Time?

For XSL to become popular in the Web community, XML must first become an industry standard in representing structured data. In addition, both XML and XSL must gain the W3C's approval and become the established standards within the industry. In the fall of 1997, Microsoft, ArborText, and Inso Corporation proposed the XSL specification to the W3C for their approval on making XSL the standard style language for XML documents.

As both XML and XSL gain popularity, a number of vendors will develop GUI (graphical user interface) tools that make creating, editing, and manipulating XML and XSL files easy. This chapter discussed one such tool in XML Styler by ArborText. So far, the Microsoft XSL ActiveX control is the only component that you can use to view the results of applying XSL stylesheets to XML data files. As XML and XSL become recognized standards in the industry, both Netscape and Microsoft are expected to provide built-in support for reading and displaying XML data in their browsers.

Chapter 9

Named Entities

*I*f you've read any DTDs or have extensive HTML experience, you've seen cryptic notations such as < or °. "Odd," you may think, "wonder what those little beasties do?" Well, they're simply a way to instruct the parser that reads and interprets XML (or HTML, for that matter) to replace these placeholders with equivalent characters or strings from the DTD, or related definitions, to render a document.

These symbols are called character or numeric *entities*. When you view an XML document with the < character entity, you see the less-than sign (<) on your computer screen, whereas the entity °, which may also be denoted as ° (if you have the right DTD), produces the degree symbol (°).

Entities are necessary for three important reasons:

➤ You use entities to represent higher-order ASCII characters in an XML viewer. *High-order characters* are those with codes above 127. Also, entities can support characters outside the ASCII set (such as non-Roman alphabet character sets and certain commonly used diacritical marks).

➤ By using entities, you can create documents that contain the special characters (such as mathematical notation) necessary for your end result (such as a heavily annotated math Web page). XML viewers can then represent those characters, which could otherwise be treated as markup by the viewer.

➤ Entities increase the portability of SGML documents. Because entities are placeholders in the SGML document instance, they can be rendered on the fly according to a particular site's requirements. An example is the &COMPANY; entity: One subcontractor could define this entity as *Federal Warehouse*, another as *Satellite Armory H-162*.

As you go through this chapter and investigate the capabilities of XML entities, you may find lots of characters and symbols that will never appear in your XML documents. If your native language isn't English, however, or if you work in a scientific environment, you find in the next few sections a lot of diacritical marks, accents, and other kinds of character modifications that will be especially useful to you. Enjoy!

Producing Special Characters

Two ingredients are necessary to make entities work in XML. First, an entity declaration for the character (or character sequence) must appear in the DTD section. This kind of declaration usually takes the form of

```
<!ENTITY Acirc "&#194;" >
<!-- capital A, circumflex accent -->
```

where the first line is the actual entity declaration that equates the string "Acirc" with the symbol denoted by the numeric character code 194. For the entity to be used in the body of an XML document, the string Â or Â must appear.

Whether in the DTD or in the document body, three characters signal the viewer that it should look up an entity string in a character table instead of simply displaying the entity string.

- **Ampersand (&):** If a string starts with &, the viewer can tell that what follows is an entity reference instead of a bunch of ordinary characters. If the next character isn't a pound sign (#), then the viewer knows that the following string is a symbol's name and must be looked up in the DTD's table of defined entity names. This construct is called a *character entity* when the reference is to a single character or a *named entity* when the reference is to a string that's more than one character long.

- **Pound sign (#):** This code flags a *numeric entity*. When the viewer happens upon a & followed by a #, the # tells the viewer that what follows next is a number corresponding to the character code for a symbol to be produced on-screen.

- **Semicolon (;):** This character ends the entity reference itself. When the viewer comes to a ;, the viewer knows that string that represents an entity has ended. The viewer then uses whatever characters or numbers follow either & or &# to perform the right kind of lookup operation and display the requested character symbol.

If the viewer doesn't recognize the information in the entity reference, it may display the original characters entered instead of generating an error message — so review your XML output! For the record, certain viewers available today produce an error message of some kind when this kind of thing happens.

Based on what you know about XML tags and what you may know about computer character sets, certain aspects of character, named, and numeric entities may surprise you. Here's a list of potential surprises:

✔ XML is case-sensitive when it comes to reproducing the string of characters for an entity. In other words, < is not the same as <! Make sure that you key in character entities exactly as shown in Tables 9-1 through 9-5. (For that reason, we often use numeric entities — it's harder to make a mistake.)

✔ Numeric codes for reproducing characters within XML come from the ISO-Latin-1 character set and Unicode numeric codes, some of which are shown later in this chapter in Tables 9-1 through 9-5. Those codes are not ASCII collating sequences. Of course, if you don't know what "ASCII collating sequences" are, then you don't really care, do you? Just focus on the characters as they appear in Tables 9-1 through 9-5 or copy the numbers that match the ISO-Latin-1 scheme; you'll get exactly what you want in whatever form your XML document is rendered.

ISO-Latin-1 Isn't a Dead Language

ISO-Latin-1 is the enigmatic name of the character set that HTML and XML use by default.

✔ *ISO* means that the set comes from the official international standards of the *I*nternational *S*tandards *O*rganization. ISO-Latin-1 has another, even more enigmatic name: ISO 8859-1. (All ISO standards have corresponding numeric tags, just to make things more confusing.)

✔ *Latin* means that the set is derived from the Roman alphabet that's used worldwide for representing text in many languages.

✔ The number *1* designates the character set number for this standard; thus, the Roman alphabet represents the first character set in this series.

XML distinguishes between two types of entities for characters:

✔ **Character entities.** These entities are strings of characters that represent specific characters. For example, < and È show a string of characters (lt and Egrave) that stand for others (< and È). (*Note:* Named entities are like character entities, except that they can represent strings that are more than one character long.)

> ✔ **Numeric entities:** These are strings of numbers that represent charac-
> ters. Numeric entities are identified by the combination &#. For ex-
> ample, < and È show a string of numbers (60 and 200) that
> stand for characters (< and È).

As the amount and kind of information presented in Web format has grown,
the need for a more extensive character entity set has become apparent.
XML supports extended entity sets that include

✔ Greek characters

✔ Special-purpose punctuation, called *general punctuation* in XML-speak

✔ Letter-like characters

✔ A general multi-alphabet character set that supports 8-, 16-, and 32-bit
characters known as Unicode (ISO10646-88 and extensions)

✔ Arrows

✔ Mathematical characters

✔ Miscellaneous technical characters

✔ Miscellaneous symbol characters

Keep in mind that the support of these character sets is new to XML. Only
viewers that support XML directly (Internet Explorer 4.0 and newer versions, plus XML-specific viewers and editors) can render the entities found
in these sets correctly.

The remainder of this chapter includes listings of many of the character
sets supported by XML. Tables 9-1 through 9-5 include each character's
name, applicable entity and numeric codes, and description. We begin with
ISO-Latin-1 because it is fully supported by all current and most older
viewers, and then we continue with some newer character sets, except for
Unicode — with more than 30,000 characters defined, it's too big to include in
this chapter.

Entity declarations, with invocation syntax, for all these character code
schemes appear on the CD-ROM. The following list provides filenames with
notes about their contents, which may be found on the CD. Please note that
we do not include the full Unicode character set listing on the CD (but you
can find places to access this information online in the sidebar titled
"Unicode Encodings," later in this chapter).

Filename	Contains XML-Compliant ENTITY Declarations for These Character Sets
`iso-lat-1.txt`	ISO-Latin-1 character set
`iso-grk-x.txt`	ISO-Greek-1 through 4 character sets
`math-chr.txt`	Mathematical characters
`tech-chr.txt`	Technical characters
`symb-chr.txt`	Common symbol characters

Creating Custom Entities at Your Command!

Producing your own entity files requires understanding the syntax of the ENTITY declaration in a DTD. To create your own versions, you would need to use the following syntax:

```
<!ENTITY <name> "&#<code>;" ><!-- <comment> -->
```

Now, in English, this means:

- ✔ *<name>* must be replaced by a unique, short, and descriptive name that will refer to the character in document text.
- ✔ *<code>* names the numeric code that designates the character.
- ✔ *<comment>* describes what is being represented by the name and the numeric code.

To help you understand what's represented by these codes and names, our tables don't list entity declarations but rather show you what these characters look like so that you can reference them properly in your XML documents.

We omit the Unicode character set because of its size. It embraces all the character sets we describe in this chapter and then some. If you want to view the Unicode character set in its entirety, check it out in the two-volume set of documents titled *The Unicode Standard: Worldwide Character Encoding*, Version 1.0, Volume 1, ISBN 0-201-56788-1, 1991, and Volume 2, ISBN 0-201-60845-6, 1992 (published by Addison-Wesley). To invoke the Unicode character set in an XML document, include an entry like the following one in your document's heading, prior to the DTD declaration:

```
<?XML version="1.0" encoding="ISO-10646-UCS-2"?>
```

This added line gives you access to all the characters you might ever conceivably want to use in any document, without requiring reference to any other external or internal entity files.

Unicode encodings

As you dig a bit further into the possibilities that Unicode delivers for XML, you'll quickly find that Unicode comes in multiple flavors and that ranges of Unicode characters correspond to specific alphabets and character sets (some of which are documented later in this chapter). If you're really curious about this topic, we can't recommend a better resource than the Unicode Consortium's *The Unicode Standard, Version 2.0*.

Unicode exists to simplify the process of translating all kinds of characters into unique, recognizable bit patterns so that computers can represent those characters in documents and on the screen accurately and quickly. The Unicode character set is also known as Universal Character Set, Version Two, usually abbreviated as UCS-2. It stands alone as a way of representing a vast array of character sets, special symbols, and all kinds of typographical elements.

For computer use, two special formats called Universal Character Set Transformation Formats (or UTFs) have been developed to accommodate arbitrarily large sets of characters in 8-bit blocks of data called *bytes*. These are

✔ UTF-7, which uses only 7 bits of data in individual bytes

✔ UTF-8, which uses all 8 bits of data in individual bytes

UTF-7 is seldom used, but you may encounter it from time to time. It is fully documented in RFC-1642 and is available for perusal at

```
www.cis.ohio-state.edu/htbin/
    rfc/rfc1642.html
```

UTF-8 was originally developed by X/Open as a way of creating a file system–safe version of Unicode, but it has since become an addendum to the ISO/IEC 10646 standard that governs Unicode. UTF preserves the original values of the entire lower order set of ASCII characters (values 0–127) but is capable of representing higher-order characters using two- to four-byte sequences, which gives Unicode a huge representational range. This is the representation form that is most commonly associated with XML and SGML and is probably what most of your documents will use.

For more information on Unicode and UTF-8, including representations of character sets viewable online, visit the Unicode Consortium's Web page at

```
www.unicode.org/
```

You may find the sections labeled "The Unicode Standard" and "Online Data" the most interesting.

Useful XML Character Sets

Now, on to the character sets that you will probably find most useful in your own XML documents.

The tables in this chapter show characters, predefined names, and numeric codes only!

Table 9-1		The ISO-Latin-1 Character Set	
Character	*Character Entity*	*Numeric Entity*	*Description*
		&#00; - &#08;	Unused
		&#09;	Horizontal tab
		&#10;	Line feed or new line
		&#11; - &#31;	Unused
		&#32;	Space
!		&#33;	Exclamation mark
"	&quot;	&#34;	Quotation mark
#		&#35;	Number
$		&#36;	Dollar
%		&#37;	Percent
&	&amp;	&#38;	Ampersand
'		&#39;	Apostrophe
(		&#40;	Left parenthesis
)		&#41;	Right parenthesis
*		&#42;	Asterisk
+		&#43;	Plus
,		&#44;	Comma
-		&#45;	Hyphen
.		&#46;	Period (full stop)
/		&#47;	Solidus (slash)

(continued)

Table 9-1 *(continued)*

Character	Character Entity	Numeric Entity	Description
0-9		0 - 9	Digits 0-9
:		&#58;	Colon
;		&#59;	Semicolon
<	&lt;	&#60;	Less than
=		&#61;	Equals
>	&gt;	&#62;	Greater than
?		&#63;	Question mark
@		&#64;	Commercial at
A-Z		A - Z	Letters A-Z (capitals)
[		&#91;	Left square bracket
\		&#92;	Reverse solidus (backslash)
]		&#93;	Right square bracket
^		&#94;	Caret
_		&#95;	Horizontal bar
`		&#96;	Grave accent
a-z		a - z	Letters a-z (lowercase)
{		&#123;	Left curly brace
|		|	Vertical bar
}		&#125;	Right curly brace
~		&#126;	Tilde
		&#127; - Ÿ	Unused
			Nonbreaking space
¡	&iexcl;	&#161;	Inverted exclamation mark
¢	&cent;	&#162;	Cent
£	&pound;	&#163;	Pound sterling
¤	&curren;	&#164;	General currency
¥	&yen;	&#165;	Yen
¦	&brvbar;	&#166;	Broken vertical bar
§	&sect;	&#167;	Section

Character	Character Entity	Numeric Entity	Description
¨	&uml;	&#168;	Umlaut (dieresis)
©	&copy;	&#169;	Copyright
ª	&ordf;	&#170;	Feminine ordinal
«	&laquo;	&#171;	Left angle quote, guillemot left
¬	&not;	&#172;	Not
−	&shy;	&#173;	Soft hyphen
®	&reg;	&#174;	Registered trademark
¯	&macr;	&#175;	Macron accent
°	&deg;	&#176;	Degree
±	&plusmn;	&#177;	Plus or minus
²	&sup2;	&#178;	Superscript two
³	&sup3;	&#179;	Superscript three
´	&acute;	&#180;	Acute accent
µ	&micro;	&#181;	Micro
¶	&para;	&#182;	Paragraph
·	&middot;	&#183;	Middle dot
¸	&cedil;	&#184;	Cedilla
¹	&sup1;	&#185;	Superscript one
º	&ordm;	&#186;	Masculine ordinal
»	&raquo;	&#187;	Right angle quote, guillemot right
¼	&frac14;	&#188;	Fraction one-fourth
½	&frac12;	&#189;	Fraction one-half
¾	&frac34;	&#190;	Fraction three-fourths
¿	&iquest;	&#191;	Inverted question mark
À	&Agrave;	&#192;	Capital A, grave accent
Á	&Aacute;	&#193;	Capital A, acute accent
Â	&Acirc;	&#194;	Capital A, circumflex accent
Ã	&Atilde;	&#195;	Capital A, tilde
Ä	&Auml;	&#196;	Capital A, dieresis or umlaut
Å	&Aring;	&#197;	Capital A, ring

(continued)

Table 9-1 *(continued)*

Character	Character Entity	Numeric Entity	Description
Æ	&AElig;	&#198;	Capital AE diphthong (ligature)
Ç	&Ccedil;	&#199;	Capital C, cedilla
È	&Egrave;	&#200;	Capital E, grave accent
É	&Eacute;	&#201;	Capital E, acute accent
Ê	&Ecirc;	&#202;	Capital E, circumflex accent
Ë	&Euml;	&#203;	Capital E, dieresis or umlaut
Ì	&Igrave;	&#204;	Capital I, grave accent
Í	&Iacute;	&#205;	Capital I, acute accent
Î	&Icirc;	&#206;	Capital I, circumflex accent
Ï	&Iuml;	&#207;	Capital I, dieresis or umlaut
Ð	&ETH;	&#208;	Capital ETH, Icelandic
Ñ	&Ntilde;	&#209;	Capital N, tilde
Ò	&Ograve;	&#210;	Capital O, grave accent
Ó	&Oacute;	&#211;	Capital O, acute accent
Ô	&Ocirc;	&#212;	Capital O, circumflex accent
Õ	&Otilde;	&#213;	Capital O, tilde
Ö	&Ouml;	&#214;	Capital O, dieresis or umlaut
x	&times;	&#215;	Multiply
Ø	&Oslash;	&#216;	Capital O, slash
Ù	&Ugrave;	&#217;	Capital U, grave accent
Ú	&Uacute;	&#218;	Capital U, acute accent
Û	&Ucirc;	&#219;	Capital U, circumflex accent
Ü	&Uuml;	&#220;	Capital U, dieresis or umlaut
Ý	&Yacute;	&#221;	Capital Y, acute accent
þ	&THORN;	&#222;	Capital THORN, Icelandic
ß	&szlig;	&#223;	Small sharp s, German (sz ligature)
à	&agrave;	&#224;	Small a, grave accent
á	&aacute;	&#225;	Small a, acute accent
â	&acirc;	&#226;	Small a, circumflex accent

Character	Character Entity	Numeric Entity	Description
ã	ã	ã	Small a, tilde
ä	ä	ä	Small a, dieresis or umlaut
å	å	å	Small a, ring
æ	æ	æ	Small ae diphthong (ligature)
ç	ç	ç	Small c, cedilla
è	è	è	Small e, grave accent
é	é	é	Small e, acute accent
ê	ê	ê	Small e, circumflex accent
ë	ë	ë	Small e, dieresis or umlaut
ì	ì	ì	Small i, grave accent
í	í	í	Small i, acute accent
î	î	î	Small i, circumflex accent
ï	ï	ï	Small i, dieresis or umlaut
ð	ð	ð	Small eth, Icelandic
ñ	ñ	ñ	Small n, tilde
ò	ò	ò	Small o, grave accent
ó	ó	ó	Small o, acute accent
ô	ô	ô	Small o, circumflex accent
õ	õ	õ	Small o, tilde
ö	ö	ö	Small o, dieresis or umlaut
÷	÷	÷	Division
ø	ø	ø	Small o, slash
ù	ù	ù	Small u, grave accent
ú	ú	ú	Small u, acute accent
û	û	û	Small u, circumflex accent
ü	ü	ü	Small u, dieresis or umlaut
ý	ý	ý	Small y, acute accent
þ	þ	þ	Small thorn, Icelandic
ÿ	ÿ	ÿ	Small y, dieresis or umlaut

Table 9-2		The Greek Character Set	
Character	*Character Entity*	*Numeric Entity*	*Description*
A	Α	Α	Capital letter alpha
B	Β	Β	Capital letter beta
Γ	Γ	Γ	Capital letter gamma
Δ	Δ	Δ	Capital letter delta
E	Ε	Ε	Capital letter epsilon
Z	Ζ	Ζ	Capital letter zeta
H	Η	Η	Capital letter eta
Θ	Θ	Θ	Capital letter theta
I	Ι	Ι	Capital letter iota
K	Κ	Κ	Capital letter kappa
Λ	Λ	Λ	Capital letter lambda
M	Μ	Μ	Capital letter mu
N	Ν	Ν	Capital letter nu
Ξ	Ξ	Ξ	Capital letter xi
O	Ο	Ο	Capital letter omicron
Π	Π	Π	Capital letter pi
P	Ρ	Ρ	Capital letter rho
Σ	Σ	Σ	Capital letter sigma
T	Τ	Τ	Capital letter tau
Y	Υ	Υ	Capital letter upsilon
Φ	Φ	Φ	Capital letter phi
X	Χ	Χ	Capital letter chi
Ψ	Ψ	Ψ	Capital letter psi
Ω	Ω	Ω	Capital letter omega
α	α	α	Small letter alpha
β	β	β	Small letter beta
γ	γ	γ	Small letter gamma
δ	δ	δ	Small letter delta
ε	ε	ε	Small letter epsilon
ζ	ζ	ζ	Small letter zeta
η	η	η	Small letter eta

Character	Character Entity	Numeric Entity	Description
θ	&theta;	&#952;	Small letter theta
ι	&iota;	&#953;	Small letter iota
κ	&kappa;	&#954;	Small letter kappa
λ	&lambda;	&#955;	Small letter lambda
μ	&mu;	&#956;	Small letter mu
ν	&nu;	&#957;	Small letter nu
ξ	&xi;	&#958;	Small letter xi
o	&omicron;	&#959;	Small letter omicron
π	&pi;	&#960;	Small letter pi
ρ	&rho;	&#961;	Small letter rho
ς	&sigmaf;	&#962;	Small letter final sigma
σ	&sigma;	&#963;	Small letter sigma
τ	&tau;	&#964;	Small letter tau
υ	&upsilon;	&#965;	Small letter upsilon
φ	&phi;	&#966;	Small letter phi
χ	&chi;	&#967;	Small letter chi
ψ	&psi;	&#968;	Small letter psi
ω	&omega;	&#969;	Small letter omega
υ	&thetasym;	&#977;	Small letter theta
ϒ	&upsih;	&#978;	Upsilon with hook
ϖ	&piv;	&#982;	Pi

Table 9-3   The Mathematical Character Set

Character	Character Entity	Numeric Entity	Description
∀	&forall;	&#8704;	For all
∂	&part;	&#8706;	Partial differential
∃	&exist;	&#8707;	There exists
∅	&empty;	&#8709;	Empty set
∇	&nabla;	&#8711;	Nabla
∈	&isin;	&#8712;	Element of

(continued)

Table 9-3 *(continued)*

Character	Character Entity	Numeric Entity	Description
∉	&notin;	&#8713;	Not an element of
∋	&ni;	&#8715;	Contains as member
∏	&prod;	&#8719;	n-ary product
∑	&sum;	&#8721;	n-ary summation
−	&minus;	&#8722;	Minus
∗	&lowast;	&#8727;	Asterisk operator
√	&radic;	&#8730;	Square root
∝	&prop;	&#8733;	Proportional to
∞	&infin;	&#8734;	Infinity
∠	&ang;	&#8736;	Angle
∧	&and;	&#8869;	Logical and
∨	&or;	&#8870;	Logical or
∩	&cap;	&#8745;	Intersection
∪	&cup;	&#8746;	Union
∫	&int;	&#8747;	Integral
∴	&there4;	&#8756;	Therefore
∼	&sim;	&#8764;	Tilde operator
≅	&cong;	&#8773;	Approximately equal to
≈	&asymp;	&#8776;	Almost equal to
≠	&ne;	&#8800;	Not equal to
≡	&equiv;	&#8801;	Identical to =
≤	&le;	&#8804;	Less than or equal to
≥	&ge;	&#8805;	Greater than or equal to
⊂	&sub;	&#8834;	Subset of
⊃	&sup;	&#8835;	Superset of
⊄	&nsub;	&#8836;	Not a subset of
⊆	&sube;	&#8838;	Subset of or equal to
⊇	&supe;	&#8839;	Superset of or equal to
⊕	&oplus;	&#8853;	Circled plus

Character	Character Entity	Numeric Entity	Description
⊗	`&otimes;`	`&#8855;`	Circled times
⊥	`&perp;`	`&#8869;`	Up tack
•	`&sdot;`	`&#8901;`	Dot operator

Table 9-4   The Miscellaneous Technical Character Set

Character	Character Entity	Numeric Entity	Description
⌈	`&lceil;`	`&#8968;`	Left ceiling
⌉	`&rceil;`	`&#8969;`	Right ceiling
⌊	`&lfloor;`	`&#8970;`	Left floor
⌋	`&rfloor;`	`&#8971;`	Right floor
⟨	`&lang;`	`&#9001;`	Left-pointing angle bracket
⟩	`&rang;`	`&#9002;`	Right-pointing angle bracket

Table 9-5   The Miscellaneous Symbols Character Set

Character	Character Entity	Numeric Entity	Description
♠	`&spades;`	`&#9824;`	Black spade suit
♣	`&clubs;`	`&#9827;`	Black club suit
♥	`&hearts;`	`&#9829;`	Black heart suit
♦	`&diams;`	`&#9830;`	Black diamond suit

If your needs require that you frequently work with character or numeric entities, you'll find that using some kind of editing tool to handle character replacements automatically makes life much easier. Also, you can use a good file-oriented search-and-replace utility as a post-processing step on your files.

Windows users can check out this ftp site for a great utility called Find-Replace: `oak.oakland.edu/fdrepl.zip`. The utility, which can be used in all flavors of Windows (including Windows 3.*x*), is contained in a Zip archive file.

The CD includes additional entity files and related XML editing tools for a variety of platforms. Check out the tools available on your favorite platform if you often need to use character codes in your pages. The tools can help you become a serious XML developer.

Part III

XML Language and Application

The 5th Wave   By Rich Tennant

AND THIS IS BUD MELLNICK WHO WRITES ALL OF OUR NATURAL LANGUAGE PROGRAMS.

GLORSPLITZ.

In this part . . .

In this part, we explore how to create special-purpose XML-based markup languages. Basically, this part is designed as a demonstration of how to use XML to create compact, powerful markup languages for meeting just about any kind of document-handling or information-delivery need. The part covers many of the most important dialects that have already been — or are currently being — defined using XML: Chemical Markup Language (CML), Channel Definition Format (CDF) language, Resource Description Framework (RDF), HTTP Distribution and Replication Protocol (DRP), Mathematical Markup Language (MathML), Web Interface Definition Language (WIDL), Synchronized Multimedia Interface Language (SMIL), and finally, Open Software Description (OSD). So, break out your spoons — it's time for alphabet soup!

Chapter 10

XML Markup Has Real Chemistry!

● ●

In This Chapter

▶ Examining an XML application

▶ Checking out XML's good chemistry

▶ Using CML

▶ Going over XML's tools, rules, and resources

▶ Understanding the CML DTD

▶ Viewing XML examples

● ●

Chemical Markup Language (CML) is an application of XML. To understand the relationship between the two, think of CML as the vocabulary and XML as the grammar. You can use CML for specialized applications, such as rendering molecular science and related technical information over both the Internet and an intranet. For example, you can use CML to draw 2-D and 3-D molecular structures. You can even publish scientific papers using CML. As such, you will find specific uses of CML over the Web for a targeted audience only.

CML is based on SGML and Java and is a relatively new object-oriented markup language developed in collaboration with the OMF (Open Molecule Foundation). Although CML is not a standard yet, all efforts indicate that the language is expected to become the standard soon.

Now, your field of expertise may not be chemistry and you probably have nothing to do with micro and macro molecules — other than what you learned about them in high school — unless it's required by your current interests. However, by reading about CML, you can gain a good understanding of XML's usefulness. By understanding CML, you can see the types of specialized applications that you can deploy using XML.

This chapter provides an overview of CML and how you can render molecular information over the Internet using this new markup language. In addition, we outline the features and advantages of using CML and the tools currently available to create, edit, and view your CML files. To gain a good understanding of CML, you must understand the CML DTD (Document Type Definition) and the CML elements (or tags) and their attributes (or properties). Gain a good understanding of these, and you can be programming CML in no time.

Molecular Technology Made Easy

To use CML, you must come to grips with molecular technology — no need to dust off your college chemistry book, though! You need to understand the molecular technology's structure and components and how they interrelate. Then you can represent such information by using the CML DTD, tags, and attributes.

This section explains some of the basic concepts of molecular technology. Using CML, you can represent the following types of molecular information:

- Inorganic crystallography
- Molecular sequence
- Molecular structure
- Organic molecules
- Quantum chemistry
- Spectra

An atom is the smallest possible unit. Atoms combined together constitute a molecule. For example, oxygen (O), hydrogen (H), carbon (C), and nitrogen (N) are all atoms. H_2O represents a molecule of water, NO_2 represents a molecule of nitrogen dioxide, and CO_2 represents a molecule of carbon dioxide. A molecular structure shows the molecule's internal representation. Figure 10-1 shows H_2O's molecular structure.

Figure 10-1:
H_2O's molecular structure.

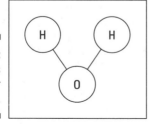

XML's Chemistry Is Good

XML is all about structured data. If you can represent data in a structured format, you can create XML files. The data can be about whatever you want to interpret and render. The markup language that you use to represent molecular information is called CML.

Because CML enables you to represent very specific data, such as molecular information, within a structured format, you also need specialized viewers to see the results. You can't use your browsers directly to view the results because browsers do not inherently support specialized XML applications such as CML.

Before we jump into the details about CML, the available tools, and the rules of the game, we want to show you some of the commonly used terms within the world of XML and CML:

- ✔ Like many other markup languages, CML is based on SGML (Standard Generalized Markup Language). As discussed in Chapter 3, SGML is a metalanguage you can use to construct new markup languages — such as CML.

- ✔ CML is an object-oriented language. At the highest level, CML includes a set of tags or elements. Each tag or element has zero or more attributes (or properties). To create and edit a CML file, you must manipulate the tags and their attributes to get the desired results.

- ✔ After a CML file is created, you can view the file with viewers, such as CMLViewer. This viewer is also available as an applet that can run within a browser, thus enabling you to view the results of the CML files within your browser.

- ✔ Any specialized application's data must be structured and follow certain rules. The vocabulary and grammar used to represent data must be something that the parser and the viewer can understand. Otherwise, the application can't be processed.

- ✔ As we discuss in Chapter 6, a DTD defines the rules of the game. Just as XML has its DTD, CML also has its DTD to which your CML must conform.

Why CML?

We can think of a number of reasons for using CML:

- ✔ Using CML has numerous advantages. CML is a platform-independent markup language, so you don't have to worry about the machine on which the application uses the CML files; you can focus on the data you want to represent and the data's structure.

✔ Like several other languages, including Java, CML is object-oriented. Think of a CML tag as an object with attributes. You can set values for these attributes.

✔ Think of CML as an ASCII representation of the database that contains information about molecular technology. Compared to other forms of information, transmitting ASCII information over the Internet is fast and easy. The client application (for example, a browser) does not really need a connection to a database back end, such as Microsoft SQL Server, Sybase Adaptive Server, Oracle, and so on. The client application retrieves and renders the data directly from the CML document.

✔ CML is not a database management system. However, you can represent both the database schema and data using CML.

Tools and Rules

CML is one of several new kids on the block. (Fortunately, we're speaking metaphorically!) CML is still in its infancy (Version 1) and is catching on quickly. Because of this, few tools are available to help you create, edit, and manipulate CML files easily.

The simplest and easiest tool to use to create and edit your application's CML files is your favorite text editor, such as Notepad, WordPad, Emacs, and so on. (Now you know why these tools still exist, even with all the advances in technology.)

While you wait for a company or individual to create a nifty little editor that makes your CML life much easier, use your favorite text editor. Yes, this doesn't seem like the best solution, but at least it is a solution.

After creating your application's CML file, run the file through a program such as a CML parser. To view the results, use a specialized application such as the CMLViewer. Written in Java, the CMLViewer is available both as an applet (that can run within a browser) and as a stand-alone application.

When writing CML code, you must abide by certain rules and regulations. Some of these rules are

✔ A CML document must include a DOCTYPE statement.

✔ Every CML element must have a starting and ending tag. For example, the ATOMS element must have a starting tag (`<ATOMS>`) and an ending tag (`</ATOMS>`). Whereas you can omit the ending tag for some HTML 4.0 elements, you cannot do so with CML (or XML) tags.

✔ You must specify the values for an attribute within quotes.

✔ Do not use white space as markup.

The CML DTD

This section discusses the nine important CML elements, their attributes, and examples of using them. Covering all the CML elements is beyond the scope of this chapter.

For complete documentation on CML, with examples, tutorials, DTDs, and the Java API, visit www.venus.co.uk/omf/cml/doc/index.html.

The nine important CML elements are

✔ <ARRAY>

✔ <ATOMS>

✔ <BONDS>

✔ <CML>

✔ <FORMULA>

✔ <MOL>

✔ <XADDR>

✔ <XLIST>

✔ <XVAR>

<ARRAY>

To represent an array of variables, use the <ARRAY> tag. You can represent both one- and two-dimensional arrays using the <ARRAY> tag. The following is an example of a one-dimensional array:

```
<ARRAY BUILTIN="ATID2">
    2 5 6 7 3 8 9 4 5 10 11
</ARRAY>
```

The following is an alternative way to represent an array of variables:

```
<ARRAY START="2.5" DELTA="0.5" SIZE="10">
    2.5 3 3.5 4 4.5 5 5.5 6 6.5 7
</ARRAY>
```

Interpret the preceding array declaration as follows: The array starts at 2.5, the increment level is 0.5, and the total number of variables within the array is 10.

Every starting <ARRAY> tag must have a matching ending </ARRAY> tag.

<ATOMS>

To represent an atom or a list of atoms within a molecule, use the <ATOMS> tag. The <ATOMS> tag has a number of attributes.

For a complete list of the attributes, visit www.venus.co.uk/omf/cml/doc/index.html.

The following is a list of some of the attributes:

- ATOMNO: Represents the atom's serial number
- ATID: Represents the atom's unique identifier
- ATTYPE: Represents the atom type
- ELSYM: Represents the atom's element symbol
- ISOTOPE: Represents the atom's isotope
- X2: Represents the atom's 2-D X coordinate
- Y2: Represents the atom's 2-D Y coordinate
- X3: Represents the atom's 3-D X coordinate
- Y3: Represents the atom's 3-D Y coordinate
- Z3: Represents the atom's 3-D Z coordinate

The following is an example of how to use the <ATOMS> tag:

```
<ATOMS>
    <ARRAY BUILTIN="X2">
        -1.342 0.137 0.8 -0.1029 -1.3289 -1.882 -1.8799
            0.438 0.464 -0.1409 0.163
    </ARRAY>
    <ARRAY BUILTIN="Y2">
        -0.527 -0.905 0.335 1.2439 0.879 -0.8419 -0.878 -
            1.471 -1.441 1.1049 2.28
    </ARRAY>
    <ARRAY BUILTIN="ELSYM">
        C C O C O H H H H H H
    </ARRAY>
</ATOMS>
```

Every starting <ATOMS> tag must have a matching ending </ATOMS> tag.

<BONDS>

To represent a chemical bond, use the <BONDS> tag. A chemical bond represents the connection between two atoms. The <BONDS> tag can contain an arbitrary number of arrays for carrying bond information. The tag supports the following attributes:

- ✔ ATID1: Represents the atom id of the first atom within the bond
- ✔ ATID2: Represents the atom id of the second atom within the bond
- ✔ BONDID: Represents the bond's unique identifier
- ✔ CYCLIC: Represents the bond's cyclicity
- ✔ ORDER: Represents the bond's order
- ✔ PARITY: Represents the bond's parity

The following example shows how to use the <BONDS> tag:

```
<BONDS>
    <ARRAY BUILTIN="ATID1">
        1 1 1 1 2 2 2 3 4 4 4
    </ARRAY>
    <ARRAY BUILTIN="ATID2">
        2 5 6 7 3 8 9 4 5 10 11
    </ARRAY>

</BONDS>
```

Every starting <BONDS> tag must have a matching ending </BONDS> tag.

<CML>

To represent a CML document, use the <CML> tag. The following code block is an example of how to use the <CML> tag.

```
<!DOCTYPE CML PUBLIC "-//CML//DTD CML//EN">
<CML TITLE="Hello CML">
</CML>
```

Every starting <CML> tag must have an ending </CML> tag.

\<FORMULA>

To represent a chemical formula, use the \<FORMULA> tag. The \<FORMULA> tag has the following attributes:

- ✔ **MOLWT:** Represents the element's molecular weight
- ✔ **STOICH:** Represents the element's *stoichiometry*, which is the element's chemical composition

The following is an example of how to represent the formula C_2OCOH_4:

```
<FORMULA>
    <XVAR BUILTIN="STOICH">
    C C O C O H H H H
    </XVAR>
</FORMULA>
```

The following example demonstrates how to use the \<FORMULA> tag to represent the chemical formula CH_2OH:

```
<FORMULA>
    <XVAR BUILTIN="STOICH">
     C H H O H
    </XVAR>
</FORMULA>
```

Every starting \<FORMULA> tag must have a matching ending \</FORMULA> tag.

\<MOL>

To represent a molecule, use the \<MOL> tag. Representing a molecule includes representing the molecule's atoms, the bonds between the atoms (if any), and the molecule's formula as shown:

```
<MOL>
   <ATOMS>
    <ARRAY BUILTIN="X2">
     -1.342 0.137 0.8 -0.1029 -1.3289 -1.882 -1.8799
        0.438 0.464 -0.1409 0.163
    </ARRAY>
    <ARRAY BUILTIN="Y2">
     -0.527 -0.905 0.335 1.2439 0.879 -0.8419 -0.878 -
        1.471 -1.441 1.1049 2.28
    </ARRAY>
```

```
    </ATOMS>
      <BONDS>
         <ARRAY BUILTIN="ATID1">
          1 1 1 1 2 2 2 3 4 4 4
         </ARRAY>
         <ARRAY BUILTIN="ATID2">
          2 5 6 7 3 8 9 4 5 10 11
         </ARRAY>
      </BONDS>
    <FORMULA>
         <XVAR BUILTIN="STOICH">
          C C O C O H H H H
         </XVAR>
    </FORMULA>
</MOL>
```

Every starting <MOL> tag must have a matching ending </MOL> tag.

<XADDR>

To represent a person or an organization's address, use the <XADDR> tag:

```
<XADDR>123 Anywhere St., Suite 765, Jacksonville, FL 32256
</XADDR>
```

You can also include the address as different components using the <XVAR> tag like this:

```
<XADDR>
    <XVAR>123 Anywhere St.</XVAR>
    <XVAR>Suite 765</XVAR>
    <XVAR>Jacksonville</XVAR>
    <XVAR>FL</XVAR>
    <XVAR>32256</XVAR>
</XADDR>
```

Every starting <XADDR> tag must have a matching ending </XADDR> tag.

<XLIST>

The <XLIST> tag is a generic container. You can include arrays, xvars, or xlists within this tag. The following is an example of how to use the <XLIST> tag to represent an array of ten chemical elements and compounds. The data that the <XVAR> tag represents is of type string:

```
<XLIST CONTENT=ARRAY SIZE=10 SUBELEMENT="XVAR">
    <XVAR TYPE=string>Oxygen</XVAR;>
    <XVAR;>Hydrogen</XVAR;>
    <XVAR;>Nitrogen</XVAR;>
    <XVAR;>Carbon</XVAR;>
    <XVAR;>Sulphur</XVAR;>
    <XVAR;>Phosphorus</XVAR;>
    <XVAR;>Sulphur Dioxide</XVAR;>
    <XVAR;>Carbon Monoxide</XVAR;>
    <XVAR;>Carbon Dioxide</XVAR;>
    <XVAR;>Nitrogen Dioxide</XVAR;>
</XLIST>
```

The following example shows how to use the <XLIST> tag to represent an array of five dates. The data that the <XVAR> tag represents is of type date:

```
<XLIST CONTENT=ARRAY SIZE=5 SUBELEMENT="XVAR">
    <XVAR TYPE=date>01-01-1998</XVAR;>
    <XVAR;>01-01-1997</XVAR;>
    <XVAR;>01-01-1996</XVAR;>
    <XVAR;>01-01-1995</XVAR;>
    <XVAR;>01-01-1994</XVAR;>
</XLIST>
```

Every starting <XLIST> tag must have a matching ending </XLIST> tag.

<XVAR>

To represent a generic variable, use the <XVAR> tag. The following code is an example of using the <XVAR> tag to represent a chemical formula:

```
<FORMULA>
    <XVAR BUILTIN="STOICH">
        H H S O O O O
    </XVAR>
</FORMULA>
```

Every starting <XVAR> tag must have a matching ending </XVAR> tag.

CML Examples

To view examples of how CML output looks, visit the site www.ch.ic.ac.uk/java/cml/. Click on any of the links. The browser, in turn, loads the applet and related Java classes. Note that some of the examples may take some time to load if they include a number of Java classes.

This section discusses three examples of CML. The first example shows you a basic CML document with no content. From there, we move into representing a molecule composed of atoms, bonds, and a formula. Finally, we look at a CML document that includes references and pointers to other CML documents.

CML document with no content

The following example demonstrates a basic CML document with no content:

```
<!DOCTYPE CML PUBLIC "-//CML//DTD CML//EN">
<CML TITLE="Abracadabra CML">
</CML>
```

Every CML document must have the first line of code as shown in the preceding example. The !DOCTYPE defines the document's type — in this case, the document type is CML. This declaration is followed by the <CML> ... </CML> tags. You define a CML document's content and attributes within these tags. The preceding code specifies no content, only an attribute TITLE for the CML document. The TITLE attribute's value is Abracadabra CML.

CML molecule code

How about another sample of CML code? The next block of code defines a molecule composed of atoms, bonds, and a formula. As the code indentation indicates, the <ATOMS>, <BONDS>, and <FORMULA> tags are contained within the <MOL> tags. The representation is hierarchical in nature. The following is an explanation of what each of these tag pairs represent in our example:

- The <MOL> tag represents a molecule.

- The <ATOMS> tag represents the atoms. It contains a number of arrays. An array can be one- or two-dimensional in nature. All the arrays in this example are one-dimensional. The array's BUILTIN attribute specifies a variable of the atom followed by a value for the variable.

- The <BONDS> tag represents the chemical bond between two atoms. Similar to the <ATOMS> tag, the <BONDS> tag also contains a number of arrays. An array can be one- or two-dimensional in nature. All the arrays in this example are one-dimensional. The array's BUILTIN attribute specifies the type of chemical bond.

✔ The `<FORMULA>` tag represents a formula. The `<XVAR>` tag represents the formula's variable. A formula can have one or more variables. The `BUILTIN` attribute specifies the variable's name followed by a value for the variable.

All of the these attributes are contained within the `<CML>` tags, thereby representing a CML document:

```
<!DOCTYPE CML PUBLIC "-//CML//DTD CML//EN">
<CML>
<MOL>
  <ATOMS>
     <ARRAY BUILTIN="X2">
     -1.342 0.137 0.8 -0.1029 -1.3289 -1.882 -1.8799 0.438
          0.464 -0.1409 0.163
     </ARRAY>
     <ARRAY BUILTIN="Y2">
     -0.527 -0.905 0.335 1.2439 0.879 -0.8419 -0.878
          -1.471 -1.441 1.1049 2.28
     </ARRAY>
     <ARRAY BUILTIN="ELSYM">
        C C O C O H H H H H
     </ARRAY>
  </ATOMS>
  <BONDS>
     <ARRAY BUILTIN="ATID1">
      1 1 1 1 2 2 2 3 4 4 4
     </ARRAY>
     <ARRAY BUILTIN="ATID2">
      2 5 6 7 3 8 9 4 5 10 11
     </ARRAY>
     <ARRAY BUILTIN="ORDER">
      1 1 1 1 1 1 1 1 1 1 1
     </ARRAY>
     <ARRAY BUILTIN="STER">
      0 0 0 0 0 0 0 0 0 0 0
     </ARRAY>
  </BONDS>
  <FORMULA>
     <XVAR BUILTIN="STOICH">
      C C O C O H H H H H
     </XVAR>
  </FORMULA>
</MOL>
</CML>
```

CML references and pointers

The following is another example of a CML document. This example shows a CML document that includes references and pointers to other CML documents using the <XLIST> and <XVAR> tags. Each <XVAR> tag has a number of attributes, including TITLE and MIME. The TITLE attribute specifies the CML document's title. The MIME attribute specifies the mime type, an Internet data type. For example, *chemical/x-cml* indicates that the document's data type is CML. In other words, the document contains data and information represented by CML tags and attributes.

```
<DOCTYPE CML PUBLIC "-//CML//DTD CML//EN">
<CML>
<XLIST TITLE="A set of other files">
   <XVAR MIME="chemical/x-cml" TITLE="A CML document">
   sample.cml
   </XVAR>
   <XVAR MIME="chemical/x-cml" TITLE="Another CML
          document">
   sample2.cml
   </XVAR>
   <XVAR MIME="chemical/x-cml" TITLE="CML protein file">
   protein.cml
   </XVAR>
   <XVAR MIME="chemical/x-jcamp" TITLE="IR Spectrum">
   ir-spectrum.jdx
   </XVAR>
   <XVAR MIME="chemical/x-jcamp" TITLE="NMR Spectrum">
   nmr-spectrum.jdx
   </XVAR>
   <XVAR MIME="chemical/x-jcamp" TITLE="Mass Spectrum">
   mass-spectrum.jdx
   </XVAR>
   <XVAR MIME="chemical/x-mdl-molfile" TITLE="MDL Molfile">
   td1y.mol
   </XVAR>
   <XVAR MIME="chemical/x-mdl-molfile" TITLE="Another MDL
          Molfile">
   td2y.mol
   </XVAR>
   <XVAR MIME="chemical/x-swiss" TITLE="Swiss Prot
          insulin">
   insulin.sw
   </XVAR>
```

(continued)

(continued)

```
    <XVAR TITLE="Authors Database">
      authors.bib
      </XVAR>
  </XLIST>
  </CML>
```

Just the Tip of the Iceberg

CML is still in Version 1. In the coming days, we can certainly expect enhancements and modifications to this relatively new markup language. With Open Molecule Foundation (OMF) backing, we can also anticipate CML becoming an industry standard for rendering molecular information over the Internet. In addition, we can expect better and more-efficient tools for creating, editing, and viewing our CML files. CML is a markup language for use over the Web. The language's specification originated on the Web.

To stay abreast of the enhancements and modifications to this new markup language, visit these Web sites:

- ✔ For more information on CML, visit `www.venus.co.uk/omf/cml/`.

- ✔ For complete documentation on CML with examples, tutorials, DTDs, and the Java API, visit `www.venus.co.uk/omf/cml/doc/index.html`.

- ✔ For a list of frequently asked questions (FAQs) on CML, visit `www.venus.co.uk/OMF/cml-1.0/doc/faq/index.html`.

- ✔ For more information on the Java-based JUMBO browser for CML documents, visit `www.venus.co.uk/~pmr/README`.

- ✔ To learn more about the Open Molecule Foundation, visit `www.ch.ic.ac.uk/omf/`.

- ✔ To find out more about the OMF, visit `www.ch.ic.ac.uk/omf/`.

Chapter 11

XML Can Channel from Many Different Sources

*C*hannel is one of the buzzwords used in the Internet community today. This chapter introduces you to the concept of channels and where and how they are being used. We introduce you to the Channel Definition Format (CDF) and show you how this XML-based format is defined in detail. We also present how it works in two of the most important applications that use CDF — Microsoft Internet Explorer 4.0 and RIO by DataChannel.

What Is a Channel?

The word *channel* seems to appear in many different contexts, some of which do not seem too have much in common. The best-known use of channel is found in television technology. We use the term *channel* in reference to television on a daily basis. Very rarely, however, do we think about what a channel really is and how it is defined.

If you are interested in sports, you tune into your favorite sports channel on TV; if it's the latest news you want, you find a 24-hour news station. In other words, a channel (in television) provides you a fixed arrangement of sources for a particular subject or type of information. History, wildlife, and science fiction channels are other good examples of such classifications.

Your choice of newspapers is similar to picking a particular channel. Do you choose a newspaper with a focus on business and finance, such as *The Wall Street Journal*, or do you choose one that covers local news and sports, such as the *Austin American-Statesman* (for those who live in Austin, Texas)?

To take this a level further, think about your local newspaper. You probably go directly to the local news, the sports pages, and the comics every day. Chances are good that you don't even have to search for your favorite sections. You know exactly where they are. Even more important, you know that the latest football scores aren't going to be in the Classified section somewhere between "Used Cars" and "Tools for Gardening."

TV channels, newspapers, books, and even supermarkets provide you with a variety of classifications. Channels on the World Wide Web use this same concept.

Describing channels

The organization and classification of Web content can be a challenging task. Two alternatives seem to be possible.

In the first approach, many services try to be the directory — the database — for the Web. Dozens of search engines and directories try be a good starting point for people who need to find specific information on the Web. However, in many cases, these services fail to present a utility. A third party (other than the content creator itself) may find it hard to provide a meaningful description and a meaningful organization of a collection of Web pages. And navigation of a Web server or a collection of Web pages is another problem. As these information services grow bigger and bigger, they become less and less useful because consumers can't find the right navigational path to a specific item or can't guess the right combination of words necessary to have a successful search against some per-site search service.

Channel-like search engine services

One big problem on the Internet is that a plethora of information related to a particular subject or keyword is available. We all know the frustration of getting 1,000 hits as a result of a search using very common and ambiguous keywords. What you actually want to do is find Web servers and pages that relate to a particular subject in a broad field.

Search engines try to approach the problem through services that may be considered channels. At Yahoo!, you find a classification scheme that starts with very broad terms of classification and allows you to navigate down a tree hierarchy that, hopefully, guides you closer and closer to the subject in which you're interested.

In the second approach, we who create Web pages, sites, and channels present the means to describe the content and the structure of a Web server explicitly and so that it is accessible for everyone. This description, the metacontent, provides a human or a software agent with information about a Web service or — to be as general as possible — a collection of Web pages.

Imagine trying to describe your company Web server verbally. You may say, "You can find pages that contain product information, pages with whitepapers, press-releases, and current job-listings." Wouldn't you like to be able to present this information to a browser, so that with just one mouse-click, a user would be at their section of choice? This is what channels are about. Channels allow you to categorize and describe your pages and to make that data available to the public. In other words, channels can be seen as a sort of site map — the road map for Web servers and Web pages.

Even more important, however, is that we can make this information available for different services — such as browsers, indexers, channel catalogs, and other forms of agents — by using a common format for describing a channel.

Smart pull and push

When surfing the Internet, your browser retrieves pages from a WWW server. This retrieval is often referred to as *pulling.* Your client (browser) pulls pages from the server to your desktop.

Using channels, you can go much further. Assume, for now, that you can use channel information in your browser — a file tells you where to find information about skiing. Now that you have this information, you can tell your browser where all the important news about skiing resides.

Your browser uses channels to gather information in one of two ways:

✔ **Smart pull:** *Smart pull* means that the browser still pulls the pages from the server, but you find two important differences:

- **Directed:** Now that you have a file that tells the browser where to find relevant information about skiing, the days and hours of searching for it are gone.

- **Automated:** You can set up the browser so that it automatically checks for new information on the skiing server. Because a channel is not just a bookmark, the browser can check more than just the home page to find out whether news that you want to know is there.

✔ **Push:** *Push* reverses the idea of traditional Web browsing. Instead of having the browser pull information from the Internet, a process on the server (or at least a process that checks the data on the server) sends all the information needed to your client. So the browser no longer has to go out to the Web — the Web comes to your browser.

The Channel Definition Format (CDF)

The Channel Definition Format (CDF) is an XML-based file format for the description of channel information. CDF was developed by Microsoft and is supported by Internet Explorer 4.0 as well as by the software of other manufacturers, such as DataChannel and PointCast.

A minimal CDF file

In the following example, we show you a very simple yet sufficient example of a CDF file that can be put on a Web server. (XML.org is a fictitious non-profit organization whose goal is to promote the use and adoption of XML technology.)

```
<?XML version="1.0"?>
<CHANNEL
HREF="http://www.xml.org/xml.html">
<TITLE>XML.Org - XML for everybody</TITLE>
<ABSTRACT>
XML.org is a non-profit organization that wants to foster
            the adoption of XML technology. XML members are
            drawn from different industries and from coun-
            tries all over the world. Here you will find all
            relevant information about XML.
</ABSTRACT>
</CHANNEL>
```

Because this generic form is found in so many applications of CDF, we explain every single part of this example. Here's our line-by-line analysis.

✔ `<?XML version="1.0"?>`: As you know, CDF is an XML application. This line is merely a way to state the same fact.

✔ `<CHANNEL> ... </CHANNEL>`: Channel is the container for all our channel information.

✔ HREF="http://www.xml.org/xml.html": Channel has one important attribute — HREF — which you probably recognize from HTML. HREF indicates a hyperlink to a resource — for example, an HTML page. Because a channel usually describes resources on the Web, such as Web pages, this HREF points to a page that is the top level and/or starting point for your collection of pages. In our example, HREF points to the top-level page of our organization's server.

✔ <TITLE> ... </TITLE>: A title in a CDF file allows us to describe the content of the channel in a few concise words.

✔ <ABSTRACT> ... </ABSTRACT>: An abstract allows you to provide a more wordy and detailed description of the information in your channel.

The title and the abstract of your channel can be very crucial to its success. They are the first things users see, and users decide whether they want to venture into your Web pages based on what's written in the title and abstract.

CDF unleashed

In the following sections, we tell you all about CDF. We provide you with a whole set of directives that specify powerful channel information. Now you can become the "Master of the Channels." (Try not to let this go to your head!)

Scheduling

You use a schedule to specify how often a channel needs to be updated. You can give a client application instructions this way; for example, you can specify how often the server should check your channel to see if new information has arrived or if something has changed. The following code is a minimal scheduling specification that updates occur once a day:

```
<SCHEDULE>
  <INTERVALTIME DAY="1"/>
</SCHEDULE>
```

The following schedule specifies updates every four hours. An update schedule starts at midnight. Thus, in this case, we would receive updates at 4 a.m., 8 a.m., 12 p.m., 4 p.m., 8 p.m., and 12 a.m.

```
<SCHEDULE>
  <INTERVALTIME HOUR="4"/>
</SCHEDULE>
```

You can specify the start and end dates of a certain schedule:

```
<SCHEDULE START="1998-01-01" END="1998-05-01">
</SCHEDULE>
```

The general format for specifying a date is this: YYYY-MM-DD.

And here's another way you can use scheduling. Say you're a content provider, and thousands of clients are accessing your server at the same time because they are all using the same CDF file with the same preset scheduling information. To avoid these peak-traffic times, a CDF file can specify a time frame within which a client can access the content to check for updates. Clients can randomly choose from the limits set by the CDF:

```
<SCHEDULE>
 <INTERVALTIME HOUR="12">
 <LATESTTIME HOUR="2">
 <EARLIESTTIME HOUR="1">
</SCHEDULE>
```

With this schedule, updates would occur between 1 a.m. and 2 a.m. and between 1 p.m. and 2 p.m.

Bibliographic description

A "bibliographic description" in the CDF standard has been described in our example CDF for XML.org. (See "A minimal CDF file," earlier in this section, for more about XML.org.) TITLE and ABSTRACT are both used to describe the content of a channel in abstract terms.

Page retrieval

You can set attributes on a channel that enable you to define how HTML pages, which are the content of channels, are downloaded to your client.

- ✔ LASTMOD: This attribute specifies the date the content of a channel was last updated. A client can check this attribute and download only pages that have been updated after the date specified in this attribute. Lastmod specifies both date and time in the canonical form of "YYYY-MM-DD THour:Minute."

- ✔ PRECACHE: This attribute determines whether content should be downloaded and stored in your clients cache. The default is "YES"; setting the attribute to "NO" prohibits precaching. PRECACHE is very important because it allows your system to download pages and make them available to you even if you are off-line.

> ✔ **LEVEL:** Using LEVEL, you can order the client to climb down the hier-
> archy that starts with the page you refer to in your channel "HREF"
> attributes. LEVEL="1" means that all pages that can be reached via one
> hyperlink "jump" will also be downloaded and cached on your client.

The following example loads all pages that have been modified after 3 p.m.
on January 1, 1998. It also fetches all pages that are two "jumps" away from
the main reference. Because PRECACHE is defaulted to "yes," the pages are
stored in the client's cache.

```
<CHANNEL HREF="http://www.xml.org/xml.html"
   LASTMOD="1998-01-01T15:00"
   LEVEL="2">
</CHANNEL>
```

Hierarchies

You can use CDF to set up hierarchies in your Web pages. For example, you
may want to have separate sections for your professional life and your
personal life on your Web page. If you travel quite a bit, you may want to
create an illustrated travel channel as a separate item. Because you travel
often, your travel channel changes frequently.

First, consider this: Describing your channel with a vague title, such as
"Travel Page," isn't a good idea. Think about how you want to organize a
travel channel description for your personal page and give it a specific title,
such as "Mike's Skiing Page."

Now you can use CDF to refine the content you have in your channel.

You can use the following code example as a starting point for your own CDF
file. We created this CDF file so that you could use it to add structure to the
collection of pages that you use to describe yourself. In this small example,
we only want to show you what a simple channel looks like. For your
convenience, we have already placed one item — your travel page — into
the CDF file. Please replace our fictitious travel agency with your personal
favorite.

```
<?XML Version="1.0"?>
<CHANNEL>
 <TITLE>My personal pages</TITLE>
 <ABSTRACT>These pages are about me, myself, and I. My
           life, my job, my travels.</ABSTRACT>
```

(continued)

(continued)

```
<ITEM HREF="http://www.travelfun.com/">
  <TITLE>Mike's Skiing Page</TITLE>
  <ABSTRACT>Here I start my travels</ABSTRACT>
</ITEM>
</CHANNEL>
```

Logo

CDF allows you to specify a logo (image) that is displayed with your channel. LOGO also enables you to specify an attribute (STYLE) for the context in which a certain logo should be used. The STYLE attribute allows these values:

- ICON: If you use this value, your logo must be 16 x 16 pixels. An icon of this size is used, for example, if you browse your channel files using Internet Explorer 4.0. In other words, if you render this information on-screen and you use a hierarchy to do that, you use this code to specify the icons. This is not important if you use an agent that only reads the CDF and uses it for building a catalog. Because Internet Explorer 4 reads the CDF and does rendering for the channel bar, Internet Explorer uses the value specified in ICON.

- IMAGE: An icon for image must be 32 x 80 pixels and is used, for example, in the Internet Explorer 4.0 channel bar.

- IMAGE-WIDE: A wide image is 32 x 194 pixels.

The CDF specification also notes that GIF and JPEG images should be used and supported as logo images. However, Internet Explorer 4.0 currently allows you to use the .ICO format (logo.ico, for example), for icon-sized logos as well.

The following code example specifies the image that should be used for an "image" style logo:

```
<LOGO HREF="http://www.myserver.com/images/logo.gif"
          STYLE="IMAGE">
```

Login

You may find channel content that requires password protection. The LOGIN statement in your CDF file directs the browser to prompt the user for authentication information when the user subscribes to a channel. This information is used for later updates.

```
<LOGIN/>
```

The following requires the user to authenticate if he or she wants to access the pages of this channel automatically:

```
<?XML version="1.0"?>
<CHANNEL>

<TITLE>Mr. Private - Secret Channel</TITLE>
<ABSTRACT>
My home page can only be accessed via a password.
</ABSTRACT>

<LOGIN/>

</CHANNEL>
```

Logging

All WWW servers today allow administrators to keep track of when and from where a certain client retrieves a particular page. Page-hit logging allows a publisher to apply the same concept to channels.

Logging can detect three different actions. You can define the "scope" as being:

- **Online:** Only pages that are read online are being reported.
- **Off-line:** Only pages that are being read off-line, from the cache, are being reported.
- **All:** This is a combination of off-line and online.

The publisher of the CDF files needs to specify the URL where the logging information is sent and how it should be uploaded. A client can use either POST or PUT to upload information. POST and PUT are different ways in which a client can send data to a Web server. POST is supported in most HTTP servers; PUT requires servers that support HTTP 1.1. In the following, we want the logs to be sent to the DataChannel server, and we want the scope to be both of the retrieval modes, online and off-line.

```
<LOGTARGET
 HREF="http://www.datachannel.com/logging"
 Method="POST"
 SCOPE="ALL">
</LOGTARGET>
```

In addition, you can also restrict the client to send only hits that are tracked after a certain date. The PURGE specification allows you to get a report that contains only hits within a certain time frame. The following statement, within a log-target specification, tells the client to consider only hits of the last 24 hours to be uploaded to the server.

```
<PURGETIME HOUR="24"/>
```

The LOG statement allows you to define which items in a CDF file should be considered for logging.

In the following code block, the CDF file instructs the browser to insert a new entry into the log-file whenever a document is being viewed.

```
<ITEM HREF="http://www.datachannel.com/news.htm">
  <LOG VALUE="document:view"/>
</ITEM>
```

Please note that in order not to abuse logging, an item can only be logged if the item shares the same URL stem with the CDF or the log target's upload URL (its HREF).

Using Internet Explorer 4.0 and CDF

To understand channels and use them in your Web site design, you need to understand how visitors to your site use channels. Microsoft Internet Explorer 4.0 was the first application to support CDF. Channel support is integrated in your Internet Explorer 4.0 browser. To enable CDF, you have to activate your channel bar through the View⇨Explorer bar command.

If you have just installed Internet Explorer 4.0 or if you have never used CDF before, you'll see a sample collection of CDF files that point to a variety of sites of different topics and subjects when you activate the channel bar, as shown in Figure 11-1.

Channels in the Internet Explorer 4.0 channel bar are, by default, arranged by subject. Click one of the icons displayed and Internet Explorer will open a set of channels that relate to the chosen topic.

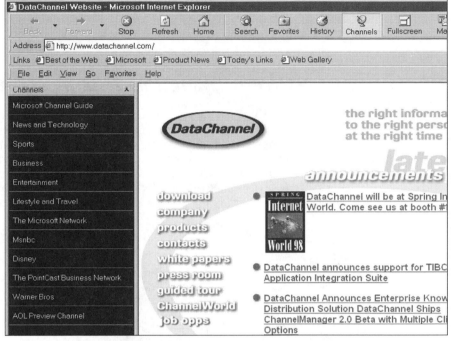

If you click <u>news & technology</u>, as shown in Figure 11-2, you get a list of
different channels, such as news magazines and other news sources. Figure 11-2
shows the channel labeled *The New York Times.*

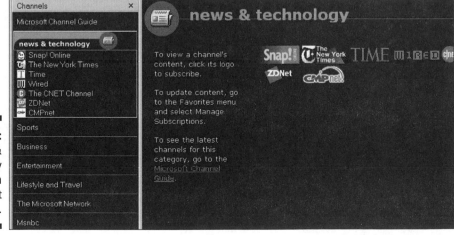

You can also browse the other items that are presented in the channel bar. Take a look at the wondrous world of information that opens up right in front of you and have some fun exploring it.

Channels from Disney to Business News

Just as indexes for WWW servers are on the Web, so are indexes that contain collections of CDF files. Just as in a newspaper, you can find channels that relate to news and technology, sports, business, entertainment, and lifestyle and travel. Microsoft is the host of Channel Guide, which is a collection of references to more than 700 different information systems that offer access to their data via CDF files. Using Internet Explorer, you can get to Channel Guide via Go⇨Channel Guide in your menu bar, as shown in Figure 11-3.

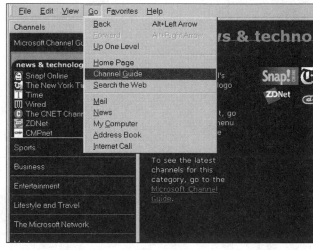

Figure 11-3: Use Go⇨Channel Guide to get cool information on your favorite topic.

Adding and subscribing

After you explore the wealth of channels that are available on the Internet, you can start using them to their full power. Before you get carried away, you first need to find out how to subscribe to channels.

When you subscribe to a channel, you have to find a reference to the CDF file of that particular channel. If you download that CDF file, for example, by following the hyperlink that points to the CDF, your browser recognizes the channel and guides you through the subscription process.

Very often, you see an icon labeled Add Active Channel, similar to the one shown in Figure 11-4. A simple click on this icon starts the subscription process for you. Occasionally, you see a text-based hyperlink that says something like <u>Click here to subscribe</u>.

Figure 11-4:
Add a channel by using this button.

Internet Explorer 4.0 enables you to customize the way you subscribe to a channel. After you click the Add Active Channel button, you see the Modify Channel Usage dialog box, as shown in Figure 11-5. You have these choices:

Figure 11-5:
The Modify Channel Usage dialog box enables you to choose a method when subscribing to a channel.

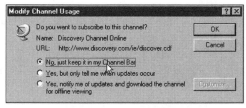

> ✔ **Add to channel bar:** The first entry in the menu is: "No, just keep it in my Channel Bar." By adding a channel to the channel bar, you include the item in the list of existing channels. If you select this option, your new channel is added. From now on, you can use this new channel as a simple entry point to the new server. However, you do not get any notification if content on the server has changed or if new content has been added.

✔ **Add and notify:** The real power of channels is experienced when you select the radio button labeled "Yes, but only tell me when updates occur." Whenever something changes in the channel, you're told about it. In addition, you can set up your system so that these notifications are sent directly to your mailbox.

✔ **Add, notify, and download:** Using this method, you can instruct Internet Explorer 4.0 to download pages when changes occur. The downloaded pages are kept cached in your browser and retrieved when needed. That way, you can read through changes when you are off-line. If you choose to customize the settings of this dialog box, you have complete control over download and update schedules.

When you select "Add, notify, and download," the first dialog box asks whether the browser should download all the pages as specified in your channels or only the starting page — a setting you specified in the HREF attribute. If you elect to download all the pages, these pages are stored on your local hard disk after the update process. They can then be viewed off-line.

Deleting a channel

To delete a channel from your channel bar, select the item you want to remove with a right mouse click. A pop-up menu gives you several choices; select the Delete entry and — go figure — you delete that selection.

A Channel for Your Home Page

After you understand both the theory of CDF and how to use CDF files in Internet Explorer 4.0, you want to understand how to create your own CDF file, right? Well, you're in luck! In this section, we provide you with a template for building a CDF file on your personal home page. This CDF file presents only a skeleton, and we encourage you to play with it and extend it until your desires are satisfied.

The first step

To use these examples, you need to have access to a Web server through which you can access the example CDF files. In our examples here, we assume that your pages are located at `E:\myhomepage` and that you access your home page via `www.myhosts.com/mcchannel`.

To start, create a simple CDF file that describes your entire home page at the top level. The following initial CDF specification also contains a schedule for updates; updates are defined to occur once a week:

1. **Open your favorite text editor and create a new file.**

   You may want to use your initials and a version number. Because you start out with the simplest one, start with 0. If your name is Mike McChannel; give it the name MMC-0.CDF.

2. **Type the following code, modified with your information, in the new text file.**

   The code is only as a template and a starting point for your own ideas. Modify the data to reflect your name and channel information. Also, please note that the following initial CDF specification contains a schedule for updates; updates are defined to occur once a week.

   ```
   <?XML version="1.0"?>
   <CHANNEL
   HREF="http://www.provider.com/mcchannel/index.htm">

   <TITLE> Mike McChannel - Personal Channel</TITLE>
   <ABSTRACT>
   Hello, I am Mike McChannel and this is my personal
           channel. Here you can find information about my
           research as well as my private life.
   </ABSTRACT>

   <SCHEDULE>
    <INTERVALTIME DAY="7"/>
   </SCHEDULE>

   </CHANNEL>
   ```

3. **Copy the CDF file to the root directory of your Web site.**

   For example, if your personal home page's root directory is E:\myhomepage, copy your CDF file to that directory. I use my initials and a version number in the name, for convenience, so my CDF file would be E:\myhomepage\MMC-0.CDF.

4. **Load the CDF file.**

   Now you want to use Internet Explorer 4.0 to point to your CDF file. Under the assumption we have established earlier, this would be www.myhosts.com/mcchannel/MMC-0.cdf.

After loading your CDF file, Internet Explorer should present to you the channel setup dialog box (described in earlier sections). The Modify Channel Usage dialog box appears.

5. **Click the appropriate radio button from the list of choices and then click OK.**

See the "Adding and subscribing" subsection of the "Using Internet Explorer 4.0 and CDF" section, earlier in this chapter, for an explanation of the options outlined in that dialog box.

After you finish with the Modify Channel Usage dialog box and click OK, your channel appears in the Microsoft Channel Guide.

Using custom icons

Look at your browser's channel bar and notice that your channel is displayed using the standard Internet Explorer 4.0 channel symbol, which looks like a satellite dish. Don't you wish your icon could be as colorful as all the other channels in your channel bar? It can be done. Keep reading!

Follow these four steps to achieve "cool icon" status:

1. **Create custom icons.**

As described in the "Logo" section earlier in this chapter, CDF supports three sizes of icons. Use your favorite image editor to create three icons in the sizes as described in the "Logo" section. In this example, we saved the files as test.ico (for an icon) and test_sl.gif (for a full-size image).

2. **Copy the icon files in the same directory as your home page.**

For example, if your personal home page's root directory is E:\myhomepage, copy your icon files to that directory.

3. **Open your CDF file with your favorite text editor (such as Windows Notepad), save it with a new version number, and modify the text by inserting the following code block.**

In my case, I saved the file as MMC-1.CDF to show that it's a new version. The following XML code (shown in bold) should go after the schedule specification and before the end of the channel description:

```
....
</SCHEDULE>

<LOGO HREF="test.ico" STYLE="ICON"/>
<LOGO HREF="test_sl.gif" STYLE="IMAGE"/>

</CHANNEL>
```

4. Load your new CDF file by following the same steps you used for MMC-0.cdf.

Please note that after your confirmation to add the new channel, Internet Explorer will realize that a channel with the same name already exists and will open a dialog box prompting you for the choice of overwriting the existing one or canceling the operation. In order to enable the new channel, you need to choose the overwrite option.

During this testing phase, you could also choose to delete your existing channel before you insert the new one. Sometimes this helps with finding the problem if none of your previous channels exist in the channel bar.

Please note that because we have just a channel and no items yet, only the logo "image" style will actually be used. However, when you add some items, you will see how this second logo specification starts playing a role. Note also that for each channel, you need to specify which logos are to be used for the channel and for items in the channel.

Make sure that your Internet settings about temporary files in your browser are set so that files are checked for updates each time a page is visited. To get to these settings, choose View⇨Internet Options⇨Settings. To get the most up-to-date information downloaded, click the radio button marked Every Visit to the Page.

Introducing hierarchy

What you have available at this point is a minimum CDF file at your home page, which is semi-satisfactory for most people. However, you may want to introduce some more hierarchical levels to your structure.

We will assume for now that your home page has two distinct parts:

- **A section about your professional life:** Here, you describe your job, tell what you like or hate about your job, and possibly even provide an on-line résumé (especially if you hate your job!). We'll assume that these pages start at "professional/index.htm."

- **A section about your personal life:** Even though you're a very hard-working person, you manage to squeeze in a personal life. In this section, you talk about your partner, your family, and maybe your pet(s). You may have family pictures that you want to share or want to tell the story of the time your cat got a glass of water stuck on his head. In our example, you store these pages starting with the page "professional/pp.html."

Insert the following text after the specification of the schedule for the top-level channel. Please note that the new elements are inserted in bold text:

```
......
</ABSTRACT>

<CHANNEL HREF="professional/index.htm">
<TITLE>Professional</TITLE>
<ABSTRACT>
Learn more about my work here.
</ABSTRACT><ITEM HREF="professional/pp.html">
<TITLE>Presentations and Publications</TITLE>
<ABSTRACT>
Read about where I have been speaking and publishing
in recent years.
</ABSTRACT>

</ITEM>

</CHANNEL>

<LOGO HREF="test.ico" STYLE="ICON"/>
<LOGO HREF="mytest_sl.gif" STYLE="IMAGE"/>
```

RIO, CDF, and Your Intranet

Previous sections of this chapter discuss channels and CDF for a variety of professional content uses or for your personal use. CDF can also be used in a very different way. The next sections show you how CDF and channels can be used in an intranet.

An *intranet* is similar to the Internet, but it is designed for use solely within an organization. Typically, an intranet consists of information created within your company plus information coming from the outside Internet. The most important aspect of an intranet is that the information is meant for consumption only within your organization.

Channels for your intranet

Intranets are usually designed to allow employees to share information in an efficient way. The most established use of an intranet is e-mail — the exchange of electronic messages between individuals. However, a lot of information for an intranet gets created for a larger audience. Content is created and must be published for a number of interested parties. The key to success is to get the right information to the right person at the right time.

Certain kinds of information should be kept centralized to avoid having dozens of different versions of documents, many of which are outdated, floating around; phone lists and human resources information are typical examples. People need to know where to find the latest news and documents without having to browse around for hours on the intranet. Ideally, you can inform all interested parties as soon as changes have occurred.

You can use RIO by DataChannel to enable the power of channels on your intranet. RIO is a database-driven application that provides you with the ability to maintain a variety of different pools of information to get the most out of your existing network system, including

- **User profiles:** A user profile, similar to the one shown in Figure 11-6, is a document that contains information about users, including groups, desktop settings, and so on. Individual users need a collection of different information sources to get all the information needed to carry out a task. Thus, an important part of a user profile is information about what channels the user is interested in.

- **Group profiles:** An organization is usually divided into groups. Groups in this sense can range from a whole department of people to a team of two people. What is important in the context of channels and intranets is that groups share a common interest in certain subjects — thus they share a common interest in certain channels.

- **Channels:** Channels are information about organized content. The content itself can be located within your intranet or on the Internet. Marketing information, sales, and human resources are typical internal sources found on the intranet. The latest data from the New York Stock Exchange and a local weather report are typically found on the Internet.

RIO combines this wealth of information to create channels that make sure that all employees get the relevant information they need. Because all information about channels is maintained centrally, you don't need to worry about out-of-date channel information on your employees' desktops. As soon as channels need to be changed, these changes can be sent and incorporated on all client systems; furthermore, users can be notified about the news.

RIO and Internet Explorer

RIO can export its channel information into a variety of formats and thus can communicate with many different applications. RIO can export its channel information to CDF out of a database and on the fly.

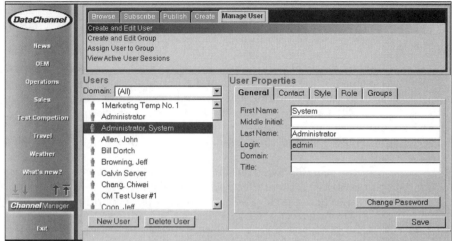

Figure 11-6:
User
profiles
maintenance.

RIO comes with its own powerful client — RIO Client. It is a Java-based application that runs on all major 32-bit browser applications. However, you may find situations in which you want to use the information maintained in RIO with other client applications.

Because RIO uses CDF, this data can be used with all the channel features in Internet Explorer 4.0. The combination of Internet Explorer 4.0 and RIO makes is possible to combine the power of centralized channel management with major browser technology.

CDF on all platforms

Unfortunately, you won't always have the opportunity to use a highly sophisticated client system, such as the RIO Client or Internet Explorer 4.0. Nevertheless, by using CDF for your channels, you can still harness all the power of such a client. Because CDF is an XML application, building your own CDF-based application (for example, your own CDF viewer) is easy. You need two things:

✔ **An XML parser:** XML parsers exist for many major programming languages and on all major platforms. Use the XML parser to read the CDF information and pass it to your tree viewer. For more information on XML parsers, see Chapter 6.

> ✔ **A tree viewer:** The tree viewer's task is to take the information from the
> parser and represent the hierarchical structure of the CDF in a visual
> tree. Tree view controls are also very common and you shouldn't have
> too much trouble finding one suitable for your system. Your job is to
> populate the tree control with the data that comes from the CDF file.
> Visit `meteora.ucsd.edu/~pierce/ncview_home_page.html` for an
> X-Windows CDF viewer called Ncview.

DataChannel is the host of the XML Development Toolkit, which is a set of
XML software components. One of the features included in the DataChannel
XDK is an example of how to use a Java-based XML processor and a Java-
based tree viewer to build your own customizable CDF viewer. Figure 11-7
shows you the DataChannel CDF viewer. This is just one example of how you
can take two existing components (an XML parser and a tree viewer) to
build a new application — a CDF viewer.

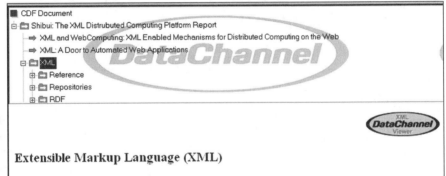

Figure 11-7:
Generic
CDF viewer.

Chapter 12

XML Is the Master of Many Resources

*T*ypically, when you enter any office, you find papers, folders, and books lying around. This type of organization makes searching and retrieving information difficult.

Wouldn't it be nice if you could organize the papers, folders, and books into some type of a library system and make the search and retrieval process easy? That is what RDF (Resource Description Framework), Web Collections, and MCF (Meta Content Framework) are all about. Using RDF to create Web Collections and MCF, you can organize information about Web resources, such as a Web page, Web sites, and so on, in a structured manner, meaning that you can represent a Web resource as an object and describe the object by specifying the properties and values for the properties. XML fits right into this because that is what XML is all about — representing structured data. Thus, Web Collections and MCF are both XML applications based on RDF.

A Web resource may be a Web page, a Web site (collection of Web pages), or any collection of electronic information. Each such resource may contain additional resources, such as images, audio, video, and more. You can describe the resources by using properties and values for the properties. For example, a Web page may include such properties as author, last modified date, and title. An image, video, or audio resource may include such properties as title, type, source, and URL. You need a way to represent this information in an organized manner, and that is what Web Collections and MCF are all about.

RDF is the foundation for processing *metadata* — which means higher-level data, or in this case the data describing the different types of Web resources. Microsoft is the primary proponent of Web Collections, although both Netscape and Apple participated in the W3C meetings on Web Collections. Netscape acquired MCF from Apple and is now the primary proponent of MCF. Which specification will emerge as the standard remains to be seen.

The information that RCF, Web Collections, and MCF represent does not necessarily imply viewer output. These specifications outline the rules for representing Web resources; how you use them for viewer output depends on your application requirements and the tools you use. A number of potential applications for Web Collections and MCF use metadata, including search engines, WebMaps, Personal Information Management (PIM) functions, scheduling, and content labeling. For example, search engines can return metadata about the Web sites within the search results. You can also use the metadata as your Web site's documentation by organizing the information in a structured manner and parsing the XML code. For that matter, you can use Web Collections and MCF to label your Web site's content, which means that you can store information such as comments, properties, and site history.

This chapter provides an overview of RDF, Web Collections, and MCF.

RDF: Not Just a Rural Route Address

The World Wide Web Consortium (W3C) defines RDF as the foundation for processing metadata. *Metadata* means higher-level data; it is the data about data. In the case of RDF, metadata is the data describing the different types of Web resources.

As the name suggests, RDF means a framework for describing Web resources. To understand RDF, you must understand the RDF data model and RDF grammar. If these terms sound confusing, consider the statement "Ed Tittel is the author of the book *HTML For Dummies*. To find more information about the book, visit `www.lanw.com/books/h4d3.htm`." You can use the RDF data model and grammar to represent this type of statement.

Think of a Web resource as an object. Because objects have properties and properties have values, you can certainly expect resources to have properties and these properties to have values.

For example, every URL has an author. The author is the URL's property and the author's name is the property's value. Microsoft Corporation is the Microsoft Web site's author. The Microsoft Web site (`www.microsoft.com`)

is the URL or Web resource. The Web site has a property: the author. This property's value is `Microsoft Corporation`. Similarly, Netscape Corporation is the Netscape Web site's author. The Netscape Web site (`www.netscape.com`) is the URL or Web resource. This Web site has a property: the author. This property's value is `Netscape Corporation`.

Understanding the RDF grammar

The RDF grammar defines the tags and their attributes that you use to represent the resources.

This section discusses some of the important RDF tags. For information on the other RDF tags and their attributes, visit `www.w3.org/TR/WD-rdf-syntax/`.

- ✔ **RDF serialization:** To define an RDF serialization (that is, an RDF initialization), use the `<RDF:serialization>`...`</RDF:serialization>` tag pair. Within the tags, define the nodes, including assertions, resources, and so on. The syntax of the RDF serialization tag pair is

  ```
  <RDF:serialization>node</RDF:serialization>
  ```

- ✔ **RDF resource:** To define an RDF resource, use the `<RDF:resource>`...`</RDF:resource>` tag pair. Specify the property for the resource within the tags. The RDF resource tag pair syntax is

  ```
  <RDF:resource idAttrib>property</RDF:resource>
  ```

  Represent the `idAttrib` as follows (note that `IDSymbol` specifies the resource's name):

  ```
  id=<IDSymbol>
  ```

- ✔ **RDF assertion:** To define an RDF assertion, use the `<RDF:assertion>`...`<RDF:assertion>` tag pair. Specify the property for the assertion within the tags. The RDF assertion tag pair's syntax is

  ```
  <RDF:assertion idAttrib>property</RDF:assertion>
  ```

  Represent the `idAttrib` as follows (note that `IDSymbol` specifies the assertion's name):

  ```
  id=<IDSymbol>
  ```

Representing a resource

Graphically, you can represent a resource as shown in Figure 12-1.

For example, you can represent the Microsoft Web site resource as shown in Figure 12-2.

You can represent the resource in Figure 12-2 using the RDF model and grammar, as shown in the following code:

```
<RDF:serialization>
    <RDF:resource http://www.microsoft.com/>
        <bib:name>Microsoft Corporation</bib:name>
    </RDF:resource>
</RDF:serialization>
```

Similarly, you can represent the Netscape Web site resource as shown in Figure 12-3.

Figure 12-1:
A resource
has
properties,
and
properties
have
values.

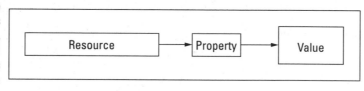

Figure 12-2:
Representing
the
Microsoft
Web site
resource.

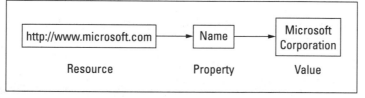

Figure 12-3:
Representing
the
Netscape
Web site
resource.

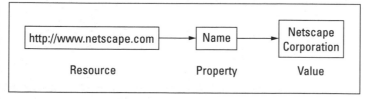

You can represent the Netscape Web site resource using the RDF grammar, as follows:

```
<RDF:serialization>
   <RDF:resource http://www.netscape.com/>
      <bib:name>Netscape Corporation</bib:name>
   </RDF:resource>
</RDF:serialization>
```

Making assertions

A resource can have more than one property. Each such property has a value associated with it, as shown in the following bit of code:

```
Resource Property1 Value1
         Property2 Value2
         Property3 Value3
```

The RDF specification defines a resource as having multiple properties and values for the properties as an assertion. The following is an example of representing an assertion. The assertion represents the resource www.microsoft.com. In addition, the assertion represents the properties name, e-mail address, and phone number for this resource. The values for these properties are Microsoft Corporation, info@microsoft.com, and +1 (800) 123-4567, respectively:

```
<RDF:serialization>
  <RDF:assertions href="http://www.microsoft.com/">
  <bib:author>
    <RDF:resource>
      <bib:name>Microsoft Corporation</bib:name>
      <bib:email>info@microsoft.com</bib:email>
      <bib:phone>+1 (800) 123-4567</bib:phone>
    </RDF:resource>
  </bib:author>
  </RDF:assertions>
</RDF:serialization>
```

The following example also demonstrates how to represent an assertion. The assertion represents the resource www.netscape.com. In addition, the assertion represents the properties name, e-mail address, physical address, and phone number for this resource. The values for these properties are Netscape Corporation, info@netscape.com, 501 E. Middlefield Road, Mountain View, CA 94043, and +1 (800) 123-4567, respectively:

```
<RDF:serialization>
 <RDF:assertions href="http://www.netscape.com/">
 <bib:author>
   <RDF:resource>
    <bib:name>Netscape Corporation</bib:name>
    <bib:email>info@netscape.com</bib:email>
    <bib:address>501 E. Middlefield Road, Mountain View, CA
           94043</bib:address>
    <bib:phone>+1 (800) 123-4567</bib:phone>
   </RDF:resource>
 </bib:author>
 </RDF:assertions>
</RDF:serialization>
```

Taking Up Web Collections

On March 9, 1997, Microsoft submitted the specification for Web Collections to the W3C and asked the consortium for its approval to make the specification an industry standard.

Using Web Collections, you can describe an object's properties within a hierarchical format. (An object may have one or more properties, and each property has a value associated with it.) For example, you can describe a Web page by describing the page's properties including the page's author, title, URL, and date last modified.

The best way to understand Web Collections is to look at an example. The following code represents the Web page object's properties, which are `Author`, `LastMod`, and `Title`. The values for these properties are `IDG Corporation`, `Wed 18 Feb 1998`, and `IDG Home Page` respectively. The attribute `profile` represents the Web page object's attribute identifying the collection. This attribute's value is `www.idg.com/`:

```
<XML>
<WEBPAGE profile="http://www.idg.com/">
 <Author value="IDG Corporation"/>
 <LastMod value="Wed 18 Feb 1998"/>
 <Title value="IDG Home Page"/>
</WEBPAGE>
</XML>
```

As you can see, a Web Collection represents a collection of properties and values for a given object. Notice that the Web Collection's definition is enclosed within the `<XML>...</XML>` tags.

You can nest a collection within another collection. Say that a Web site has multiple levels of pages. You can represent such a Web site in the form of a hierarchical tree. For example, the home page for the Web site www.samachar.com is a meta-level collection of the different news sites for the Indian community, as shown in Figure 12-4.

You can enclose a Web Collection within the pair of <XML>...</XML> tags as shown:

```
<XML>
<WEBPAGE profile="http://www.idg.com/">
 <Author value="IDG Corporation"/>
 <LastMod value="Wed 18 Feb 1998"/>
 <Title value="IDG Home Page"/>
</WEBPAGE>
</XML>
```

All the remaining Web Collections examples in this chapter are shown enclosed within the pair of <XML>...</XML> tags.

Each URL link in the SAMACHAR site represents a Web Collection. Figure 12-5 shows the SAMACHAR site's graphical representation.

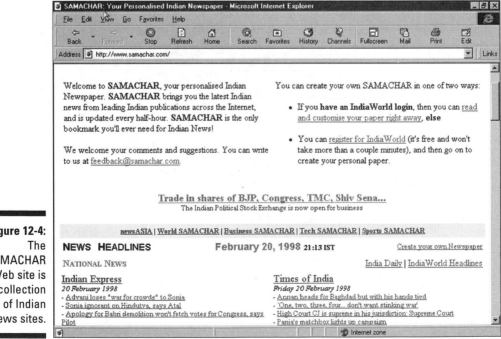

Figure 12-4: The SAMACHAR Web site is a collection of Indian news sites.

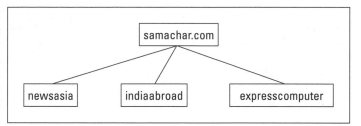

Figure 12-5:
Representing the SAMACHAR site graphically.

You can represent the SAMACHAR Web Collection using XML as follows:

```
<XML>
<WEBMAP profile="http://www.samachar.com">
 <Author value="India World"/>
 <Feedback value=feedback@samachar.com/>

   <Page about="http://www.newsasia.com">
    <Author value="India World"/>
    <LastMod value=="Sun, 01 Feb 1998 10:21:18 GMT"/>
    <Title value="News Asia"/>
    <Slogan value="All the Asian News… just 1 click away"/>
    <Schedule value=DAILY/>
   </Page>

   <Page about="http://www.indiaabroadonline.com/">
    <Author value="India World"/>
    <LastMod value=="Mon, 09 Feb 1998 08:14:18 GMT"/>
    <Title value="India Abroad Online"/>
    <Schedule value=MONTHLY/>
   </Page>

   <Page about="http://www.expressindia.com/bpd/ec/">
    <Author value="Indian Express Group"/>
    <LastMod value=="Tue, 17 Feb 1998 7:15:10 GMT"/>
    <Title value="Express Computer"/>
    <Slogan value="The Weekly Update on Information Tech-
            nology"/>
    <Schedule value=WEEKLY/>
   </Page>

</WEBMAP>
</XML>
```

After the SAMACHAR site's representation is complete, the site's search engine, for example, can use this representation to return information about the site's components. For example, if a user is interested in learning more about the Indian Express Group, the search engine returns additional information about the Indian Express Group such as author, title, update schedule, and so on.

A Web Collection can have one or more of the following attributes:

- ✔ **about:** The attribute provides additional information about the Web Collection. Typically, the about attribute points to a URL, as shown in this bit of code:

```
<Page about="http://www.mycompany.com/products.htm">
```

- ✔ **href:** To pass a value by reference, use the href attribute, as shown here:

```
<WEBPAGE profile="http://www.microsoft.com/">
 <Author href="http://www.microsoft.com/about"/>
 <Title value="Microsoft Home Page"/>
</WEBPAGE>
```

- ✔ **id:** The id attribute uniquely identifies the collection, as shown by the following:

```
<WebPage id="MyPage">
```

- ✔ **profile:** The profile attribute identifies the collection, as shown here:

```
<WEBPAGE profile="http://www.idg.com/">
 <Author value="IDG Corporation"/>
 <LastMod value="Wed, 18 Feb 1998"/>
 <Title value="IDG Home Page"/>
</WEBPAGE>
```

- ✔ **type:** Using the type attribute, you can specify the value's type. The WebMap page is a Web page of type MyPage, as shown in this bit of code:

```
<WebMap type="MyPage">
```

- ✔ **value:** The value attribute specifies the property's value, as shown here:

```
<WEBPAGE profile="http://www.idg.com/">
 <Author value="IDG Corporation"/>
 <LastMod value="Wed, 18 Feb 1998"/>
</WEBPAGE>
```

As the Web Collections specification evolves, we expect Microsoft to add more attributes to the specification.

Building Meta Content Framework

Meta Content Framework (MCF) is the Netscape equivalent of the Microsoft Web Collections. You can use MCF to describe a Web page by describing the page's properties — including the page's author, title, URL, and date last modified. Netscape submitted the MCF specification to the Consortium on June 6, 1997, for the same reasons that Microsoft submitted Web Collections.

You can use MCF to represent the Web sites as a collection of objects and properties. MCF provides a structured way to represent Web resources. The following code is an example of representing a Web page by using MCF:

```
<WebPage>
    <LastMod>1/9/1998</LastMod>
    <Title>IDG Home Page</Title>
    <URL>http://www.idg.com</URL>
    <Author unit="IDG Corporation"/>
</WebPage>
```

As you can see, MCF uses XML to describe the Web resources. The preceding MCF representation describes a Web resource: IDG Corporation's home page. This representation includes the properties Last Modified, Title, URL, and Author. The respective values for these properties are: 1/9/1998 (a number), IDG Home Page (a string), http://www.idg.com (a URL), and IDG Corporation (a unit). A unit refers to another object or resource. In this case, the author property refers to a Corporation object. The following is an example of defining the Corporation object:

```
<Corporation id="IDG Corporation">
    <name>International Data Group</name>
    <email>info@idg.com</email>
</Corporation>
```

As you can see, the Corporation object includes a couple of properties (name and email) and an attribute (id). The values for name and email properties are of type string. The id attribute represents a unique identifier for the object.

You can also represent the preceding Web page resource as follows:

```
<WebPage>
    <LastMod>1/12/98</LastMod>
    <Title>IDG Home Page</Title>
    <url>http://www.idg.com</url>
    <Author>IDG Corporation<Author/>
</WebPage>
```

In this case, the `Author` property does not point to another object. Rather, the `Author` property's value is the string `IDG Corporation`. The preceding code is a simple, straightforward representation and does not include nested objects.

The following code is representative of the SAMACHAR Web site, which we show in Figure 12-4. In the earlier section "Taking Up Web Collections," we discuss how the Web site is viewed within the Web Collections standard proposed by Microsoft. To compare and contrast MCF with Web Collections, we chose to use MCF to represent the SAMACHAR Web site. Take a look at the MCF example below and compare it with the Web Collections example in the preceding section:

```
<WebPage id="samachar.com">
    <URL>http://www.samachar.com</URL>
    <Feedback>feedback@samachar.com</Feedback>
    <Author>India World</Author>
</WebPage>

<WebPage id="newsasia">
    <URL>http://www.newsasia.com</URL>
    <Parent unit="samachar.com"/>
    <Author value="India World"/>
 <LastMod value=="Sun, 01 Feb 1998 10:21:18 GMT"/>
 <Title value="News Asia"/>
 <Slogan value="All the Asian News... just 1 click away"/>
 <Schedule value=DAILY/>
</WebPage>

<WebPage id="indiaabroad">
    <URL>http://www.indiaabroadonline.com</URL>
    <Parent unit="samachar.com"/>
    <Author value="India World"/>
 <LastMod value=="Mon, 09 Feb 1998 08:14:18 GMT"/>
 <Title value="India Abroad Online"/>
 <Schedule value=MONTHLY/>
</WebPage>
```

(continued)

(continued)

```
<WebPage id="expresscomputer">
    <URL>http://www.expressindia.com/bpd/ec/</URL>
    <Parent unit="samachar.com"/>
    <Author value="Indian Express Group"/>
  <LastMod value=="Tue, 17 Feb 1998 7:15:10 GMT"/>
  <Title value="Express Computer"/>
  <Slogan value="The Weekly Update on Information Technol-
            ogy"/>
  <Schedule value=WEEKLY/>
</WebPage>
```

Representing the SAMACHAR Web site using MCF includes representing each URL as an entity by itself and then establishing the relationships between them. Representing the SAMACHAR Web site using Web Collections includes representing the entire site as an entity by itself with the relationships between the different URLs embedded within this entity.

Describing the properties

The code example shown in the preceding section describes the IDG Corporation Web page and includes such properties as LastMod, Title, URL, and Author. With MCF, you can define the domain and range for such properties. A domain specifies the scope of the attribute, and the range specifies the attribute's data type.

The following code is an example of defining the domain and range for the LastMod property. The domain specifies the unit to which the property applies. The range specifies the property's type. Keep in mind that both domain and range are part of the MCF specification. Use them to specify the scope and data type of the properties. For example:

✔ The LastMod property's domain is WebPage (that is, the resource you defined within the preceding section using MCF), and the range is a string, as shown here:

```
<PropertyType id="LastMod">
 <domain unit="WebPage"/>
 <range unit="String"/>
</PropertyType>
```

✔ The Title property's domain is WebPage and the range is a string, as shown here:

```
<PropertyType id="Title">
 <domain unit="WebPage"/>
 <range unit="String"/>
</PropertyType>
```

✔ The URL property's domain is WebPage, and the range is a string, as shown here:

```
<PropertyType id="URL">
 <domain unit="WebPage"/>
 <range unit="String"/>
</PropertyType>
```

✔ The Author property's domain is Corporation, and the range is a string, as shown here:

```
<PropertyType id="Author">
 <domain unit="Corporation"/>
 <range unit="String"/>
</PropertyType>
```

✔ The name property's domain is Corporation, and the range is a string, as shown here:

```
<PropertyType id="name">
 <domain unit="Corporation"/>
 <range unit="String"/>
</PropertyType>
```

✔ The email property's domain is Corporation, and the range is a string, as shown here:

```
<PropertyType id="email">
 <domain unit="Corporation"/>
 <range unit="String"/>
</PropertyType>
```

The domain and range properties are part of MCF's evolving vocabulary.

Understanding MCF's built-in properties

The MCF specification continues to evolve, and presently the specification includes very few built-in properties. A built-in property is a property that the specification already provides for you to use. As MCF evolves, the specification will include additional built-in properties. This is important to understand because as the specification includes additional built-in properties, the specification's scope will expand, letting you represent Web resources in more detail.

Here are some of MCF's built-in properties:

✔ name: To assign a name to a property, use the `<name>` property:

```
<PropertyType>
 <name>Author</name>
 <domain unit="Corporation"/>
 <range unit="String"/>
</PropertyType>
```

✔ description: To describe a property, use the `<description>` property:

```
<PropertyType id="Author">
 <description>Author's name</description>
 <domain unit="Corporation"/>
 <range unit="String"/>
</PropertyType>
```

✔ propertyType and superPropertyType: To represent a hierarchical relationship between two properties, use the superPropertyType property. Using these properties, you can represent an object's instances. You can use PropertyType to define a generic property and then use superPropertyType to define a specific property. For example, a person is a generic property, and an author is an instance of the Person object:

```
<PropertyType id="Person">
 <domain unit="Human Being"/>
 <range unit="String"/>
</PropertyType>
<PropertyType id="Author">
 <description>A type of person</description>
 <superPropertyType unit="Person"/>
</PropertyType>
```

Tools, Rules, and Resources

At present, the simplest and easiest tool to create and edit your application's Web Collection and MCF files is your favorite text editor. No good GUI tools are available at the moment that you can use to manipulate Web Collections and MCF files. Hopefully, this will change in time as both Web Collections and MCF files gain recognition within the industry.

After creating the Web Collections and MCF files, you must run the files through a parser. Just as you write programs using tools such as Visual Basic and Visual C++, and just as you must run the programs through the compiler for accuracy and verification, a Web Collections or MCF parser parses the Web Collections or MCF file for the same reasons. Upon success-ful parsing, you can view the results via a specialized viewer application. At the moment, no good WC and MCF parsers are available. Hopefully, this will change in time as both Web Collections and MCF files gain recognition within the industry.

Presently, no Web Collections or MCF viewers are available. As these children of XML develop further and gain in popularity, we can expect a number of vendors to create such tools.

Design guidelines and rules of the game

When playing with Web Collections and MCF, you must play the game by its rules. In addition, you should follow certain design guidelines when generat-ing the Web Collections or MCF representation for a Web resource:

- ✔ You must include the starting and ending tags for every element. For example, the `PropertyType` element must have a starting tag (`<PropertyType>`) and an ending tag (`</PropertyType>`). Similarly, the `Page` element must have a starting tag (`<Page>`) and an ending tag (`</Page>`), and so on.

- ✔ Indent your code properly. This improves code readability and mainte-nance, especially in the case of representing a hierarchical structure of information.

- ✔ To generate the equivalent Web Collections or MCF representation for a Web resource, identify the resource's properties and their correspond-ing values. Organize the information about the resources hierarchically, identifying the relationships among the elements.

Additional resources

If you're interested in Web Collections, Meta Content Framework (MCF), or the W3C's Resource Description Framework (RDF), check out these sites:

- ✔ You can find out more about Web Collections by visiting `www.w3.org/TR/NOTE-XMLsubmit.html`.

- ✔ For more information on Meta Content Framework, visit `www.sil.org/sgml/gen-apps.html#mcf`.

- ✔ The RDF home page is `www.w3.org/RDF/`. For a working draft of the RDF, visit `www.w3.org/TR/WD-rdf-syntax/`. For a list of frequently asked questions about the RDF, visit `www.w3.org/RDF/FAQ`. For more information on MetaData, visit `www.w3.org/Metadata/`.

Chapter 13

XML Doubles Up on Web Sites

● ●

In This Chapter

▶ Understanding the Distribution and Replication Protocol (DRP)

▶ Delivering DRP and automatic information

▶ Making DRP effective

▶ Needing DRP

▶ Examining how DRP works

▶ Looking at samples of DRP content and applications

▶ Checking out the technical specifications of DRP

● ●

*I*n this chapter, we cover the HTTP Distribution and Replication Protocol (DRP) and how it functions within XML standards. We also discuss how DRP improves automatic information delivery — a necessary component for any documentation or software that changes over time, and a staple of XML programming. After that, we discuss what makes DRP effective, why it's needed, and how it works. In addition, we include a sample of a DRP application and coding specifications for its use.

DRP Provides Automatic and Efficient Delivery

Today, organizations worldwide are looking for more effective, less costly ways to deploy, manage, and update an ever-increasing collection of software, data, and Web content to service the information-handling needs of their employees, business partners, and customers. By improving the efficiency and performance of the Web, DRP lets companies use the Web more effectively and efficiently. DRP provides this performance improvement by:

✔ Enabling more efficient channels, software distribution, and Web browsing

✔ Speeding download time for data channels and reducing server load, which eliminates the "Web crawling" and file-by-file downloads that tend to slow many subscription-based channels

✔ Supporting differential updates, which makes software distribution more efficient and eliminates the current practice of downloading an entire file when only a small portion of it needs to be updated

✔ Enabling faster and more enjoyable Web browsing — especially over oh-so-slow modem connections — by speeding the delivery of multiple Web page elements

Based on a Marimba technology, and originally developed and deployed as part of Castanet, DRP simplifies file version updates and provides powerful replication for scalability. DRP uses advanced checksum technology, which creates a fingerprint of information, to assure accurate delivery of requested applications and data.

We refer to checksums quite often in this chapter. A *checksum* is a complex value that's calculated based on a file's composition before it is sent and then recalculated after delivery; if the values match, the assumption is that the data was delivered accurately, because even a one-bit change between sent and received versions will change the checksum value that's calculated.

You probably have a lot of questions regarding the basics of DRP. Well, the best source for this information — as is the case for most technologies — is a Web-based FAQ. Marimba (one of DRP's creators) maintains a great list of frequently asked questions and answers about DRP. So, instead of taking our word for it, get the information straight from the horse's mouth at `www.marimba.com/faq/drp-faq.html`.

Technical Specifications of DRP

DRP's design goals are to make it easy to identify and isolate elements in a hierarchical collection of files and to deliver only those elements that are necessary to bring a client's collection in compliance with an image on a server. If this "mix and match" metaphor makes sense, so will the rest of this explanation of DRP from a technical perspective.

So, you may ask, how does DRP identify and isolate these elements? Basically, DRP uses a token, called a *content-identifier,* to identify individual pieces of content. A content-identifier token is made up of one or more Uniform Resource Identifiers (URIs), which are separated by commas. URIs are combined into a single content-identifier to form a unique identifier for an entire hierarchy of files. According to the DRP spec, the syntax for a content-identifier is as follows:

```
content-identifier ::= URI ( "," URI )*
```

In English, this production rule means that a content-identifier must include at least one URI, and if more than one URI is included, a comma must separate any two URIs.

The asterisk notation means that the combination of a comma, followed by a URI, can repeat zero or more times, as explained in Chapter 4.

Typically, a checksum algorithm is used to generate a content-identifier for each piece of content. A *checksum algorithm* is a mathematical function used to calculate a number, or a series of numbers and letters to represent the number and sequence of bits in any given file. These numbers represent a mathematical signature or fingerprint for each file. In the DRP protocol, two specific algorithms are used to identify a file's content to ensure extra reliability:

✔ **MD5:** The Message Digest (MD5) is a well-known algorithm from RSA — an acronym for Rivest, Shamir, and Adelman, the founders of RSA Data Security, Inc., a technology licensing company that specializes in encryption and security. MD5 is used to compute a 128-bit checksum for any file or object. (See www.rsa.com/pub/rfc1321.txt for details on the implementation of the MD5 algorithm.)

According to the specification, you can generate a Universal Resource Name (URN), which defines a way of uniquely identifying any object anywhere on the Internet and which is a special type of URI, for any 128-bit MD5 checksum as follows:

```
MD5-URN = "urn:md5:" base64-number
```

✔ **SHA:** The Secure Hash Algorithm (SHA) from the National Institute of Standards and Technology is similar to the MD5 algorithm. The checksums generated by SHA are 160 bits long and have different properties, as described at csrc.nist.gov/fips/fip180-1.txt. The following code describes the method used to generate a URN using a SHA checksum:

```
SHA-URN = "urn:sha:" base64-number
```

Content is encoded through the use of base64 encoding by both MD5- and SHA-based URIs. This is done by encoding every three bytes of the checksum into four characters, each of which contains six bits of information. It is important to note that base64 numbers can include the characters / and +.

When these characters are included in a URN checksum, it is not necessary to escape them when they appear in a checksum URN, even though they are treated specially in the URN syntax specification.

When a content-identifier's URI designates common checksum algorithms such as MD5 or SHA, you can easily check the completeness of the content. However, if the URIs don't designate a common checksum algorithm, the content-identifier has to be regarded as an *opaque string* (which is a string whose content cannot be verified) and the URIs can only be used to provide addressing information. These examples are all valid content-identifiers:

```
urn:md5:FNG4c6MJLdDEY1rcoGb4pQ==
urn:md5:HUXZLQLMuI/KZ5KDcJPcOA==
urn:sha:thvDyvhfIqlvFe+A9MYgxAfm1q5=
```

The previous examples and the remaining code examples in this chapter are taken from the DRP note, written by Arthur van Hoff of Marimba, Inc., John Giannandrea of Netscape, Inc., Mark Hapner of Sun Microsystems, Inc., Steve Carter of Novell, Inc., and Milo Medin of At Home Corp. The note is posted on the W3C's Web site at `www.w3.org/TR/NOTE-drp`, and the W3C retains all copyrights associated with the note.

If you are working with an application that will not allow duplicates for any one URN, you can create unique content-identifiers by using a collection of appropriate URIs. For example, if version numbers are included as part of the content, make sure the version number is a unique identifier. Do this by adding the URL of the object that the version number describes in the content-identifier, in addition to the checksum URN. The next two examples of URNs include URLs as the initial part of those URIs.

```
http://www.acme.com/images/
        foo.gif,urn:md5:FNG4c6MJLdDEY1rcoGb4pQ==
http://www.acme.com/Example/,urn:x-version:5
```

A content-identifier is often embedded in an HTTP header, and therefore, the URIs in the content-identifier must not contain reserved characters, which have meaning to an HTTP server. These reserved characters include spaces, commas, plus signs, equal signs, or ampersands. All reserved characters should be encoded as stipulated in the URI specification; thus, in the following example, the %20 represents an encoded or "escaped" space.

```
ftp://www.acme.com/Hello%20World
```

Index format

DRP uses an index, or data-structure, to describe the exact condition of a set of data files. The index plays two important roles:

- ✔ It describes the hierarchical structure of the files, capturing and preserving directory structures.
- ✔ It provides version, size, and type information for each file in the collection.

Generally, an index provides a picture of the condition of a set of files at one particular moment in time. As the files change, so should their index.

Usually, an index is stored in a computer's memory as a tree data structure. However, if clients and servers are to share this information via HTTP, the index can be described in XML. The index DTD used by the DRP protocol is part of its specification, which is as follows:

```
<!-- XML DTD for the DRP Protocol -->
    <!ELEMENT index      (file | dir)*
           >
    <!ATTLIST index      id              CDATA
          #IMPLIED       >
    <!ATTLIST index      base            CDATA
          #IMPLIED       >
    <!ELEMENT file       EMPTY
           >
    <!ATTLIST file       path            CDATA
          #REQUIRED      >
    <!ATTLIST file       id              CDATA
          #IMPLIED       >
    <!ATTLIST file       size            CDATA
          #IMPLIED       >
    <!ATTLIST file       mime            CDATA
          #IMPLIED       >
    <!ATTLIST file       info            CDATA
          #IMPLIED       >
    <!ELEMENT dir        (file | dir)*
           >
    <!ATTLIST dir        path            CDATA
          #REQUIRED      >
```

Using this DTD, we created this example of an index that describes a hierarchical set of files. To begin with, it describes a collection of directories and files that may be diagrammed like this:

```
    Name          Size      MD5  Checksum
root-level
 home.html      12,345    PEFjWBDv/sd9alS9BYuXOw==
 layer1.js      32,112    W25YCu3toJt3ZsDsHIZmpg==

subdirectory: images
 acme.gif        4,532    +hbZN5XfU6QAJB1RF1/KSQ==
 banner.gif     10,452    tr3X+oN3r9kqvsiyDSSjjg==

subdirectory: java/classes
 scroll.java    14,323    xjBkgWouS6p6FTUMIkx/Zg==
 gui.jar       540,321    tcUzwODKut3SiTpmpAsi8g==
```

In other words, we have a collection of files that includes an HTML document (file ends in .html) and a JavaScript program (file ends in .js) in the root of the hierarchy, beneath which two subdirectories reside. In the /images subdirectory, two graphics (.gif) files occur, and in the java/classes subdirectory, a Java source code file (name ends in .java) and a Java archive file (name ends in .jar) occur. These may represent only a small set of changed files that DRP can map into a much larger set of subdirectories beneath the root itself.

But, in the following code, note how DRP opens the index of elements with the <index> tag, and then opens each subdirectory reference with a <dir> tag; in each case, the closing tag (</index> or </dir>) provides an explicit indication when that structure closes, so we can tell exactly what's in the root (everything up to the first <dir> tag) and what's in each subdirectory referenced.

```xml
<?XML VERSION="1.0" RMD="NONE"?>
<index>
<file path="home.html" size="12345" id="urn:md5:PEFjWBDv/
          sd9alS9BYuXOw=="/>
<file path="layer1.js" size="32112"
          id="urn:md5:W25YCu3toJt3ZsDsHIZmpg=="/>
<dir path="images">
<file path="acme.gif" size="4532"
          id="urn:md5:+hbZN5XfU6QAJB1RF1/KSQ=="/>
<file path="banner.gif" size="10452"
          id="urn:md5:tr3X+oN3r9kqvsiyDSSjjg=="/>
</dir>
<dir path="java/classes">
<file path="Scroll.java" size="14323"
          id="urn:md5:xjBkgWouS6p6FTUMIkx/Zg=="/>
<file path="gui.jar" size="540321"
          id="urn:md5:tcUzwODKut3SiTpmpAsi8g=="/>
</dir>
</index>
```

Index retrieval

When you use DRP, an index for a specific hierarchy is retrieved through a specific URL for that index. This index can be stored in any file and can be retrieved using a normal HTTP GET request. The *MIME* type of the index file allows clients to treat the index as a special file that provides meta information about other files. (MIME stands for Multipurpose Internet Mail Extensions and provides a taxonomy of Internet file types that applications can use to identify the contents of files; a DRP index has a specific type that identifies what it is and how it is to be used.)

After it is properly identified, a DRP index can be used by a client to automatically download the files that are specified therein. In the example from the preceding section of this chapter, reading that particular index file within a DRP client application would cause all of the file referenced therein to be read and copied into the root and the other specified subdirectories mentioned.

An index file can be contained in any ordinary text file on an HTTP server, but an index can also be generated dynamically, perhaps by some application that walks a targeted directory tree and generates the index file on the fly. In such a case, it's not necessary to ensure that a new index gets constructed each time the target directory tree changes, because the index is always generated based on what's present in the directory tree.

An index need not necessarily be generated from a file system; it could also represent hierarchical data from a different source, such as a database.

After an index is downloaded the first time, the client can update the content easily by simply downloading a new version of the index and making a quick comparison between the newly downloaded version and the initial version. The client can determine exactly which files it needs to download because each file has a unique entry in the index. This ensures that only a minimal set of files is downloaded, saving valuable bandwidth and time.

Index base URL

You typically want to locate the index file in the root directory of the file hierarchy that it describes. In such cases, the base URL for the files in the index is the same as the base URL for the index itself. A base URL defines the root for a set of HTTP references and, therefore, establishes a frame of reference for relative file accesses from that base. This notion descends directly from the HTML <BASE> tag.

The index file should not be listed in the index itself. This creates a circular reference, which may cause some parsers to loop back into the index infinitely and never return from spinning around in circles!

An index can expressly point to another absolute or relative base URL via the base attribute of the index tag, allowing an index to illustrate files located in a different directory or even on a different server. So, an index located at this address

```
www.acme.com/Examples/index.xml
```

defines the base URL of the index as

```
www.acme.com/Examples/
```

unless the base attribute of the index tag is declared differently.

Given the base URL that occurs on the preceding line, this means that the index described in the code block in the "Index format" section earlier in this chapter actually refers to the following absolute file references:

```
www.acme.com/Examples/home.html
www.acme.com/Examples/layer1.js
www.acme.com/Examples/images/acme.gif
www.acme.com/Examples/images/banner.gif
www.acme.com/Examples/java/classes/Scroll.java
www.acme.com/Examples/java/classes/gui.jar
```

Index expiration

Unless specified by metadata, the DRP client program must observe the `Expires` field included in the HTTP reply of the index request. This determines how long the index remains valid. When an index does expire, a new version should be downloaded by the client. By reading the value of the `Expires` field in the HTTP reply for any index request, DRP provides a simple mechanism to schedule updates for indexes.

In some cases, additional metadata will be available that can provide more detailed information for scheduling updates of the index and the content it describes. This usually requires additional XML programming that parses for specific metadata or that makes access to other fields in a server's HTTP replies.

For more information on this topic, please consult Robin Cover's excellent discussion of DRP, which is available at `www.sil.org/sgml/xml.html#xml-drp`.

Index caching

HTTP proxies are allowed to cache indexes only if the HTTP header says so. In general, an HTTP proxy should treat indexes in the same manner as other normal files. HTTP Version 1.0 and 1.1 include several cache control tools that can be used to direct the caching of indexes.

Information about both versions of HTTP is available on the W3C Web site at
`www.w3.org/Protocols/`.

A server that generates personalized indexes with the same base URL must
flag such indexes as "not cacheable" using standard HTTP mechanisms as
defined in the HTTP Versions 1.0 and 1.1 protocol specifications. That's
because different users may use the same base URL and one user's
personal index could differ from another's, depending on what software
they run and how they've configured their machines. This flagging prevents
such an occurrence by forcing the server to download the index each time
it's requested, thereby avoiding the problem of delivering an incorrect
index to the wrong user.

Content-based addressing

When a client requests an index file, it obtains a full description of the
structure and state of a collection of data files. When a client has a index, it
can decide exactly which files should be downloaded, and also determine
the total size of the download. The client's ability to determine exactly
which files should be downloaded allows the end user to issue several GET
requests and retrieve all the files at once.

Several extensions to the HTTP have been proposed by the HTTP-NG
working group and as part of the HTTP Pipelining proposal that can be used
to make the download of multiple files more efficient. Here, NG stands for
"Next Generation" and represents research work underway at the W3C to
define a new and improved version of HTTP. For more information on this
topic, please visit this W3C Web page: `www.w3.org/Protocols/HTTP-NG/`.

The new work that's underway, both for HTTP-NG and HTTP Pipelining,
concerns itself with endowing HTTP with the ability to access and deliver
multiple files at once, instead of the one-at-a-time transfer capabilities inherent in HTTP 1.0 and 1.1. The ability to combine multiple files in a single
transfer is expected to improve delivery, partly because it reduces the number
of TCP connections required to effect delivery and partly because it allows
data-streaming techniques to be used to speed up the delivery process.

Because clients can store data files in a disk cache, they can examine
multiple indexes and determine if any of the indexes point to files with the
same content-identifiers. If the indexes do, the client can simply retrieve a
copy of the file from the cache, instead of downloading it a second time.
This common procedure is used when different sites refer to the same
images or libraries. In effect, this practice prevents redundant downloads.

By eliminating redundant downloads, the overhead of downloading commonly used data and software components is greatly reduced. Clients use
content-identifiers to determine which files are identical, even if they are

stored on separate servers. The savings in overhead will be exactly equal to the combined size of those redundant files that would otherwise have to be transferred repeatedly, if unnecessarily.

Indexes are not required to include a content-identifier for each file, and the content-identifiers may be deleted for any or all files in the index. Servers can elect to omit content-identifiers for dynamically generated files, such as live audio. If the content-identifier is absent, files are retrieved using a regular `GET-IF-MODIFIED` request. When clients compare indexes, those files that don't have content-identifiers should always be considered different from their previous incarnations and treated as new versions for every access.

Content-ID header field

Now that obtaining an index for a large set of files is possible, we need a mechanism that will help us obtain the correct version of each of the files that need downloading.

Each file's correct version is determined by its content-identifier, as indicated in the index. Ultimately, the successful distribution of applications depends on the correct version of each file being obtained, not just the current version.

When a client requests a file, it can include the content-identifier in the HTTP `GET` request to the server, as in this example:

```
GET /Example/home.html HTTP/1.1
Content-ID: urn:md5:PEFjWBDv/sd9alS9BYuXOw==
```

The `Content-ID` header field, new to HTTP, specifies the correct version of the requested file. The server uses the content-identifier in the `Content-ID` field to decide whether the requested version of the file can be sent to the client. When the server replies to the client, the content-identifier specified in the `Content-ID` should match the one specified in the `GET` request. If the correct version of the file is not available, the server should respond with the dreaded error `404 File Version Not Found`.

Note that this 404 error is bit different from the ones you're used to seeing on the Web. The message now includes the word "Version" indicating that it isn't necessarily the file that isn't available, but instead the necessary version of the file isn't available. A subtle but important difference.

If a content-identifier is not specified in the HTTP `GET` request, the server must return to current version of the file, as in a normal HTTP request. The server's reply should include the `Content-ID` field if the client's DRP application knows the correct content-identifier for the file that is returned. When a server cannot interpret a `Content-ID` field, it should reply with the most current version of the requested file.

The server is not required to specify a `Content-ID` in its reply, and the client must make sure that the reply contains the correct content-identifier if a `Content-ID` field is included. When the requested content-identifier contains a URN with a verifiable checksum, the client should always recompute that checksum to make sure that the correct content is returned.

Differential downloads

When a file is updated on the server, it is downloaded by each client that needs the new version. Updates to files often affect only small portions of a file. Thus, the most efficient way to deliver updates is for the server to reply only with those parts of the file that have changed. This requires use of the differential GET request.

Differential-ID header field

Clients can use indexes received from servers to conclude what changes have been made to a collection of files. The index also helps the client decide which files were modified, not just created or deleted.

If a file has been modified, the client can deliver for that file a differential `GET` request that includes:

 ✔ The content-identifier for the version of the file requested
 ✔ The content-identifier for the version of the file already stored on the client machine

In addition to the `Content-ID` field in the `GET` request, a differential request also includes a `Differential-ID` field that specifies the content-identifier of the file the client already has, as in this example:

```
GET /Example/home.html HTTP/1.1
Content-ID: urn:md5:PEFjWBDv/sd9alS9BYuXOw==
Differential-ID: urn:md5:3FS2oCnWPZptpNO5oKBemA==
```

Then, when a server receives this kind of `GET` request — one that includes a `Differential-ID` field — it looks inside its cache for both versions of the requested file (as specified by the content-identifiers listed in the `Content-ID` and `Differential-ID` fields of the request). If both versions are present, the server can figure out the difference between the two files and return the differences by themselves in a patch file to be applied to the client version, rather than copying the entire file to the client.

When a server replies with a differential update, it must include both the content-identifier of the resulting file in the `Content-ID` field, as well as the content-identifier of the file to which the update should be applied in the `Differential-ID` field.

As with changes from one version to another, if an HTTP server does not have access to the version of the file indicated by the differential content-identifier, it can ignore that identifier and return the entire file instead. Also, if the differences file is not smaller than the original file, the server can elect to the send the original file instead.

A client can detect when a differential update is returned by examining the reply's MIME type. After verifying the `Content-ID` and `Differential-ID` fields in that reply, the client can apply the differences file to its current version of the file to generate the desired version.

To ensure interoperability, you must specify a well-known format that can be used to describe differences between two version of any file. The default differences file format is the `GDIFF` format, which is defined in a separate proposal. Any DRP client can specify additional acceptable differencing formats using the HTTP `Accept` header field.

A simple server can choose to ignore differential `GET` requests altogether and simply reply with the entire contents of any requested file. Note that although the example uses the `Content-ID` field to specify the desired version of a file, this field can be omitted to obtain a differential update to the most recent version. The server should return a `304 Not Modified` reply if the requested resource has not changed.

Differential index retrieval

The process of obtaining the most up-to-date index must be efficient because clients poll for updates repeatedly. Sending the entire index each time an `INDEX` request is made would be wasteful, especially because there is often little or no change between requests. Also, indexes can contain many files and can be rather large.

To avoid repeated downloads of a complete index, clients can use a differential `GET` request to obtain indexes. In response to a differential `INDEX` request, the server can reply with the differences file between the client's index and the server's current index.

The server decides what content-identifier to use for each index. Each content-identifier must identify the index uniquely. One way of doing this is to construct an identifier from a checksum computed on the index; another way is to combine the URL of the index with a version number. Note that a differencing algorithm can be defined that performs a structural comparison of two indexes, rather than a textual comparison. Either way, the idea is to be able to identify different versions between client and server, and to deliver the latest differences from the server to the client to keep them synchronized.

HTTP proxy caching

It is possible to make an HTTP proxy aware of the Content-ID and Differential-ID fields in HTTP requests and replies. The proxy can avoid accidentally returning the wrong version of a requested file because the content-identifier is included in each GET request. Retrieving the wrong version from an intermediate proxy can cause serious problems when distributing important applications or data.

The proxy must use the content-identifier field to uniquely identify the content being transferred. The same piece of content, even when downloaded from multiple locations, is likely to have the same content-identifier. The proxy can check this value to avoid redundant downloads.

In addition, a proxy can use the Differential-ID header field to reply to differential GET requests. If both versions of the file are in the proxy's cache, the proxy can compute the differential reply locally, without requiring access to the originating server.

Backward compatibility

The DRP protocol works efficiently with existing HTTP-enabled environments. Some special precautions need to be taken to make sure that older proxy servers don't interfere with the version handling strategy used by DRP.

HTTP 1.0 proxy caching

To prevent the inaccurate caching of data files in HTTP 1.0 proxies, servers should identify all files returned to an HTTP 1.0 client or proxy as not cacheable. This can be done using the Pragma and/or Expires fields, as defined in the HTTP 1.0 specification.

To correctly cache files in an HTTP 1.1 proxy, the server can use the Vary field in the HTTP reply, which should be set to Content-ID. This example of a reply includes a Content-ID:

```
HTTP/1.1 200 OK
Vary: Content-ID
Content-ID: urn:md5:PEFjWBDv/sd9alS9BYuXOw==
```

If the request also contains a `Differential-ID`, the `Vary` header field should be set to `Content-ID,Differential-ID`. This example of a reply to a differential `GET` request contains a `Differential-ID`:

```
HTTP/1.1 200 OK
Vary: Content-ID,Differential-ID
Content-ID: urn:md5:PEFjWBDv/sd9alS9BYuXOw==
Differential-ID: urn:md5:3FS2oCnWPZptpNO5oKBemA==
```

Using this strategy, you can clearly see that client requests that specify a `Content-ID` are cached appropriately by an HTTP 1.1 proxy. However, when the `Content-ID` is omitted, the proxy will not match the request and will download the requested file from the server each time a request is made.

Using the `Vary` header provides the best performance for HTTP 1.1 without weakening any of the caching guarantees required by the DRP protocol.

Compatibility with existing servers

The DRP protocol is set up to not require server support. The index can be specified using a normal file on a server that describes part of or an entire site. Generating an index file using a simple program that scans the file system is easy.

The client can use the index file to determine which files to download from the site using normal HTTP requests. If the server does not provide special DRP support, no guarantees can be given about file version handling. However, if the index file specifies content-identifiers for each file, the client can use these to verify that it has obtained the correct version by recomputing the appropriate checksums.

The aforementioned technique permits DRP to be used with a number of existing URL types, such as `ftp:` and `file:`, without alteration.

The HTTP Distribution and Replication Protocol provides significant added value to the HTTP protocol. DRP enables the distribution and replication of data files in a simple and efficient manner. DRP is a widely applicable technology and is appropriate for the distribution of HTML-based content, as well as important applications and data.

Chapter 14

Marking XML by the Numbers

● ●

In This Chapter

▶ Creating an XML application

▶ Understanding the advantages of using MathML

▶ Using MathML to render mathematical information over the Internet

▶ Creating MathML presentation markup

▶ Using MathML content markup

▶ Examining some MathML examples

▶ Exploring MathML tools, rules, and resources

● ●

MathML is a relatively new object-oriented markup language based on XML. Although MathML is not a standard yet, all efforts indicate that the language is headed in that direction. In this chapter, we take an in-depth look at MathML and how you can render mathematics over the Internet by using this new markup language. In addition, this chapter outlines the features and advantages of using MathML and the tools available that you can use to create, edit, and view your MathML files. Gain a good understanding of the MathML tags and their attributes, and you will be programming in MathML in no time.

Like CML (Chemical Markup Language — see Chapter 10), Mathematical Markup Language (MathML) is also an application of XML. You can use MathML for specialized applications such as rendering mathematical content and notation over both the Internet and an intranet. For example, you can represent mathematical expressions such as $x + 2$, $x^2 + y^2$, $(x + 4)y$, and so on over the Web by using MathML.

Although your field of expertise may not be mathematics, you can still read this chapter and gain insight into MathML, which can help you gain a good understanding of XML's usefulness.

The XML/MathML Relationship

XML is all about structured data. If you can represent data in a structured format, you can create XML files. The data can be about anything you want to interpret and render: software products, books and publishers, molecular information, and so on.

The markup language you use to represent the mathematical information is called MathML. Because you can represent very specific data such as mathematical notation and content in a structured format using MathML, you also need specialized viewers to view the results. You can't use your browsers (Netscape Navigator and Internet Explorer) directly to view the results.

The specialized application's syntax, grammar, and vocabulary are different because the browsers do not inherently support specialized XML applications like MathML. However, you can configure your browser to execute an external helper application that reads and interprets MathML files. Presently, no significant MathML viewers, helper applications, or parsers are on the market. As the markup language develops and gains popularity, we can expect a number of vendors to develop such tools.

MathML Definitions

Before we jump into the details about MathML, the available tools, and the rules of the game, we want to cover some of the commonly used terms in the world of XML and MathML. First, you must understand that XML is based on SGML, which is a metalanguage used to construct new markup languages like MathML, CML, and so on.

As we discuss in Chapter 3, a *metalanguage* is a language about a language. When you create or edit a MathML file, you manipulate the MathML tags and their attributes to achieve the desired results. After you create a MathML file, you can view the file by using a MathML viewer.

MathML, like any XML-based language, has a DTD — see Chapter 6 for the details on DTDs. A MathML file must conform to the DTD; otherwise, the MathML file is invalid and the MathML parser and viewer will not process it.

The following code listing gives you a quick look at a sample MathML code for the expression $x^2 + x - 4$. Follow these simple steps to create the equivalent MathML code for a given expression:

1. **Represent the expression as a binary tree structure, as shown in Figure 14-1.**

2. **Apply the appropriate MathML tag to every node of the tree and group the nodes together appropriately as needed.**

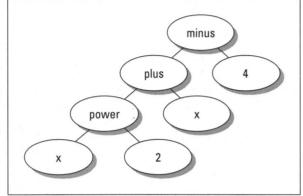

Figure 14-1:
The binary tree representation of the expression $x^2 + x - 4$.

```
<MROW>
  <MROW>
   <MI>x</MI>
   <POWER/>
   <MI>2</MI>
  </MROW>
  <PLUS/>
  <MI>x</MI>
  <MINUS/>
  <MN>4</MN>
</MROW>
```

Using MathML

Although you can use HTML to represent text and graphics over the Web, you can use MathML to represent notations including mathematical, trigonometric, geometric, and rational expressions, as well as calculus, polynomials, and the like, over the Web. HTML's target audience is typically anyone and everyone who uses the Web, whereas MathML's target audience includes researchers, mathematicians, students, engineers, technicians, and so on.

MathML includes two types of markup: presentation and content.

MathML presentation markup

Using MathML presentation markup, you can mark a mathematical notation's expression structure. The MathML presentation markup includes two types of elements: the elements that declare the type of the data (`<MI>`, `<MN>`, and so on) and the elements that denote the layout definition, including fractions, rows, and scripts (`<MROW>`, `<MFRAC>`, and so on).

The following lists some of the presentation markup tags and examples of how you can use them. This section does not list the attributes of the tags because this is not intended to be a complete reference.

For a complete list of the presentation markup tags and their attributes, visit www.w3.org/TR/WD-math-970515/section3.html#sec3.

✔ **The `<MI>` Tag:** To represent identifiers such as variables, function names, and symbolic constants, use the `<MI>` tag. For example:

```
<MI>x</MI>
<MI>D</MI>
<MI>sin</MI>
```

✔ **The `<MF>` Tag:** To represent a *fence* (such as a set of parentheses), use the `<MF>` tag. The F within the `<MF>` tag stands for fence. For example:

```
<MF>(</MF>
<MF>)</MF>

<MF>[</MF>
<MF>]</MF>
```

✔ **The `<MN>` Tag:** To represent numeric data, use the `<MN>` tag like so:

```
<MN>1.2</MN>
<MN>.234</MN>
<MN>3.2e10</MN>
```

✔ **The `<MO>` Tag:** To represent a mathematical operator, use the `<MO>` tag as shown in the following example:

```
<MO>+</MO>
<MO>--</MO>
<MO>.AND.</MO>
<MO>.NOT.</MO>
<MO>.OR.</MO>
```

✔ **The** `<MTEXT>` **Tag:** To represent arbitrary text, use the `<MTEXT>` tag as follows:

```
<MTEXT>Remarks:</MTEXT>
<MTEXT>/* Comments */</MTEXT>
```

✔ **The** `<MS>` **Tag:** To represent a string literal within an expression, use the `<MS>` tag.

✔ **The** `<MSPACE/>` **Tag:** To represent a blank space of any size, use the `<MSPACE/>` tag.

✔ **The** `<MTABLE>` **Tag:** To represent a table or matrix, use the `<MTABLE>` tag.

✔ **The** `<MTD>` **Tag:** To specify a table or matrix's element, use the `<MTD>` tag. You can use the `<MTD>` tag only within an `<MTABLE>` tag.

✔ **The** `<MTR>` **Tag:** To represent a table or matrix's row, use the `<MTR>` tag. You can use the `<MTR>` tag only within an `<MTABLE>` tag.

Presentation markup layout definition

This section lists some of the presentation markup layout definition tags and examples of how you can use them. This section does not list the attributes of the tags because this is not intended to be a complete reference.

For a complete list of the layout definition tags and their attributes, visit `www.w3.org/TR/WD-math-970515/section3.html#sec3`.

✔ **The** `<MERROR>` **Tag:** To display the contents as an error message, use the `<MERROR>` tag. For example:

```
<MERROR>This is an error message</MERROR>
```

✔ **The** `<MFRAC>` **Tag:** To represent fractions, use the `<MFRAC>` tag like so:

```
<MFRAC>5 6</MFRAC>
```

✔ **The** `<MROOT>` **Tag:** For all other types of roots such as a cube root, use the `<MROOT>` tag as follows:

```
<MROOT>5 3</MROOT>
<MROOT>123 5</MROOT>
```

✔ **The** `<MROW>` **Tag:** To horizontally group together a number of subexpressions, use the `<MROW>` tag as shown here:

```
<MROW>
  <MSUP>
    <MI>x</MI>
    <MN>2</MN>
  </MSUP>
  <MO>+</MO>
  <MI>x</MI>
  <MO>-</MO>
  <MN>4</MN>
</MROW>

<MROW>
  <MI>PV</MI>
  <EQ/>
  <MN>1</MN>
  <OVER/>
  <MROW>
    <MN>1</MN>
    <PLUS/>
    <MI>r</MI>
  </MROW>
</MROW>
```

✔ **The** `<MSQRT>` **Tag:** To represent square roots, use the `<MSQRT>` tag. For example:

```
<MSQRT>5</MSQRT>
<MSQRT>9</MSQRT>
```

✔ **The** `<MSTYLE>` **Tag:** To apply style changes to the content, use the `<MSTYLE>` tag as shown here:

```
<MSTYLE maxsize="2">
  <MI>a</MI>
  <MO><OVER/></MO>
  <MI>b</MI>
</MSTYLE>
```

Presentation markup for symbol script definition

This section lists some of the presentation markup symbol script (attaching a script to a base) definition tags and examples of how you can use them. Superscripts and subscripts are examples of symbol scripts. This section does not list the attributes of the tags because this is not intended to be a complete reference.

For a complete list of the symbol script definition tags and their attributes, visit www.w3.org/TR/WD-math-970515/section3.html#sec3.

- **The** `<MSUB>` **Tag:** To attach a subscript to a base, use the `<MSUB>` tag. The syntax is `<MSUB>base subscript</MSUB>`. The following shows how you implement it:

  ```
  <MSUB>6 3</MSUB>
  ```

- **The** `<MSUBSUP>` **Tag:** To attach a pair of superscript and subscript to a base, use the `<MSUBSUP>` tag. The syntax is `<MSUBSUP>base sub-script superscript</MSUBSUP>`. For example:

  ```
  <MSUBSUP>2 2 4</MSUBSUP>
  ```

- **The** `<MSUP>` **Tag:** To attach a superscript to a base, use the `<MSUP>` tag. The tag's syntax is `<MSUP>base superscript</MSUP>`. For example:

  ```
  <MSUP>2 4</MSUP>
  ```

- **The** `<MOVER>` **Tag:** To attach an overscript to a base, use the `<MOVER>` tag. The syntax is `<MOVER>base overscript</MOVER>`, and you implement it as follows:

  ```
  <MOVER>2 2</MOVER>
  ```

- **The** `<MUNDER>` **Tag :** To attach an underscript to a base, use the `<MUNDER>` tag. The syntax is `<MUNDER>base underscript</MUNDER>`. For example:

  ```
  <MUNDER>2 2</MUNDER>
  ```

- **The** `<MUNDEROVER>` **Tag:** To attach a pair of underscript and overscript to a base, use the `<MUNDEROVER>` tag. The syntax is `<MUNDEROVER>base underscript overscript</MUNDEROVER>`. For example:

  ```
  <MUNDEROVER>2 5 2</MUNDEROVER>
  ```

MathML content markup

You use MathML content markup to encode a mathematical expression's underlying content. Although the presentation markup is for rendering (in other words, presentation), the content markup is for encoding the meaning of elementary mathematical expressions. For MathML content markup, you can use the `<EXPR>` tag.

Arithmetic and algebraic elements

Table 14-1 lists the different arithmetic and algebraic elements and their MathML tags.

Table 14-1	Arithmetic and Algebraic Elements
Operation	*MathML Tag*
Addition	`<PLUS/>`
Subtraction	`<MINUS/>`
Division	`<OVER/>`
Multiplication	`<TIMES/>`
To the power of	`<POWER/>`
Exponentiation	`<EXP/>`
Remainder	`<REM/>`
Factorial	`<FACTORIAL>`
Maximum	`<MAX>`
Minimum	`<MIN>`

The following subsections show examples of how to use arithmetic and algebraic statements and equations in MathML.

Simple algebraic statement

Here's an example of how you use the basic arithmetic and algebraic elements to create a simple algebraic statement in XML. The expression in question is

```
(x*2 + x - 4) / (x - 2)
```

The binary tree structure for this statement is shown in Figure 14-2.

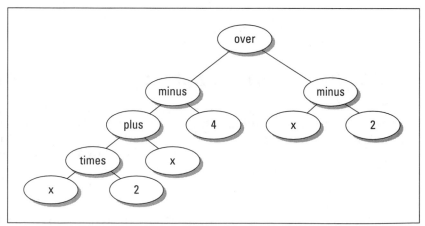

Figure 14-2:
The binary tree representation of the expression $(x*2 + x - 4)/(x - 2)$.

To create the equivalent MathML representation, represent each node within the tree with the appropriate MathML tag.

The expression includes a numerator and a denominator. As a result, you can use the <MROW> ... </MROW> tag to represent each of them. Again, within the numerator, you can represent $x*2$ by using the <MROW> ... </MROW> tag.

To represent the identifier x, use the <MI> ... </MI> tag. To represent the numbers *2* and *4,* use the <MN> ... </MN> tag. In addition, to represent the plus, minus, multiplication, and division operators, use <PLUS/>, <MINUS/>, <TIMES/>, and <OVER/> with the <MO> ... </MO> tag.

The following code block shows the MathML representation of this statement:

```
<MROW>
 <MROW>
  <MROW>
   <MI>x</MI>
   <MO><TIMES/></MO>
   <MN>2</MN>
  </MROW>
  <MO><PLUS/></MO>
  <MI>x</MI>
  <MO><MINUS/></MO>
  <MN>4</MN>
 </MROW>
 <OVER/>
 <MROW>
  <MI>x</MI>
  <MO><MINUS/></MO>
  <MN>4</MN>
 </MROW>
</MROW>
```

Complex algebraic statement

Here's an example of how you use the basic arithmetic and algebraic elements to create a complex algebraic statement in XML. The expression in question is

```
(x(x + 1) + y(y - 1)) / xy
```

We show the binary tree structure for this statement in Figure 14-3.

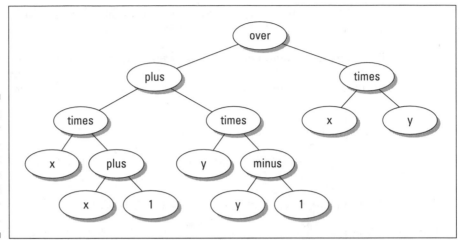

Figure 14-3:
The binary
tree repre-
sentation
of the
expression
$(x(x + 1) +$
$y(y − 1))/xy$.

To create the equivalent MathML representation, represent each node within the tree with the appropriate MathML tag. The expression includes a numerator and a denominator. As a result, you can use the ⟨MROW⟩ ... ⟨/MROW⟩ tag to represent each of them. Again, within the numerator, you can represent $x + 1$ and $y − 1$ by using the ⟨MROW⟩ ... ⟨/MROW⟩ tag.

To represent the identifier x, use the ⟨MI⟩ ... ⟨/MI⟩ tag. To represent the number 1, use the ⟨MN⟩ ... ⟨/MN⟩ tag. In addition, you represent the plus, minus, multiplication, and division operators, by using ⟨PLUS/⟩, ⟨MINUS/⟩, ⟨TIMES/⟩, and ⟨OVER/⟩ tags.

The MathML representation for this statement is as follows:

```
<MROW>
 <MROW>
  <MI>x</MI>
  <TIMES/>
  <MROW>
     <MI>x</MI>
     <PLUS/>
     <MN>1</MN>
  </MROW>
  <PLUS/>
  <MI>y</MI>
  <TIMES/>
  <MROW>
     <MI>y</MI>
     <MINUS/>
     <MN>1</MN>
```

```
   </MROW>
   </MROW>
   <OVER/>
   <MROW>
      <MI>x</MI>
      <TIMES/>
      <MI>y</MI>
   </MROW>
   </MROW>
```

Algebraic equation

Here's an example of how you use the basic arithmetic and algebraic elements to create an algebraic equation in XML. The expression in question is

```
PV = 1 / (1 + r)
```

You can see the binary tree structure for this equation in Figure 14-4.

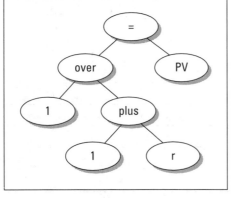

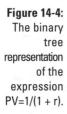

Figure 14-4:
The binary tree representation of the expression PV=1/(1 + r).

To create the equivalent MathML representation, represent each node within the tree with the appropriate MathML tag. The expression's right side includes a numerator and a denominator. Use the <MROW> ... </MROW> tag to represent the denominator. Within the denominator, you can represent *1 + r* by using the <MROW> ... </MROW> tag.

To represent the identifiers *PV* and *r,* use the <MI> ... </MI> tag. To represent the number *1,* use the <MN> ... </MN> tag. In addition, to represent the plus and division operators, use <PLUS/> and <OVER/> tags. Also, to represent equality, use the <EQ/> tag.

The MathML representation for this equation is as follows:

```
<MROW>
   <MI>PV</MI>
   <EQ/>
   <MN>1</MN>
   <OVER/>
   <MROW>
      <MN>1</MN>
      <PLUS/>
      <MI>r</MI>
   </MROW>
</MROW>
```

Basic content elements and set theory

Table 14-2 lists the basic content elements and their MathML tags. Table 14-3 lists the different set relations and their MathML tags.

Table 14-2	Basic Content Elements
Element	*MathML Tag*
A user-defined function	`<FN>`
A generic separator	`<SEP/>`
Such that separator	`<ST/>`
A generic inverse for functions	`<INVERSE/>`
Applying a function explicitly to the arguments	`<APPLY/>`
A scoping element	`<EXPR>`
An equation or a relation	`<E>`
An interval constructor	`<INTERVAL>`

Table 14-3	Set Relations and Their MathML Tags
Relation	*MathML Tag*
Set	`<SET>`
Union	`<UNION/>`
Intersection	`<INTERSECT/>`
Is In	`<IN/>`

Relation	MathML Tag
Is Not In	`<NOTIN/>`
Is a Subset	`<SUBSET/>`
Is a Proper Subset	`<PRSUBSET/>`
Is Not a Proper Subset	`<NOTPRSUBSET/>`

Here's an example of how you use the basic content elements and the set theory elements. The expression in question is

```
A UNION(B INTERSECTION C)
```

Check out the binary tree structure for the expression in Figure 14-5.

Figure 14-5:
The binary tree representation of the expression A UNION (B INTERSECTION C).

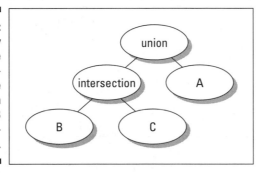

To create the equivalent MathML representation, represent each node within the tree with the appropriate MathML tag. The expression uses the set theory operators union and intersection. To represent them, use the `<UNION/>` and `<INTERSECTION/>` tags.

To represent the identifiers _A, B,_ and _C,_ use the `<MI>` ... `</MI>` tag.

Because the union of _A_ is with the intersection of _B_ and _C,_ represent the intersection of _B_ and _C_ within the `<EXPR>` ... `</EXPR>` tags.

In addition, represent the entire expression within another set of `<EXPR>` ... `</EXPR>` tags.

The following code shows the MathML representation of the expression:

```
<EXPR>
 <MI>A</MI>
 <UNION/>
 <EXPR>
     <MI>B</MI>
     <INTERSECTION/>
     <MI>C</MI>
 </EXPR>
</EXPR>
```

Linear algebra

Table 14-4 lists the different linear algebraic functions and their MathML tags.

Table 14-4 Linear Algebraic Functions and Their MathML Tags

Function	MathML Tag
Vector	`<VECTOR>`
Matrix	`<MATRIX>`
MatrixRow	`<MATRIXROW>`
Inverse of a matrix	`<MATRIXINVERSE>`
Determinant	`<DETERMINANT>`

Here's an example of using MathML markup for a linear algebra expression. The expression in question is:

$$A = \begin{vmatrix} 1 & 0 & 1 \\ 0 & 1 & 0 \\ 1 & 1 & 0 \end{vmatrix} + \begin{vmatrix} 1 & 0 & 0 \\ 0 & 1 & 1 \\ 1 & 0 & 1 \end{vmatrix}$$

You can see the binary tree structure for the expression in Figure 14-6.

Figure 14-6:
The binary tree representation of a linear algebraic expression.

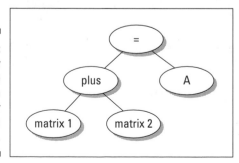

To create the equivalent MathML representation, represent each node within the tree with the appropriate MathML tag. The linear algebraic expression includes addition of a couple of matrices. To represent a matrix, use the `<MATRIX>` tag. To represent a row within the matrix, use the `<MATRIXROW>` tag. To represent the separation between any two elements within the matrix, use the `<SEP/>` tag.

To represent the numbers *0* and *1,* use the `<MN>` ... `</MN>` tag pair. To represent the identifier *A,* use the `<MI>` ... `</MI>` tag pair. Contain the entire expression within the set of `<E>` ... `</E>` tag pair. The `<E>` ... `</E>` tag pair represents an equation in this case. To represent the equality, use the `<EQ/>` tag.

The MathML representation for the expression is as follows:

```
<E>
 <MI>A</MI><EQ/>
 <MATRIX>
  <MATRIXROW>
   <MN>1</MN><SEP/>
   <MN>0</MN><SEP/><MN>1</MN>
  </MATRIXROW>
  <MATRIXROW>
   <MN>0</MN><SEP/>
   <MN>1</MN><SEP/><MN>0</MN>
  </MATRIXROW>
  <MATRIXROW>
   <MN>1</MN><SEP/>
   <MN>1</MN><SEP/><MN>0</MN>
  </MATRIXROW>
 </MATRIX>
 <PLUS/>
 <MATRIX>
  <MATRIXROW>
   <MN>1</MN><SEP/>
   <MN>0</MN><SEP/><MN>0</MN>
  </MATRIXROW>
  <MATRIXROW>
   <MN>0</MN><SEP/>
   <MN>1</MN><SEP/><MN>1</MN>
  </MATRIXROW>
  <MATRIXROW>
   <MN>1</MN><SEP/>
   <MN>0</MN><SEP/><MN>1</MN>
  </MATRIXROW>
 </MATRIX>
</E>
```

Relations

Table 14-5 lists the different mathematical relations and their MathML tags.

Table 14-5	Mathematical Relations and Their MathML Tags
Relation	*MathML Tag*
=	`<EQ/>`
!=	`<NEQ/>`
>	`<GT/>`
<	`<LT/>`
>=	`<GEQ/>`
<=	`<LEQ/>`

Here's an example of how to use the relations tags. The expression in question is

```
B > (C <= D)
```

You can check out the binary tree structure for this expression in Figure 14-7.

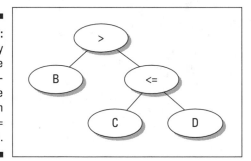

Figure 14-7: The binary tree representation of the expression B > (C <= D).

To create the equivalent MathML representation, represent each node within the tree with the appropriate MathML tag. The expression uses the relational operators > (greater than) and <= (less than or equal to). To represent those operators, use the `<GT/>` and `<LEQ/>` tags, respectively. To represent the identifiers *B, C,* and *D,* use the `<MI>` ... `</MI>` tag pair. To represent the relation within the parentheses, use the `<E>` ... `</E>` tags. You use the `<E>` ... `</E>` tags to represent an equation or relation. In addition, represent the entire expression within another set of `<E>` ... `</E>` tags.

The MathML representation for the expression is as follows:

```
<E>
 <MI>B</MI>
 <GT/>
 <E>
  <MI>C</MI>
  <LEQ/>
  <MI>D</MI>
 </E>
</E>
```

Sequences and series

Table 14-6 lists the different sequences and series elements and their MathML tags.

Table 14-6	Sequences and Series Elements
Element	**MathML Tag**
Sum	`<SUM/>`
Product	`<PRODUCT/>`
Limit	`<LIMIT/>`
Tends-to	`<TENDSTO/>`

Here's an example of using MathML tags to show sequences and series elements. For this example, the expression is

```
limit x tends to 0
```

To create the equivalent MathML representation, represent each node within the tree with the appropriate MathML tag. To represent the limit, use the `<LIMIT/>` tag. To represent the identifier x, use the `<MI>` ... `</MI>` tag pair. To represent the number 0, use the `<MN>` ... `</MN>` tag pair. Here's the MathML code:

```
<EXPR>
 <LIMIT/>
 <MI>x</MI><TENDSTO/><MN>0</MN>
</EXPR>
```

Statistics

Table 14-7 lists the different statistical functions and their MathML tags.

Table 14-7	Statistical Functions and Their MathML Tags
Function	**MathML Tag**
Average	`<MEAN>`
Median	`<MEDIAN>`
Mode	`<MODE>`
Variance	`<VAR>`
Standard deviation	`<SDEV>`
Moment	`<MOMENT>`

To create the equivalent MathML representation of

```
standard deviation of x
```

represent each node within the tree with the appropriate MathML tag. To represent the standard deviation, use the `<SDEV>` and `</SDEV>` tags. To represent the identifier x, use the `<MI>` ... `</MI>` tags. The MathML code for this example is as follows:

```
<SDEV>
  <MI>x</MI>
</SDEV>
```

Trigonometry

Table 14-8 lists different trigonometric functions and their MathML tags.

Table 14-8	Trigonometric Functions and Their MathML Tags
Function	**MathML Tag**
Sine	`<SIN/>`
Cosine	`<COS/>`
Tangent	`<TAN/>`
Arcsine	`<ARCSIN/>`
Arccosine	`<ARCCOS/>`
Arctangent	`<ARCTAN/>`
Hyperbolic sine	`<SINH/>`
Hyperbolic cosine	`<COSH/>`
Hyperbolic tangent	`<TANH/>`

Function	MathML Tag
Secant	`<SEC/>`
Cosecant	`<COSEC/>`
Cotangent	`<COTAN/>`
Hyperbolic secant	`<SECH/>`
Hyperbolic cosecant	`<COSECH/>`
Hyperbolic tangent	`<COTANH/>`

You can use MathML to show trigonometric equations. In this example, the expression is

```
t = cos(x + a) + tan(y / b)
```

Figure 14-8 shows the binary tree structure for this equation.

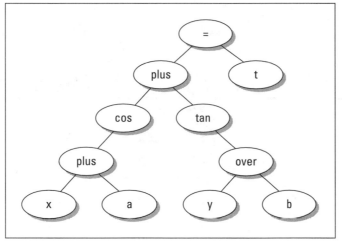

Figure 14-8: The binary tree representation of the expression t = cos (x + a) + tan(y / b).

To create the equivalent MathML representation, represent each node within the tree with the appropriate MathML tag. The expression's right side includes a summation of a couple of trigonometric calculations. To represent each trigonometric calculation, use the `<MROW>` ... `</MROW>` tag pair.

To represent the identifiers *t, x, a, y,* and *b,* use the `<MI>` ... `</MI>` tag pair. To represent the plus and division operators, use `<PLUS/>` and `<OVER/>`. To represent equality, use the `<EQ/>` tag.

The MathML representation for the example equation is as follows:

```
<MROW>
 <MI>t</MI>
 <EQ/>
 <COS/>
 <MROW>
  <MI>x</MI>
  <PLUS/>
  <MI>a</MI>
 </MROW>
 <PLUS/>
 <TAN/>
 <MROW>
  <MI>y</MI>
  <OVER/>
  <MI>b</MI>
 </MROW>
</MROW>
```

Understanding calculus

Table 14-9 lists the different calculus functions and their MathML tags.

Table 14-9	Calculus Functions and Their MathML Tags
Function	**MathML Tag**
Logarithm	`<LOG>`
Natural logarithm	`<LN>`
Derivative	`<DIFF>`
Partial derivative	`<PARTIALDIFF>`
Total derivative	`<TOTALDIFF>`
Definite integral	`<INT>`
Lower limit of integral	`<LOWER>`
Upper limit of integral	`<UPPER>`
Bound variable	`<BVAR>`
Degree within nth derivative	`<DEGREE>`

You can use MathML to describe calculus problems. In this example, the expression is

```
Log (a / b)
```

The binary tree structure for this expression appears in Figure 14-9.

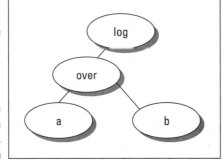

Figure 14-9:
The binary
tree
representation
of the
expression
log (a / b).

To create the equivalent MathML representation, represent each node within the tree with the appropriate MathML tag. Because the expression is used to calculate the logarithm, use the `<LOG>` ... `</LOG>` tag pair. The expression includes *a* divided by *b;* therefore use the `<OVER/>` tag for the division operator and the `<MI>` ... `</MI>` tag pair to represent the identifiers *a* and *b*.

The MathML representation for this calculus expression is:

```
<LOG>
   <MI>a</MI>
   <MO><OVER/></MO>
   <MI>b</MI>
</LOG>
```

Understanding the expression from the markup

This section includes an example that demonstrates how you can derive the mathematical expression from a given MathML representation. The representation in question is as follows:

```
<MROW>
   <MI>x</MI>
   <MO><POWER/></MO>
   <MN>2</MN>
</MROW>
<MO><PLUS/></MO>
<MI>a</MI>
<MO><PLUS/></MO>
<MI>b</MI>
```

The binary tree structure for this expression appears in Figure 14-10.

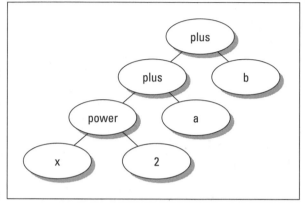

This example demonstrates how you can derive the mathematical expression from a given MathML representation. There is one set of <MROW> ... </MROW> tags followed by two plus operators and two literals (*a* and *b*). Within the set of <MROW> ... </MROW> tags, the expression is *x* times *2* followed by +*a* and +*b*. So the expression is

$$x^2 + a + b$$

MathML Tools, Rules, and Resources

MathML is a new markup kid on the block, and as such is still in its infancy. Not a great many tools are available in the market today that you can use to create, edit, and manipulate MathML files easily.

The simplest tool that you can use to create and edit your application's MathML files is your favorite text editor — Notepad, WordPad, Emacs, and so on. (Now you know why these tools still exist.) While you wait for a company or individual to create a nifty little editor that will make your MathML life much easier, you can use your favorite text editor to work with such files.

After you create your application's MathML file, you must run the file through the MathML parser. In the same way that you write programs using tools such as Visual Basic and Visual C++ and then run them through the compiler for accuracy and verification, the MathML parser parses the MathML file for accuracy and validity. If the file graduates with an A+, you get the parser's go ahead to do whatever you like with the file.

To view the results of your MathML document, you must again use a specialized application. Presently, no MathML viewer is available in the market. As the markup language develops and gains popularity, we can expect a number of vendors to develop such tools.

Design guidelines and rules of the game

When playing with MathML, you must play the game by its rules. In addition, you should follow certain design guidelines when generating the equivalent MathML representation for a given mathematical expression:

- Every element must have a starting and ending tag. For example, the <MI> element must have a starting tag (<MI>) and an ending tag (</MI>). Although you can omit the ending tag for some HTML 4.0 elements, you cannot do so with MathML tags.

- Indent your MathML code properly. This improves code readability and maintenance.

- To generate the equivalent MathML representation from a given expression, choose one of these methods:

  - Follow the expression from left to right and write the equivalent MathML content or presentation markup. Make sure you follow the first guideline in this list — that is, include the starting and ending tags for every MathML element.

  - First represent the expression in the form of a binary tree structure. Then "walk" down the binary tree and identify the MathML tags that you can use to represent each node within the tree.

- To verify whether the MathML representation that you have generated is correct, try generating the expression back from the MathML representation. If the expression that you generate is the same one you started with, your MathML representation is correct.

Additional resources

You can find more detailed information about the topics discussed in this chapter at these sites on the Web:

- For a working draft of the Mathematical Markup Language: `www.w3.org/TR/WD-math-970515/`.

- For a complete list of the presentation markup tags and their attributes: `www.w3.org/TR/WD-math-970515/section3.html#sec3`.

- For a list of the content markup tags and their attributes: `www.w3.org/TR/WD-math/chap4_1.html`.

Chapter 15
Look Out! XML Gets Dynamic

*W*eb Interface Definition Language (WIDL) is an XML application that is relatively new and object oriented. WIDL is not a standard yet, and whether WIDL becomes a Web automation standard remains to be seen. But its implications on Web automation are important enough to warrant coverage of WIDL in this book, for the following reasons:

✔ WIDL has a very good chance of becoming a standard.

✔ WIDL embodies the concept of Web automation and what you can do with it.

In this chapter, we take an in-depth look at WIDL and how you can enable Web automation by using this interface definition language. In addition, this chapter outlines the features and advantages of using WIDL and the tools currently available that you can use to create, edit, and view your WIDL files.

Before embarking on Web automation, make sure that you evaluate your company's or your own current processing methods and needs. This evaluation can help you determine whether Web automation will help alleviate the problems and save your company time and money. If your company has a slew of staff transcribing data from the Web into your company's internal applications manually, you could save time and money by using Web automation and WIDL. In addition, your company can analyze and manipulate the data from the Web using Web automation and WIDL.

Business as Usual

To introduce the concept of WIDL, we start with a real-world example. Assume that a new employee is joining your company. Here's what she goes through:

1. The first department that the employee reports to is human resources. The human resources department enters the employee's information into their system. Typically, this includes the employee's demographic information, such as last name, first name, middle initial, social security number, date of birth, and so on.

2. The employee is sent all the way across town to register with the payroll department and provide the same information. The employee gladly does this because getting paid is a priority.

3. The employee then is instructed to call the benefits department and again provide the same information! (She's getting tired, and so are we. How about you?)

Okay, all three of these departments have received almost exactly the same information. Wouldn't it be wonderful, less time-consuming, and more efficient if the human resources department's system could automatically enter the new employee's information in both the payroll and benefits systems? The new employee saves time because she doesn't need to call the different departments at different times, and the employees working in the payroll and benefits departments save time because the new employee information is entered in their systems automatically.

Similarly, whenever an employee leaves the company, the human resources department's system enters the information regarding the employee's termination in the payroll and benefits departments' systems automatically.

Such automation is possible! It is done by using WIDL. The purpose of WIDL is to implement Web automation. Groovy, huh?

WIDL Tools

A few WIDL tools are available right now. A company called webMethods (www.webmethods.com) leads the race when it comes to promoting Web automation using WIDL. webMethods provides Web automation software that enables rapid integration with and direct access to Web data from within business applications.

You can download a free copy of the Web automation toolkit from the company's site at `www.webmethods.com/products/toolkit/userguide/download.html`.

If you would like to see a demo of Web automation first, visit the site at `www.webmethods.com/products/toolkit/userguide/demos.html` and follow these steps:

1. Click Web Automation Demos and then click Overview.

2. Click Intelligence Reporter.

After you click, you get to see an example that demonstrates an intelligence reporter in action. The reporter automates searches across multiple news services.

3. Type your search criteria and click the news service that the reporter should search against.

For example, type **IDG** in the *search term 1* text field and click TechWeb, PCWeek, InfoWorld, and NewsDotCom, as shown in Figure 15-1. Voilà! The reporter returns a list of matching items.

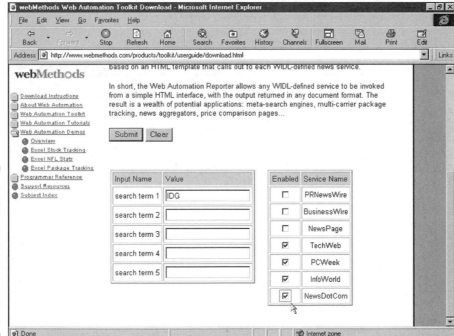

Figure 15-1: Searching for IDG within the Web sites TechWeb, PCWeek, InfoWorld, and NewsDotCom.

4. Click Submit.

The reporter returns with a fresh page displaying the search results, as shown in Figure 15-2. To enter a new search criteria, click New Query.

The news reporter uses a WIDL that defines an *interface* to each of the specified news sites. An interface is a method or protocol of communication used with the news site servers.

The Basics of WIDL

You want to know about WIDL? Well, first, you must understand what *Web Interface Definition Language* is. We all know what the *Web* is. *Interface Definition* means defining a method or protocol of communication. *Language* means the language you can use to define the method or protocol. Thus, WIDL is the language you can use to define a protocol of communication with the Web. Within the communication, you can expect a transfer of data.

To show how the definition applies in the real world, we include in this section some steps on how to install and review a demo from the webMethods Web site. The demo demonstrates how an application, such as Microsoft Excel, can interface with the Web in real time and retrieve the data that the user requests.

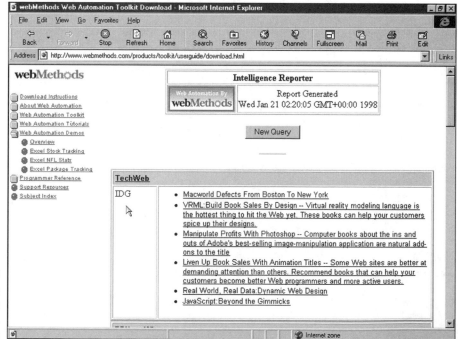

Figure 15-2: The search results.

In this example, Microsoft Excel is the user or presentation interface and the Web is the data source. The example demonstrates the retrieval of the latest U.S. National Football League (NFL) statistics on the team of your choice from the Web site at www.nfl.com.

This example works on Windows 95 and Windows NT platforms only. Also, to run this example, you must install Microsoft Excel on your computer.

To install and run the demo files, follow these steps:

1. **Connect to the webMethods site at** www.webmethods.com/products/toolkit/userguide/demos.html.

2. **Click Web Automation Demos in the menu bar on the left; then click Excel NFL Stats.**

3. **To download the demo, click the hypertext link.**

    The demo files are in a zip file, which must be extracted; the extraction automatically creates a folder called *NFL* on your hard drive at C:\Nfl.

4. **Switch to the DOS prompt.**

    To do so, select Run from the Start menu on your Windows 95 (or NT) desktop. The Run dialog box appears, as shown in Figure 15-3.

Figure 15-3:
Switching
to DOS with
the Run
dialog box.

5. **Type** command **in the Open text field and then click OK.**

    Windows 95 (or NT) displays the DOS prompt.

6. **Switch to the directory \nfl by typing** cd nfl.

    You should see C:\Nfl>, where C: is the letter for your hard drive. If not, type **cd\nfl**.

7. **Type** install **as shown in Figure 15-4 and press Enter.**

    The installation program uses the registration server on your system to register the ActiveX control wmContext.dll with your system. The installation program calls a couple of different registration servers, one for Windows 95 and the other for Windows NT. If you run the installation program under Windows 95, the program displays the results, as shown in Figure 15-5. (The harmless error message you see on the screen is because the install file tries to execute a Windows NT command under Windows 95.)

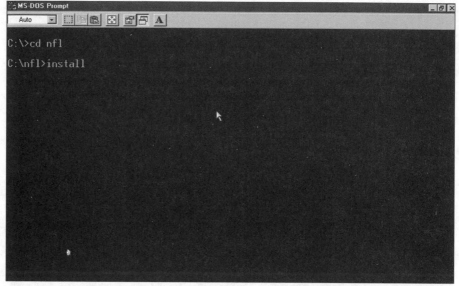

Figure 15-4:
Installing
the
webMethods
demo.

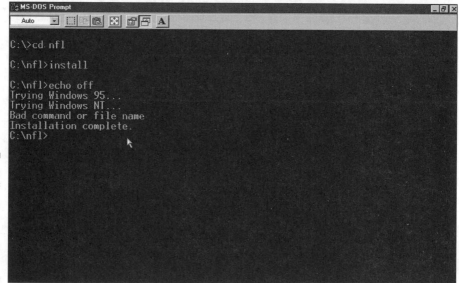

Figure 15-5:
Results of
executing
the
install.bat
file under
Windows 95.

8. Return to Windows, determine the version of Microsoft Excel you have on your system, and double-click the appropriate file.

If you have Excel for Windows 95 (Excel 7), double-click NFL95.xls. If you have Microsoft Excel 97, double-click NFL97.xls. These files exist within the C:\Nfl directory. Figure 15-6 shows NFL97.xls.

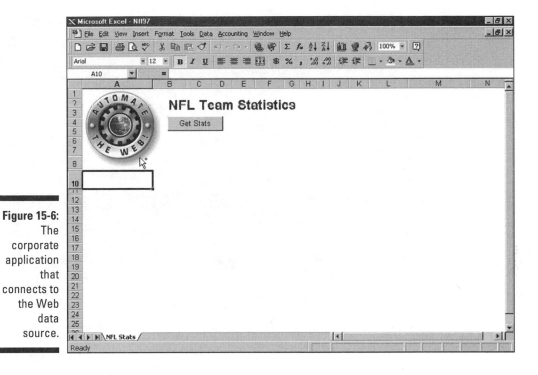

Figure 15-6:
The corporate application that connects to the Web data source.

9. **To retrieve the statistics on your favorite NFL team, click Get Stats.**

   Excel displays the NFL Stats dialog box.

10. **In the text box, type your favorite team's name, and then click OK.**

    We typed in **Jaguars**, as shown in Figure 15-7.

Figure 15-7:
Specifying the NFL team name.

If you're not already connected to the Internet, the program prompts you to do so. After you connect to the Internet, the program retrieves the statistics on the team and displays them, as shown in Figure 15-8.

11. **Click the Get Stats button again and type in an invalid NFL team name, such as** Bulls.

    The program returns and displays an error message, as shown in Figure 15-9.

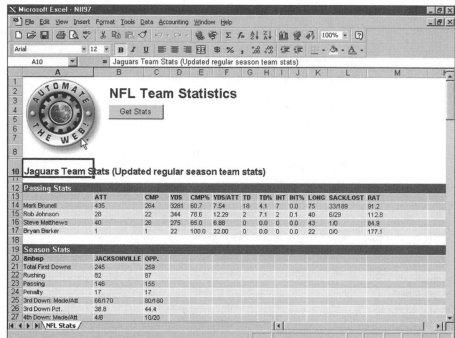

Figure 15-8:
Displaying
the team
statistics
for the
Jacksonville
Jaguars.

Figure 15-9:
Specifying
an invalid
NFL team
generates
an error
message.

From this example, you can see how an application communicates with the Web. The Web provides the data, and the application is the GUI (graphical user interface) that presents the data to the user. The WIDL interface makes this possible. The WIDL files include a collection of Web services, which are nothing more than a bunch of simple function calls.

As you can see, applications such as Microsoft Word, Microsoft Excel, and Microsoft PowerPoint can communicate with the Web using the WIDL interface. To play with some of the other WIDL demos, visit this URL: www.webmethods.com/products/toolkit/userguide/demos.html. Here's a sample of what you can find:

✔ **Excel stock tracking**. This example demonstrates a Microsoft Excel spreadsheet accessing live data from the Nasdaq stock quote Web page (www.nasdaq.com).

✔ **Excel package tracking**. This example demonstrates a Microsoft Excel spreadsheet accessing the package tracking sites of Airborne, DHL, Federal Express, and UPS.

Although these demos use Microsoft Excel as the application to access the Web data, you can use other applications, such as Microsoft Word, Microsoft PowerPoint, or almost any of your client/server applications.

Using WIDL

As discussed in the preceding section, a WIDL file includes definitions of the services. Imagine that the service is like a function call. In addition to the function name, you define the function's input and output parameters. Similarly, you define the input and output parameters for a service; therefore, a WIDL file includes

✔ Each service's location (the URLs)

✔ Input parameters to the service

✔ Output parameters that the service returns

In the example discussed in the section "The Basics of WIDL," earlier in this chapter, the service's location is www.nfl.com. The input parameter to the service is the NFL team's name. The output parameter that the service returns is the information displayed by Microsoft Excel.

WIDL's primary purpose is integration with business applications. In the past, these business applications were probably written in Visual Basic, C++, Java, or some other complicated programming language. WIDL provides the middle-tier interface between these business applications and the Web.

As you can see in Figure 15-10, the WIDL architecture is three-tiered. The first tier is the corporate application, the second tier contains the WIDL interface files, and the third tier is the data source, typically the Web. The WIDL files include the definitions for the services required by the corporate application.

One common application of WIDL is the multicarrier package tracking and shipment ordering service. Think about the components needed to implement a package tracking and shipment ordering service. Within your company, who would benefit from such a service? Practically every department that sends and receives packages through the leading carriers, including Federal Express, Airborne Express, UPS, and DHL, would benefit from the service. One way that you could provide such a service is to design a client/server application specifically for this purpose.

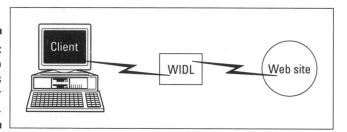

Figure 15-10:
Web automation's three-tier architecture.

Designing such an application could take a lot of time, money, and resources — especially if your company implements various hardware platforms (Windows, Macintosh, UNIX, and so on). Not only would you have to design, develop, and test the application for one platform, you'd also need to deploy the application company-wide. That's a lot of work when all you want to do is provide a way for users to check the shipment status of a package from a leading carrier's Web site. Wouldn't it be wonderful to provide a way to check the shipment status from the existing corporate applications? WIDL comes into the picture here.

Defining a set of services using WIDL

Suppose you want to define a service that checks the shipment status of the packages shipped via the three major carriers: Federal Express, UPS, and Airborne Express. You want to follow these general steps:

1. **Define the service.**

2. **Specify the input parameter for each service.**

   In the example of creating a tracking service, the input parameter is the tracking number and the output parameter is the shipment status.

3. **Consolidate all the services into a single WIDL file, and call this file** `tracking.widl`.

   The `tracking.widl` file uses the standard methods for communicating with the different Web sites (for example, `www.fedex.com`, `www.ups.com`, `www.airborne.com`). The standard methods for communication over the Web are HTTP (HyperText Transfer Protocol) and HTTPS (Secure HyperText Transfer Protocol).

4. On the corporate application side, you must provide the interface hooks for the corporate application to invoke the services (function calls) that you defined within the `tracking.widl` **file.**

Providing interface hooks for the corporation application means providing a connection between the corporation application and the `tracking.widl` file. The corporation application, in turn, uses the connection to call the functions you define within the `tracking.widl` file.

Check out Figure 15-11 to see what we mean.

The preceding list explains the general process of creating the tracking system. You use WIDL elements to create the WIDL file that is the linchpin for the whole system. The next few sections explain the WIDL elements in detail and give examples of how you use the elements to create your WIDL-based tracking system.

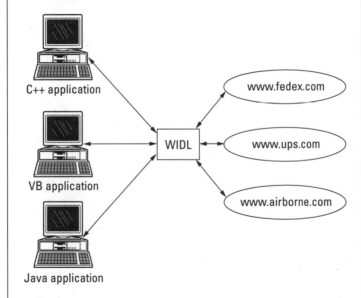

Figure 15-11:
The architecture for automating shipment tracking.

Understanding WIDL elements

Because WIDL is a markup language, it includes XML tags. You can use the WIDL tags to define an interface. Next, because an interface is made up of services, you can define services for the interface using the WIDL tags. Then you can specify the bindings (input, output, and internal variables), success or failure conditions for the output bindings, and a targeted region for displaying the results within the HTML or XML document for each service.

Presently, the WIDL specification includes six XML tags: `<WIDL>`, `<SERVICE/>`, `<BINDING>`, `<VARIABLE/>`, `<CONDITION/>`, and `<REGION/>`.

The `<WIDL>` tag

To define an interface, use the `<WIDL>` tag. An interface may contain multiple services and bindings. The example discussed in the preceding section defines a tracking interface that includes a collection of services interacting with the Web sites of the leading courier companies. Table 15-1 describes the attributes of the `<WIDL>` tag.

Table 15-1	Attributes for the `<WIDL>` Tag
Attribute	*Description*
NAME	Specifies the interface's name
VERSION	Specifies the WIDL version
TEMPLATE	Specifies the interface's specification
BASEURL	Specifies the base URL
OBJMODEL	Specifies the object model used to extract the data elements from the HTML and XML documents

The following shows how you declare the interface for the shipment tracking example by using the `<WIDL>` tag. The `<WIDL>` element must have a starting tag (`<WIDL>`) and an ending tag (`</WIDL>`):

```
<WIDL NAME="tracking" VERSION="1.0"></WIDL>
```

The `<SERVICE/>` tag

The `<SERVICE/>` tag is used to define a service. A service consists of input and output bindings. In the case of the shipment tracking example, the retrieval of the shipment status of a Federal Express or Airborne package is an example of a service. All these services together constitute an interface. Table 15-2 describes the attributes for the `<SERVICE/>` tag.

Table 15-2	Attributes for the `<SERVICE/>` Tag
Attribute	*Description*
NAME	Specifies the service's name
URL	Specifies the URL containing the service
METHOD	Specifies the HTTP method (GET or POST) for accessing the service

Attribute	Description
INPUT	Specifies the binding to be used to define the service's input parameters
OUTPUT	Specifies the binding to be used to define the service's output parameters
AUTHUSER	Specifies the user name
AUTHPASS	Specifies the password
TIMEOUT	Specifies the amount of time before the service times out
RETRIES	Specifies the number of times to retry the service before failing

The following code is an example of declaring a Federal Express service using the <SERVICE/> tag:

```
<SERVICE NAME="FedEx" METHOD="GET"
    URL="http://www.fedex.com/cgi-bin/track_it"
    INPUT="FedExInput"
    OUTPUT="FedExOutput"
/>
```

This next code is an example of declaring a UPS service using the <SERVICE/> tag:

```
<SERVICE NAME="UPS" METHOD="GET"
    URL="http://www.ups.com/tracking/tracking.cgi"
    INPUT="UPSInput"
    OUTPUT="UPSOutput"
/>
```

The <BINDING> tag

To define a binding, use the <BINDING> tag. A binding specifies the input and output variables. In addition, a binding specifies the conditions for a service's successful completion. Table 15-3 describes the attributes for the <BINDING> tag.

Table 15-3	Attributes for the <BINDING> Tag
Attribute	**Description**
NAME	Specifies the binding's name
TYPE	Specifies the type of binding (input or output)

The following code shows an example of declaring an input binding using the <BINDING> tag. The <BINDING> element must have a starting tag (<BINDING>) and ending tag (</BINDING>):

```
<BINDING NAME="FedExInput" TYPE="INPUT">
    <VARIABLE NAME="fedex_track_num" TYPE="String"
            FORMNAME="fedex_trk_num"/>
    <VARIABLE NAME="dest_city" TYPE="String"
            FORMNAME="fedex_dst_city"/>
    <VARIABLE NAME="dest_state" TYPE="String"
            FORMNAME="fedex_dst_state"/>
    <VARIABLE NAME="dest_zip" TYPE="String"
            FORMNAME="fedex_dst_zip"/>
</BINDING>
```

This next group of code shows an example of declaring an output binding using the <BINDING> tag:

```
<BINDING NAME="FedExOutput" TYPE="OUTPUT">
    <REGION NAME="region1" START="doc.font['Updated
            News*']" END="doc.font['See also*']" />
    <CONDITION TYPE="SUCCESS" TYPE="String"
            REFERENCE="doc.s[0].text"/>
    <CONDITION TYPE="FAILURE" TYPE="String" REFERENCE="
            doc.s[1].text"/>
    <VARIABLE NAME="delivery_date" TYPE="String"
            REFERENCE="doc.d[0].text"/>
    <VARIABLE NAME="delivered_to" TYPE="String"
            REFERENCE="doc.d[1].text"/>
</BINDING>
```

The <VARIABLE/> tag

The <VARIABLE/> tag is used to define a variable. The <VARIABLE/> tag is a child of the <BINDING> tag. By using the <VARIABLE/> tag, you can define the input, output, and internal variables, which are the variables that a service uses to submit the HTTP requests. The service also uses the variables to extract data from HTML and XML documents. Table 15-4 describes the attributes for the <VARIABLE/> tag.

The <VARIABLE/>, <REGION/>, and <CONDITION/> tags end with a slash because they are all children of the <BINDING> tag. All other tags exist on their own; they are not the child tags of any other tag.

Table 15-4	Attributes for the `<VARIABLE/>` Tag
Attribute	**Description**
NAME	Specifies the variable's name
VALUE	Specifies the variable's value
USAGE	Specifies whether the variable is used internally within WIDL or to pass header information within an HTTP request
TYPE	Specifies the variable's data type and dimension
FORMNAME	(Input variable) Specifies the variable name to be submitted by using the GET or POST method
OPTIONS	(Input variable) Captures the options of check boxes, radio buttons, and list boxes
REFERENCE	(Output variable) Specifies the object reference used to extract the data elements from the HTML, XML, or text documents
MASK	(Output variable) Specifies the mask to strip away unwanted labels and other text from the target data items
NULLOK	(Output variable) Specifies that output variables can have a null value

For examples of using the `<VARIABLE/>` tag, see the code examples for the `<BINDING>` tag, earlier in this section.

The `<CONDITION/>` tag

The `<CONDITION/>` tag defines a success or failure condition. Like the `<VARIABLE/>` tag, the `<CONDITION/>` tag is also a child of the `<BINDING>` tag. The `<CONDITION/>` tag lets you define the success and failure conditions for the binding of the output variables, specify the error messages that the server returns if the service fails, enable alternate binding attempts if the default binding attempt fails, and more. Table 15-5 describes the attributes for the `<CONDITION/>` tag.

Table 15-5	Attributes for the `<CONDITION/>` Tag
Attribute	**Description**
TYPE	Specifies whether the condition is checking for a binding's success or failure
REFERENCE	Specifies the object reference used to extract the data elements from the HTML or XML documents

(continued)

Table 15-5 *(continued)*

Attribute	Description
MATCH	Specifies the text pattern to be compared with the object reference that the REFERENCE attribute specifies
REBIND	Redirects the binding attempt by specifying an alternate output binding
SERVICE	Specifies the service to be invoked
REASONTEXT	Specifies the error message when the service fails
REASONREF	Specifies a reference to the object element returned as an error message when the service fails
WAIT	Specifies the amount of time to wait before attempting to retrieve a document after the server returned a server busy error
RETRIES	Specifies the number of times to retry the service before failing

For an example of using the <CONDITION/> tag, see the code examples for the <BINDING> tag, earlier in this section.

The <REGION/> tag

The <REGION/> tag is used to define a targeted region within an HTML or XML document for an output binding. Like the <VARIABLE/> and <CONDI-TION/> tags, the <REGION/> tag is also a child of the <BINDING> tag. The <REGION/> tag is used to extract the data from the results that the server returns and to display them within the document's specified regions. Table 15-6 describes the attributes for the <REGION/> tag.

Table 15-6   **Attributes for the <REGION/> Tag**

Attribute	Description
NAME	Specifies the region's name
START	Specifies an object reference that determines the start of the region
END	Specifies an object reference that determines the end of the region

To see how the <REGION/> tag is used, look at the second code example for the <BINDING> tag, earlier in this section.

WIDL Tools, Rules, and Resources

Presently, a couple of interesting tools for Web automation are available to you. Both tools, the Web Automation Toolkit and Web Automation Reporter, are from webMethods.

Web Automation Toolkit

This tool is for developers. The toolkit provides an integrated development environment for creating, editing, and managing WIDL files. The development environment is *integrated* because the toolkit provides the ability to create, edit, and manage WIDL files — all within a single environment. By using the toolkit, you can

✔ Create WIDL files

✔ Generate Weblets from WIDL files for the following languages and tools:

- Java
- JavaScript
- C++
- Microsoft Visual Basic 5
- Microsoft Excel 95
- Microsoft Excel 97

✔ Integrate Weblets into corporate applications

✔ Browse Web data sources

A Weblet is an object that integrates with the corporate application and calls the methods on a remote Web server. In other words, the corporate application accesses the Web data source using the Weblet.

You can download a free copy of the toolkit's Windows version (`toolkit21.exe`) from the webMethods Web site at `www.webmethods.com/products/toolkit/userguide/download.html`. The toolkit is available for Windows (`toolkit21.exe`), Macintosh (`toolkit21.tar.gz`), and UNIX (`toolkit21.zip`) platforms. To run the Web Automation Toolkit on Macintosh and UNIX platforms, you need JDK (Java Development Kit) from Sun Microsystems (`java.sun.com`). JDK is not needed to run the Web Automation Toolkit on the Windows platform.

Before you download the free copy of the toolkit, register it with the company. Upon registration, the company e-mails you a license key. The license key is for 365 days and is renewable. To access the toolkit, you must use the license key.

The toolkit comes with several samples; Figure 15-12 shows the service definition TrackAirborneExpress for the shipping interface within the toolkit. Other sample WIDL files include homeloan, currencies, and news. You find the samples in the `\Toolkit\samples` directory of your Web Automation Toolkit installation. As the figure shows, the toolkit provides a visual interface that you can use to define the services and bindings (including variables, conditions, and regions) for your application's interface to the Web.

To generate the Weblet, select the appropriate language or tool from the Generate menu. In addition to the Weblet and other related files, the toolkit creates a `readme.txt` file. To integrate the Weblet in your corporate application, follow the instructions in the `readme.txt` file. For example, to create the Weblet for Microsoft Excel 97, select Visual Basic⇨Excel 97 from the Generate menu. The toolkit, in turn, creates the following files for the shipping interface:

- `ShippingTrackAirborneExpressXL97Readme.txt`
- `ShippingTrackAirborneExpressXL97.cls`
- `ShippingTrackAirborneExpressXL97.bas`
- `Shipping.widl`

For instructions on integrating the Excel Weblet with Microsoft Excel 97, read the `ShippingTrackAirborneExpressXL97Readme.txt` file.

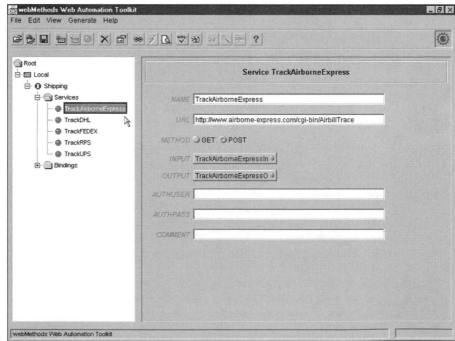

Figure 15-12:
The
TrackAirborne-
Express
service
definition.

Web Automation Reporter

You can use the Web Automation Reporter to retrieve information from Web data sources at periodic intervals. The reporter can automatically log into the remote system, submit the input criteria, and collect and present the results in HTML format. Think of the Web Automation Reporter as a reporting agent at your command.

The Web Automation reporter is a 100-percent pure Java application that dynamically generates reports based on an HTML template. The HTML template, in turn, calls each of the WIDL-defined services. In other words, you can invoke the WIDL-defined services directly from an HTML interface by using the Web Automation Reporter.

You can use the Web Automation Reporter within a number of applications including news aggregators, package tracking, meta-search engines, and so on. Although the Web Automation Reporter is a pure Java application, no Java programming is required on your part.

Additional resources

Many online resources are available to provide you with all the information that you want to know about WIDL but were afraid to ask. Here are some that we've found that should be helpful:

- ✔ For more information on WIDL, visit www.webmethods.com.
- ✔ To download the Java Development Kit for Sun, Windows 95, and Windows NT platforms, visit java.sun.com/products/jdk/1.1/index.html.
- ✔ To download the Java Development Kit for all other platforms, visit java.sun.com/cgi-bin/java-ports.cgi.

WIDL's Moving On

WIDL continues to evolve. We expect that enhancements and modifications to this relatively new interface definition language are coming soon. In addition, we expect better and efficient Web automation software. webMethods has submitted the WIDL specification to the World Wide Web Consortium (www.w3.org) for approval on making the specification a standard for accessing Web data from within business applications.

Chapter 16

XML Makes Movie Magic

Multimedia on the World Wide Web has been a hot topic since the early days of browser technology. Including embedded multimedia content on Web pages has been a challenging task for a long time. The different forms of media, such as text, images, video, and audio components, are not a novelty anymore, but they still have various requirements for the browser and for network protocols. This chapter takes you through the fog of Web-based multimedia.

Synchronizing Multimedia

Web pages, especially commercial ones, are scattered with different state-of-the-art multimedia augmentations — a movie file showing off the latest product, an audio track trying to get people into the right mood, and fancy graphics to attract the surfer's eye. Each of these components is very powerful by itself, but put them together and you can see the full power of synchronized multimedia in all its glory. You absolutely must synchronize your multimedia presentation, or you end up with something near the equivalent of garbage.

Channel++ News

What does synchronization mean? Look at a real-life example of an ordinary news program to get an understanding of the role and importance of multimedia and multimedia synchronization.

A news broadcast typically starts with a fancy tune that awakens even the most tired computer scientist. After the initial audio blast come the main headlines. First, the video footage starts and informs us of some scandal in the political arena. While we listen to it, a ticker-like text banner scrolls across the screen, showing us the headline in textual form. Next, we are in the middle of the action and the narrator covers about two-thirds of the TV screen while he lists all the possible effects of the scandal on the political climate.

For a while, we can see the face of the poor fellow who is suddenly the focus of the public eye. His name is shown at the bottom of the picture (see Figure 16-1). A list of the possible effects appears at the left side of the screen. Whenever the anchorman starts a new item, a checklist-type summary is added to the list on the left.

Figure 16-1:
The basic concept of a multimedia presentation on television.

This is just one example of synchronized multimedia. Next time the news comes on TV, look at the broadcast this way — it can be very educational. Usually, one person controls it all. One stressed-out individual in the control room of the TV station has a script that tells him or her exactly how all those different forms of media work with each other. Every broadcast element is laid out second by second, and every visual image demonstrates the importance of geometry and layout in presentation.

Before we get into the details of controlling a broadcast, we must look at those typical components that we deal with on TV and — although not coordinated as intricately — on the Web.

A few components make up the universe

A television news broadcast is a very complicated scenario, with many different components making up the whole experience. We can identify a few basic components and use them to make similar entertainment for our senses on the Web.

- ✔ **Audio:** The reporter speaking about the latest news and the tunes at the beginning of a news show are examples of audio components that play an important part in not only a news program, but also many other forms of presentation. Well-coordinated audio is essential to the experience.

- ✔ **Video:** Video is basically a consecutive arrangement of pictures. In the news example, the anchorman has to wait for the video footage to finish before he can start talking in the studio — a simple example of synchronization.

- ✔ **Images:** Images and graphics are an important part of information exchange between human beings. A very important challenge for us is to align images with all the other forms of media we employ on the Web, as well as on TV.

- ✔ **Text:** What can we say about text? Plain text has been the ruling medium on the Web for a long time. Text identifying a graphic, ticker-like banners, and lists of items used to summarize and emphasize information are important elements.

  On the Web — a Web destined to provide accessibility — text is very important, because its format is the easiest to translate into other forms. For example, text can be translated into audio so that people with visual disabilities can still use the whole spectrum of information and are not left out of this new universe of information.

SMIL Basic Concepts

Synchronized Multimedia Integration Language (SMIL) has been designed to allow integration of a collection of multimedia objects in a synchronized fashion. SMIL enables the creation of presentations (such as the TV example we outline in the previous section of this chapter). SMIL is designed to bring multimedia components together on the Web.

One of the groovy features of SMIL is that the entire presentation is coordinated in an easy-to-read description. The syntax that is used by SMIL is — surprise, surprise, Sergeant Carter! — the eXtensible Markup Language (XML). And, by the way, SMIL is pronounced "smile." Thus, we're not surprised that a prototype application that has been announced for SMIL is called GRINS.

The following list contains some of the principles and design goals that guided the design of SMIL:

- **URLs for all media-resource references:** Because we are on the Web, all objects we use for a SMIL presentation have to be found online. URLs are the means for locating resources on the Web. Thus, all objects used in SMIL have to be addressable via URLs.

- **Synchronized media objects:** Synchronizing is, of course, where all the power and goals of SMIL lie. A SMIL presentation description must be able to synchronize objects based on start and end times (such as "Start A after B has finished") and on temporal parameters (such as "Five seconds after the audio file has started, show picture *X* in the bottom-right corner of the screen").

- **Video recorder–like operations:** A human interacting with a SMIL presentation can use and operate it as if working a VCR. Stop, play, forward, and reverse should all be available via SMIL. In addition, all media components must react to these operations in a synchronized fashion.

- **Hyperlinks in presentations:** What would the Web be without hyperlinks? Nonexistent, more than likely. SMIL provides designers with the ability to specify hyperlinks that are associated with multimedia objects. SMIL goes one step further than traditional HTML hyperlinking by providing some of the extended hyperlinking facilities specified by the XML standard.

SMIL has been designed with only a few basic ideas in mind. We explain these ideas in the subsections of this section by focusing on the basic framework for a SMIL presentation and on two concepts — parallel and sequence — that are most important for you to know. Simply put, *parallel* presentations combine multiple components simultaneously to provide a complete picture; *sequence* refers to a presentation that comes in a series of individual steps.

To understand the examples that follow in this chapter, you need to be aware that SMIL refers to media types by using a generic element type: `<ref .../>`. To improve readability, SMIL provides synonyms for this element type that are named after certain media types:

```
<audio> ... </audio>
<video> ... </video>
<text> ... </text>
<img> ... </img>
```

SMIL does not make any assumptions about what actual format you use to represent your audio, video, and images. The SMIL proposed standard does define the tags (for example, <audio> is for audio files, <video> for video files, and so forth), but the standard doesn't mandate a particular format for a given tag. You can decide to use the WAV file format for sound, the MPEG file format for video, and the GIF, JPEG, and/or PNG file formats for images.

A framework for SMIL

A SMIL description is embedded within the SMIL tag. SMIL documents have two parts: a head and a body — kinda like humans, only different. Each of these parts may contain special XML instructions, such as comments and processing instructions. The head of a document is denoted by the head element type, the body by the body element type.

```
<smil>
  <head>
    <!-- here's the head part -->
  </head>
  <body>
    <!-- here's the body part -->
  </body>
</smil>
```

At the head

The head section of a SMIL document is used to describe layout-related aspects of our presentation and include some meta-information about the presentation.

```
<smil>
  <head>
    <!-- here goes layout and metadata -->
  </head>
  <body>
    <!-- here goes the body content -->
  </body>
</smil>
```

Using a layout specification, the author of a SMIL document can define how his or her multimedia objects should be laid out on the screen. If the author does not want to explicitly define what the layout should be like, then the application running the SMIL specification decides itself on how to do the layout. Later in this chapter, we provide an entire section about layout specification, so we don't go into details here.

Metadata that can provide for a SMIL document is open-ended. The official form for describing some metadata in SMIL is

```
<meta
  name="TheNameOfAVariable"
  content="TheValueOfTheVariable"
/>
```

This way of specifying metadata may look familiar to you. You add meta-information to HTML documents the same way.

SMIL has some predefined names for metadata:

- ✔ `sync`: The synchronization of a SMIL presentation can be defined as hard or soft. *Hard* means that a SMIL interpreter must adhere to the timing rules for parallel presentations of media objects exactly as defined. *Soft* gives some freedom during the execution. If this value is not specified, an implementation-dependent value is used. (Don't worry, we explain what parallel presentation means in the "Parallel" subsection later in this section.)

- ✔ **title:** Use `title` to give your presentation a name. The standard doesn't specify the semantics of naming presentations, but it is likely that SMIL programs take that information and put it into the title part of your window. Sound familiar? This functions just like the title tag in your HTML documents.

- ✔ `pics-label`: *PICS* stands for Platform for Internet Content Selection. PICS labels are used to give better control over what content can be accessed by which audiences. Originally, PICS was created to help parents control what their children should and shouldn't see. (For once, we're actually referring to real children and real parents instead of referring to the hierarchies of object-oriented programming.)

For more information about PICS, please refer to `www.w3.org/PICS/labels.html`.

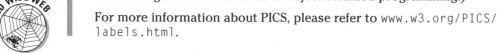

At the body

You can define three different presentation styles in the body of a SMIL presentation, two of which are of particular importance for you — parallel and sequence. *Parallel* is used to describe how two objects are presented at the same time and how their beginnings and endings relate to each other. *Sequence* is the simple, or sometimes not so simple, "first A, then B" method. Because the concepts of parallel and sequence are such a basic part of SMIL, we discuss those concepts in separate sections.

Parallel

Very often, we see the parallel presentation of different media objects. In our "Channel++" news example at the beginning of this chapter, the image of Mr. X and the video stream of the anchorman appear at the same time. For our purposes, we can also say that the anchorman's appearance was the parallel presentation of both the video footage and an audio presentation (the voice of the anchorman).

A timing diagram

We want to introduce you to a type of diagram that we use quite often to help explain the concepts of SMIL. The diagram is shown in Figure 16-2.

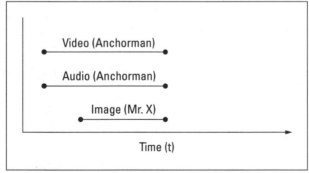

Figure 16-2:
Simple
parallel
media
objects.

When we talk about SMIL presentations, keep in mind the following questions:

✔ **What video objects do we talk about?** In this case, we talk about video, audio, and image objects. Often, we omit the concrete name of the media object and just refer to its media type.

✔ **When does the presentation start or end?** As you can see in our example earlier in this chapter, the video and audio objects start and end at the same time. The image object starts later but ends at the same time as the other two components.

✔ **What is the time frame?** In the preceding Figure 16-2, you can see the time arrow that appears left to right across the bottom of the figure. That arrow gives us some orientation and makes the diagram easier to read.

Parallel — inside out

A parallel block is indicated by the `<par>` tag. For example, an audio object and an image object for parallel can be described as:

```
<par>
  <audio .../>
  <img   .../>
</par>
```

The end of a presentation

Nothing goes on forever; everything has to end sometime. By default, the ending time of a parallel presentation is the maximum end time of all objects in the described presentation. The presentation's designer can, however, have more control over the ending time.

The optional attribute `endsync` specifies that the end of the parallel section depends on the specific end time of one of its children. The `endsync` attribute can take two discrete values and has a generic form as well:

✔ `last:` This value makes the presentation end when the last object finishes. A parallel presentation does not finish until this last object has finished its job (see Figure 16-3).

✔ `first:` This value is the opposite of `last`. As soon as one of the participating objects has finished, the overall group finishes.

✔ `id-ref:` The presentation's designer can make the duration of this parallel group dependent on the ending of a specific object (which is designated by its ID).

The following bit of code is a simple example of a parallel presentation that is ended when the first of its embedded objects ends (see Figure 16-4):

```
<par endsync="first">
  <audio video .../>
  <video audio .../>
  <img .../>
</par>
```

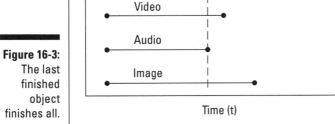

Figure 16-3:
The last finished object finishes all.

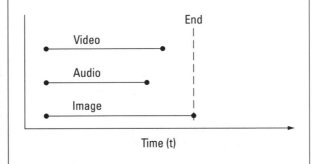

Figure 16-4:
The first finished object finishes all.

Sequence

A sequence defines a set of objects that have to be executed in sequential order. For example, first we see Video A, and then we see Video B. The general form for a sequence is as follows:

```
<seq>
  <!-- first object -->
  <!-- second object -->
</seq>
```

The first object begins its presentation at the time the overall sequence element is scheduled to start. The rest of the objects start whenever their predecessor ends. The overall sequence ends when the last member has finished its presentation (see Figure 16-5).

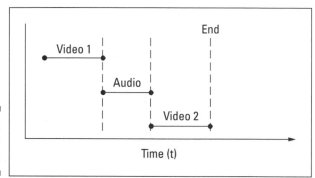

Figure 16-5: A simple sequence.

Advanced Synchronization

SMIL provides a few very powerful attributes that you can apply to media objects in general, as well as on more-abstract schedule specifications, such as parallel or sequence presentations. For example, you can make a multi-media object start five seconds after the previous object is finished, but you can also make a sequence start five seconds after another sequence is finished. The synchronization attributes can be applied in both cases.

Begin *and* end *attributes*

The begin and end attributes change the default begin time and end time of an element. Depending on what type of object these attributes are applied to, they have different semantics. The values that these attributes can take are either offset values or qualified events. We talk about qualified events a bit later in this chapter, in the section "Event-based synchronization." First, we discuss offset values.

In sequences

In a sequence, the offset determines the time between the end of the predecessor object and the start of the next object. The following code is a simple example of a sequence for an audio file and a video file. The video file begins two seconds after the audio file is finished (see Figure 16-6).

```
<seq>
  <audio .../>
  <video begin="2s" .../>
</seq>
```

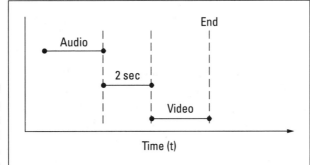

Figure 16-6:
Sequence
and delayed
start.

In parallels

If the parent of a media object is a parallel specification (see Figure 16-7), then the `begin` attribute specifies a delay with respect to the overall beginning time of the parallel object.

```
<par>
  <audio ... />
  <video begin="5s" .../>
</par>
```

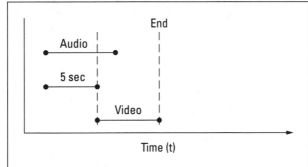

Figure 16-7:
Parallel and
delayed
start.

Event-based synchronization

One very powerful synchronization mechanism promises to provide the ability to synchronize objects based on the events of other objects. Objects can be synchronized with others that are *siblings* — in other words, members of the same sequence or parallel specification.

Three events are defined for each element of an SMIL presentation:

- begin: Whenever an element becomes active, this event is triggered.

- end: This event ends when a certain element becomes inactive.

- clock-val: You can associate an event with the status of a clock in a presentation. A SMIL presentation knows two different types of clocks. A media object (such as video, audio, and so on) comes with a media clock. This clock can be different from the actual SMIL presentation clock.

  Network congestion or delay due to expensive rendering operations can cause this difference. Sequence and parallel run according to the presentation clock. If a parallel element is described as finishing with a particular media type, via endsync, the clock of the parallel element is associated with the clock of the media object.

Look at an example:

```
<par>
  <audio id="audio1" begin="6s" ... />
  <img  begin="id(audio1)(begin)+3s" ... />
</par>
```

How do we read this example? We have two media objects — an audio object and an image object — that run in parallel. The audio presentation starts six seconds after the overall parallel is scheduled to run. Three seconds after the audio clip has started, referred to via its ID, the image is displayed. In Figure 16-8 we show you the timing diagram.

Layout Specifications

The SMIL specification states that a variety of different layout specification formats can be used in conjunction with a SMIL presentation. However, SMIL comes with a proposal for a simple layout specification mechanism.

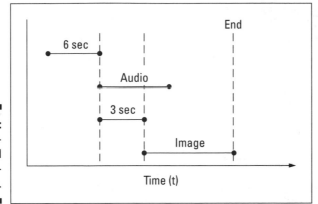

Figure 16-8:
Event-
based
synchroni-
zation.

SMIL uses the concept of channels to specify layout. A channel defines (if applicable to the media object) the position, size, and scaling of a media object. Overlapping channels are handled by a process called *clipping*. Clipping is the process of handling images that are too large or too small to fit perfectly into a given region — a window, for example.

Every defined channel must have a unique ID by which it is identified. If you don't want to bother with specifying a layout for your presentation, you can just use the default layout by including the following code fragment in your SMIL description:

```
<layout type="text/smil-basic"></layout>
```

Getting the proportions right

A channel's position is defined by the following values:

- ✔ **top:** Top is defined as the distance to the top of the rendering area. Top can be specified as either an absolute value or a percentage. If specified as a percentage, the resulting value is relative to the width of the screen. The default value is zero.

- ✔ **left:** Left describes the distance to the left corner of the rendering window. Like the top value, left can be specified as an absolute value or a percentage. If specified as a percentage, the height of the rendering window is taken as the value to relate to (see Figure 16-9).

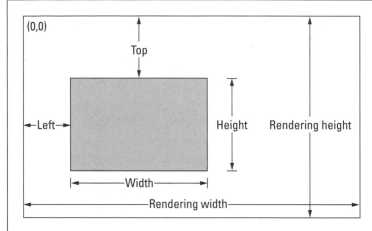

Figure 16-9:
Defining
screen
coordinates.

The proportions of a channel are defined by its width and height:

✔ width: This tag, if available, defines the width of a media object. The number can be either absolute or relative. If no value is specified, width is defined as the space between the left position and the right corner of the rendering area.

✔ height: This tag is the counterpart to width, and it follows the same rules as width. If no height is specified, it is calculated as being the space between the top coordinate and the bottom of the rendering area.

The art of clipping

Clipping is the magic that deals with situations in which the object's actual dimensions don't correspond to the proportions defined in the channel definition. SMIL provides a set of attributes that can be used to control the strategy of clipping if such a thing happens. The attribute name is clip and the possible values are:

✔ meet **(default):** Tells the presentation software to scale an object while preserving its aspect ratio until either the height or the width of the media object fits the channel. For example, if you have an object of width 10 and height 20 (aspect ratio 1:2) and you want to scale it to width 5, you need to set the height to a value of 10 so that the image still looks natural (see Figure 16-10).

Empty space is added to the media object at its corners, if needed, so that the object can be centered within the channel.

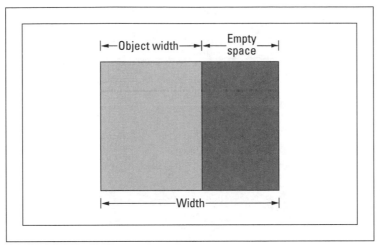

Figure 16-10:
Clipping
with filling.

✔ **slice:** As the word may suggest, slice takes the following approach: A media object is scaled, maintaining its aspect ratio until either the width or the height fits the channel's proportions. Overflow width is cut off at the right corner of the object; overflow height is cut from the bottom (see Figure 16-11).

✔ **fill:** Behaves in a way similar to the standard HTML image tag (<IMG>). It stretches the width and the height of the media object so that it fits the proportions of the channel.

✔ **visible:** This value means that an element's width and height are enlarged to contain all of its rendered content.

✔ **hidden:** The semantics of this value are very similar to those for the slice value. The only difference is that the SMIL software does not adjust width or height to fit the object, at least with respect to one of the axes. Clipping is performed without making this initial scaling adjustment.

✔ **auto:** This value leaves it up to the application to deal with images that don't fit. The application decides what to do with them.

✔ **scroll:** Scroll indicates that scrollbars should be added to the channel. Scrollbars should be added regardless of whether or not the object is too large for the specified channel proportions. Adding scrollbars prevents problems in case of dynamic environments.

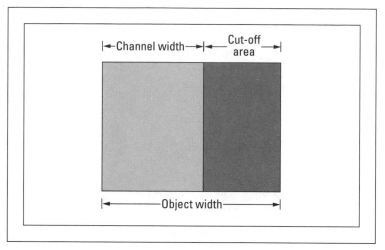

Figure 16-11:
Slice to fit.

Switching Allows for Alternatives

Often, a presentation description like SMIL should provide a way to describe a set of alternatives from which a selection may be made based on user-input or environment variables. SMIL uses the `switch` primitive to provide this feature.

SMIL switching is based on a few predefined attributes. But, in the spirit of XML, designers can specify their own switching attributes. In addition to those listed here, implementations can support additional types of attributes through the use of custom attributes.

Bitrate

We would all like to have fiber optics in our homes; however, the reality is that many users are restricted to the less-expensive bandwidth. Especially for multimedia presentations like SMIL, bandwidth is important. Bitrate allows the designer of a presentation to provide alternative media objects depending on the bandwidth of the consumer. This way, we can come much closer to a good trade-off between speed, size, and quality of the output.

For modem users, a typical bitrate would be 14,400 bps (bits per second), 28,800 bps, or 56,000 bps (unless you're lucky enough to be running an ISDN line, in which case a typical bitrate would be 128,000 bps). With this type of information, the application could, based on what it knows about the download speed of its environment, choose a particular object. Alternatively, it could prompt the user to choose an object. Code to check bitrate and define appropriate media objects for downloading looks something like the following:

```
<switch>
  <par bitrate="14400">
    <!-- some media objects -->
  </par>
  <par bitrate="28800">
    <!-- some media objects -->
  </par>
  <par bitrate="56000">
    <!-- some media objects -->
  </par>
</switch>
```

Language

Because the World Wide Web *is* worldwide, we have to deal with different languages. If you want to provide a presentation that you can send to your friends and/or business partners in the United States, Germany, and Japan, you must be able to switch between certain objects depending on their suitability for a certain language.

The lang attribute in SMIL is not like the lang attribute in XML. In XML, that attribute deals with the encoding of languages. In SMIL, it merely provides a list of selections.

SMIL has chosen a proposal for a standard for specifying languages called RDF 1766. The following code is the syntax for these language specifications:

```
<switch>
  <audio src="interview-in-french" language="fr"/>
  <audio src="interview-in-german" language="de"/>
  <audio src="interview-in-english" language="en"/>
</switch>
```

Screen size

Providing multimedia presentations that are suitable for every type of display area is very hard, if not impossible. This task is tedious for images, but it's even more tedious for multimedia stuff. SMIL enables you to specify a switch for the available screen size of your presentation. The number you use indicates the number of pixel units that you have available on your screen. Values such as 640 x 480 or 1280 x 1024 may sound familiar to you. (Anybody remember 320 x 200?) The following code shows you how to specify the screen size values:

```
<switch>
  <par screen-size="640X480">
    <!-- Media objects for 640x480 -->
  </par>
  <par screen-size="1280X1024">
    <!-- Media objects for 1280x1024 -->
  </par>
</switch>
```

Screen depth

The depth of a screen's color palette is an output-medium characteristic that makes it difficult for a designer to provide a "one-size-fits-all" solution. Typical values for screen depth are 8, 16, and 32. We can actually use the example from the preceding section and augment it with attribute values for screen-depth:

```
<switch>
  <par screen-size="640X480" screen-depth="32">
    <!-- Media objects for 640x480 -->
  </par>
  <par screen-size="1280X1024" screen-depth="16">
    <!-- Media objects for 1280x1024 -->
  </par>
</switch>
```

Advanced Hyperlinking

SMIL defines a link element, similar to the <LINK> tag in HTML, that provides a designer with the ability to describe navigational links between objects. The linking concepts of SMIL are based on those discussed in XLL (eXtensible Linking Language).

SMIL takes some basic concepts of XLL and puts restrictions on them. If you're not familiar with XLL or its terms, check out the XLL section at Robin Cover's Web site, `www.sil.org/sgml/xll.html`.

SMIL restricts links to in-line links. Links are also limited to being uni-directional, single-headed links. In other words, all links have one source and one target. You may have seen the same type of link in HTML with the A element type. All SMIL links have an implicit attribute `acutate="user"`. See Chapter 19 for more information about XLL.

Links in SMIL

A simple example for a SMIL link looks like this:

```
<a href="http://www.somewhere.com/object.smi">
    <video
        src="rtsp://else.com/graph.imf"
        channel="window-1"
    />
</a>
```

In the preceding example, we define a link to a new presentation. The new presentation replaces the old one. Replacing the old object with a new one is the default behavior for a link in SMIL. SMIL allows you to have more control and better control of this behavior.

The `show` attribute has three possible values:

✔ `replace`: This is the default value. In the preceding example, you see this default value in action. Replace the current presentation with the new one that we refer to via the link.

✔ new: "New" means we start the presentation in a new context. For example, a new SMIL presentation window would be opened and the presentation would be started automatically.

```
<a href="http://www.somewhere.com/object.smi"
        show="new">
  <video
        src="rtsp://else.com/graph.imf"
        channel="window-1"
  />
</a>
```

✔ **pause:** Pause is specific to SMIL and is not part of XLL. The old presentation pauses and the new presentation starts in a new context. The designer must also provide the user with the means to restart the paused presentation.

Anchors for enhanced image maps

Anchors in SMIL provide functionality that can be compared to the image maps from HTML. A rectangular area of an image (see Figure 16-12) is associated with a hyperlink. Clicking on that area makes the browser follow the hyperlink, thus taking you to a new page.

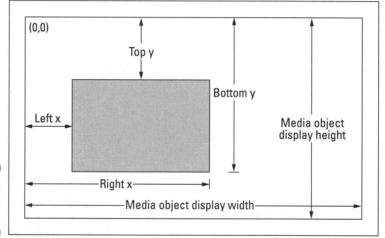

Figure 16-12: Defining an anchor.

The coordinates for an anchor can be defined in either an absolute value or a relative value as a percentage. Coordinates are specified as quadruples (a list of four values) — first the left x coordinate, then the right x coordinate, then the top y coordinate, and finally the bottom y coordinate. Here's an example that uses absolute and relative values:

```
<video src="http://www.somewhere.net/show">
  <anchor href="http://www.here.org/"
          coords="0%,0%,50%,50%"/>
  <anchor href="http://www.datachannel.com/presentations"
          coords="30,20,120,100"/>
</video>
```

In our example, we have two areas in a video. One is defined via percentage, the other one as absolute pixel values.

Unleashing the full power of anchors

We remember a presentation in which the speaker, after about 120 slides, came to a one-sentence slide that said "Now, enough introduction." We don't have to go that far. We want to show some combined examples that demonstrate how you should specify sophisticated anchors by applying the information presented earlier in this chapter.

```
<video src="http://www.somewhere.net/show">
  <anchor href="http://www.here.org/"
          begin="0s" end="7s"
  />
  <anchor href="http://www.datachannel.com/presentations"
          begin="7s" end="10s"
  />
</video>
```

Here, we combine the range for a media object with an anchor. For the first seven seconds, a click would take us to www.here.org/. Ten seconds into the presentation, the target anchor would be www.datachannel.com/presentations.

We can also use anchors as a point of reference. Given an ID, anchors can be referred to from other presentations. For example, in one presentation, we declare:

```
<a href="http://www.datachannel.com/demo#norbert">
  <video src="rtsp://somewhere.com/xml.imf"/>
</a>
```

In another, we say:

```
<video src="http://demo.datachannel.com/NorbertAndXML">
  <anchor id="norbert" begin="0s" end="5s"/>
  <anchor id="ernst" begin="5s" end="10s"/>
</video>
```

With this code, we have established a link between a video about XML and the first five seconds of a video featuring some guy named Norbert who wants to talk about XML.

A Little SMIL (e) for You

Now that we've covered the most important features of SMIL, look back at the original example that we started with in the section "Synchronizing Multimedia." Our anchorman just waits to be SMILified and transmitted over the Web.

```
<smil>
  <head>
    <layout>
      <channel id="Mr-X-Image" left="0" top="0"
               width="100" height="100"/>
      <channel id="Mr-X-text" left="0" top="100"
               width="100" height="20"/>
      <channel id="Channel++Logo" left="0" top="120"/>
      <channel id="Anchorman" left="100" top="0"/>
    </layout>
  </head>
  <body>
    <seq>
      <!-- We start the show with the Channel++ background,
           and the jingle starts two seconds after we see
           the background for the first time. The first
           part finishes three seconds after the jingle is
           over.
      -->

      <par end="id(jingle)(END)+3s">
        <img src="http://www.channel++.com/background"/>
        <snd id="jingle" begin="2s"
             src="http://www.channel++.com/jingle"/>
      </par>
      <!-- Next is the picture of Mr. X in the top-left
           corner, with his name underneath. In the bottom-
           left corner, we have the Channel++ logo. The
           right part of the screen is covered with the
           anchorman. The sound footage starts five seconds
           after the anchorman appears on the screen. The
           screen continues to display these elements until
           five seconds after we finish the video.
      -->
      <par end="id(anchorman)(END)+5s">
        <!-- Because we are on the Web now, a clock on
             Mr. X's image opens a new window with his
             bio. -->
```

```
        <a href="http://www.cia.org/bios/Mr.X" show="new">
          <img   src="http://www.pictures.com/celebrities/
          Mr.X/"
              channel="Mr-X-Image"/>
        </a>
        <video id="anchorman"
              src="http://www.channel++.com/newsfeed/studio/
          mr-x"
              channel="Anchorman"/>
        <text  src="http://www.channel++.com/newsfeed/
          studio/mr-x-label"
              channel="Mr-X-text"/>
        <snd src="http://www.channel++.com/newsfeed/studio/
          mr-x.snd"
              begin="5s"/>
      </par>
    </seq>
  </body>
</smil>
```

Chapter 17

To XML, Software Is an Open Book

. . . .

In This Chapter

▶ Examining the Open Software Description (OSD)

▶ Why OSD was built with XML

▶ Exploring specific uses and benefits of OSD

▶ Introducing the OSD vocabulary

▶ Using "pull" or "push" models of software distribution on the Web

▶ How OSD works with the Channel Definition Format (CDF) and software push

▶ The OSD references in plain English

. . . .

*I*nstalling software on a single computer or on a network has become a huge chore in recent years, giving even the most experienced computer guru nightmares. Imagine what software developers and vendors go through. Issues of platform and operating system types, as well as whether to use disk or CD-ROM as a distribution medium, make for a very interesting, and stressful, software distribution world. Surely, a better way exists. According to Microsoft and Marimba, the secret is XML.

The Open Software Description (OSD) is an XML vocabulary developed jointly by Microsoft and Marimba to provide a nonproprietary, Internet-based method of software distribution. OSD uses markup to describe the many and varied software components, and its ultimate goal is to deliver software over the Internet and intranets to multiple platforms running heterogeneous operating systems quickly and smoothly. How cool!

In this chapter, we cover OSD and how it works. In addition, we examine the XML tags that describe application components and the technology that makes OSD possible. This chapter can get pretty technical, so grab a cup of coffee, sit in a comfortable chair, open your favorite XML tool, and get ready to push and pull your software!

OSD shines a bright light on the future of upgrades

Taking a quick jaunt down memory lane, we remember that floppy disks were the original primary medium for software distribution (shudder!). The diskette method of software and data transfer was used by both companies and individuals, and it usually required lots of floppies and some poor sap to sit and switch out disk after disk. Not a happy memory for most of us.

In the not-so-distant past, CD-ROMs began to take over as the primary medium for software and data distribution. We all remember when Wing Commander was released on multiple CD-ROMs (shudder, take two!), right? Granted, CD-ROMs are a much better medium for software distribution because of their digital nature and their ability to store a much greater amount of data than a floppy disk. Unfortunately, it now seems that CD-ROMs may go the way of the floppy as a software distribution medium, as applications and data continue to consume massive amounts of storage media. These issues set the stage for the arrival of OSD.

What Is OSD?

When OSD is used to describe a software package, the package can be delivered automatically (via push technology). This process makes the previously bumpy installation process as smooth as silk for users and makes for timely software upgrades. To make things even better, cross-platform installation problems become a thing of the past (in theory). The world of computing is rapidly moving toward the networked environment and away from the lonely stand-alone modus operandi. Even the singular PC in someone's living room becomes part of a larger network after it's logged onto the Internet. Thanks to this move to an interconnected computer world, networks themselves have turned into the most effective medium for software and data distribution. CDs and floppies are out; network cables are in.

Because cables are a part of every network, the cost of distribution is built right in to an existing entity. Gone are the overhead costs associated with producing CDs and floppies. Using networks for software distribution and installation alleviates the need to create them at all.

When software is distributed on CDs and floppies, it must be *pulled* from the medium by the user. Software doesn't just jump up and install itself from a CD-ROM. Even though CDs hold tons more data than floppies, someone still has to monitor the installation of software on every computer. You still have the appointed disk switcher, even though the disks are round instead of square. This type of software distribution is the *pull* method.

Network distribution of software has the potential to do things via the *push* method. When software (or data) is pushed across a network, the action doesn't have to be initiated by the user. Instead, the push can start from the system administrator's end. Although this concept isn't new to the networked world, the existing push models of software distribution are proprietary to the network software and certainly wouldn't work over the Internet or a TCP/IP-based intranet. Push installation has some real advantages, including the following:

✔ **Push software isn't plagued by cross-platform distribution problems.** The only version sent to the client computer is one that is supported by the platform. If it's incompatible with the platform, it's rejected.

✔ **Push software can be installed hands-free.** Users don't even have to be around for their software to be installed, and the days of disk switching of any kind are shuttled to the pages of history.

✔ **Push software is upgraded in a timely fashion from a specific location.** Users are no longer responsible for locating and installing software as new releases and patches are made available. Instead, the burden of updating falls to the software.

Using OSD, you can describe how a variety of software packages should be installed from a central server onto a group of computers of different platforms, running a variety of operating systems (assuming that the software is designed to run on those platforms and operating systems). You can use OSD to install software components — as well as Java packages and standalone applications — that run on any operating system configured for Java.

Why XML for OSD?

The developers of OSD chose XML as their metalanguage because it provides extensive methods for depicting structured data in a hierarchical fashion. In English, this means that XML makes it possible to draw (figuratively or literally) a picture of the tree-like organization of data that has been structured in a specific way, like software packages. OSD had to be able to symbolize parts of a software package's structured hierarchy, as well as describe how the different parts were dependent upon one another. XML is flexible enough to allow OSD developers to create their own markup.

What does this mean in the real world? Often, when software packages are updated, not every part of the package needs to be changed, only portions. Although it is possible to overwrite the entire package, essentially replacing unchanged information with exact copies of itself, that isn't very efficient, and because OSD's primary method of dissemination is network-based, it's important that only those parts of a package that need to be changed are updated. Using this method, time and bandwidth aren't wasted downloading and installing duplicate data.

When software is installed for the first time, a complete installation isn't always necessary. Certain client computers may only need certain parts of the software. However, it's crucial that all the critical pieces and parts — those that are dependent upon one another — are all installed. OSD provides a mechanism for describing these relationships so that all the necessary modules of a software package are installed, even when a full installation isn't performed. And this is all done without human supervision. XML provides a robust and extensible environment for describing software packages and creates an economical method for installing and updating software.

Good Things Come with OSD

OSD can be used as a solution for several different needs:

- ✔ **To create stand-alone XML documents:** Because OSD is an XML vocabulary, it can be used to create valid XML documents that define the conditional relationship between different software components for different operating systems and languages. These documents include instructions for downloading and installing only the required software components based on the configuration of the client computer and the software that has already been installed on it.

- ✔ **To provide additional information for an archive file:** Java Archive (JAR) or Cabinet (CAB) files can include information described by OSD. The OSD document will probably include additional requirements for installing the software, as well as alternative instructions for installing or using any of the archive's files. This is especially handy because both JAR and OSD files are platform- and OS-independent, so they go together like hand and glove.

- ✔ **To include information about software needed to view Web pages:** Plug-ins, helper applications, and external applications all play key roles in allowing Web developers to include non-HTTP (HTML and graphics) files in their Web pages.

However, if the user doesn't have the correct plug-in or helper application, he can't see the information as the developer intended, if at all. OSD can be used to provide information about additional software needed to view Web pages. Look for APPLET and OBJECT tags to reference OSD resources that provide more information about additional software requirements sooner than later. Because it's all markup (which is text-based), OSD will one day be able to sit beside HTML on a Web page. Because OSD is designed to install software without help from the user, OSD documents may possibly be configured to automatically download and install any software the user is missing directly from the Internet. Although this last use is quite a way down the road — security and user issues will have to be addressed first — it shows the potential prowess of OSD.

✔ **To automatically distribute software:** Used in combination with push applications, OSD can be configured to download software to a user's machine automatically. Because OSD is designed to describe software in detail, only needed software components will be downloaded and installed. Documents written for the Channel Definition Format (CDF — see Chapter 11 for additional information) can point directly to an OSD document to provide information about which software components to install. CDF is responsible for the push itself, whereas OSD specifies the data that is pushed. The use of OSD to automatically trigger software installation won't be limited to Web-based technologies. It can also be used with proprietary distribution environments, such as Castanet from Marimba, to configure automatic software downloads.

Using OSD to Describe Software

OSD describes software dependencies — how components of software packages work together and with components from other packages — using what's known in the technobabble world as a directed graph. *Directed* indicates that OSD can tell which software package requires another and vise versa. *Graph* means that each software package is depicted as a node (or component) and each component can be a stand-alone package or require additional software components to function properly. When the components are distributed, the distribution name is the same as the name given to the node. The dependency specifies what nodes need what software elements to work.

Whew! Take a second to come up for air after that heavy discussion of dependencies, graphs, and nodes. Ugh.

Okay, we feel much better now. Using OSD, you can describe one or more dependencies for any given software component, including dependencies that are related directly to platform, OS, CPU, architecture, and language of the computer deciphering the OSD document. Each OSD document describes a single level of dependency information. If you have more than one set of dependency information, the OSD document must reference another file that describes the next level of dependency. Technically, this can go on and on, with one document linking to another, until a very large dependency graph is formed. In general, the bigger and more complex a document, the more OSD documents will be needed to describe its inner workings and component relationships.

We realize that all this talk of dependencies and graphs is a bit overwhelming, but what you need to understand is this: Those who take the time to learn OSD have the capability to tailor software programs to each user's unique needs — without sitting at computer after computer fiddling with configuration and preference files. To do so, an OSD developer must know very specific information about the OS, platform, and CPU of the client computer, as well as the programming language of the application that reads the OSD's instructions.

The following code samples and all other code and specification information included in the chapter are excerpts from the Open Software Description Format Note posted on the W3C's Web site at www.w3.org/TR/NOTE-OSD written by Arthur van Hoff of Marimba, Inc., and Hadi Partovi and Tom Thai of Microsoft, Inc. The W3C retains the copyright on all of these materials, as described in the W3C's document copyright notice found at www.w3.org/Consortium/Legal/copyright-documents.html, to wit: Copyright © World Wide Web Consortium (Massachusetts Institute of Technology, Institut National de Recherche en Informatique et en Automatique, Keio University). All Rights Reserved.

The following code sample shows how OSD describes dependencies. To help take some of the mystery out of the code, we've included our own descriptive comments using the ** . . . ** notation. Please note that these are our comments and not part of the original OSD Note.

For additional information, see the section titled "The OSD Reference," later in this chapter.

```
<SOFTPKG NAME="com.foobar.www.Solitaire" VERSION="1,0,0,0">
**Names the software to be opened and its location.**


<TITLE>Solitaire</TITLE>
**Gives the exact title of the software.**


<ABSTRACT>Solitaire by FooBar Corporation</ABSTRACT>
<LICENSE HREF="http://www.foobar.com/solitaire/
             license.html/">
**Gives License location and abstract information.**


<!--FooBar Solitaire is implemented in native code for
             Win32, Java code for other platforms -->
  <IMPLEMENTATION>
  <OS VALUE="WinNT">
    <OSVERSION VALUE="4,0,0,0"/>
    </OS>
  <OS VALUE="Win95"/>
```

```
<PROCESSOR VALUE="x86"/>
<LANGUAGE VALUE="en"/>
**Gives the Operating System specifications**

<CODEBASE HREF="http://www.foobar.org/solitaire.cab"/>
</IMPLEMENTATION>
<IMPLEMENTATION>
<IMPLTYPE VALUE="Java"/>
<CODEBASE HREF="http://www.foobar.org/solitaire.jar"/>
**Gives location of Java object code and solitaire program
         location.**

<!-- Java needs the DeckOfCards object -->
<DEPENDENCY>
<CODEBASE HREF="http://www.foobar.org/cards.osd"/>
</DEPENDENCY>
</IMPLEMENTATION>
</SOFTPKG>
**Gives location of Java object (deck of cards) that is
         needed by the software package.**
```

A client must read the OSD file in its entirety to determine which implementations and dependencies are pertinent, based on the client's configuration.
In addition, the client may have to download additional OSD files. For
example, the filename cards.osd names another OSD file that provides
information about second-level dependencies. After the client has downloaded this additional OSD file, it will have the whole picture (dependency
graph) to work from. It will then be able to download only the needed
software components and install the software package.

Use HTML to give OSD a push

Earlier, we said that *pull* means that the user has to initiate an action, such
as download or installation, and *push* means that actions occur without the
requisite user initiation. Although OSD exists to make the automation of the
download and installation process a breeze, users must still open the HTML
page that initiates the push process. For example, the <OBJECT> tag can be
used to let the user know that a new or updated version of a software
package is available. If the user's browser or agent is OSD-aware and the
<OBJECT> tag points to an OSD resource, the browser can download and
update the software components automatically, assuming that the user has
given permission for OSD to activate downloads. The HTML used to reference an OSD document in conjunction with the <OBJECT> tag looks like this:

```
<OBJECT CLASSID="clsid:9DBAFCCF-592F-101B-85CE
          00608CEC297B"
          VERSION="1,0,0,0"
          CODEBASE="http://www.acme.com/test.osd"
          HEIGHT=100 WIDTH=200 >
</OBJECT>
```

The <APPLET> tag can be used in much the same way:

```
<APPLET code=foo.class id=testid width=320 height=240>
    <PARAM NAME=useslibrary VALUE="test">
    <PARAM NAME=useslibraryversion VALUE="0,0,0,1">
    <PARAM NAME=useslibrarycodebase VALUE="test.osd">
</APPLET>
```

Details on the <OBJECT> tag in HTML 4.0 can be found at www.w3.org/TR/ WD-html40/html140.txt. Details on the <APPLET> tag in HTML 3.2 can be found at www.w3.org/TR/REC-html32.html.

For a friendly description and lots of good examples of the OBJECT and APPLET tags in motion, look for *HTML 4 For Dummies* in your local or online bookstore, or visit the *HTML 4 For Dummies* Web site at www.lanw.com/ books/html4dum/h4d4e/html4dum.htm.

You can point to an OSD file directly using the CODEBASE attribute in the <OBJECT> tag and the useslibrarycodebase parameter in the <APPLET> tag; or use the same attributes to point to an archive package such as a CAB or JAR that includes an OSD file and any additional software files.

With CDF, software gets pushy

Even when an OSD file is referenced from an HTML page, the user must still navigate his way to the page to allow the OBJECT or APPLET tags to begin software download and installation. At its root level, this method still uses the pull paradigm because the user has to surf the Web to start the process. As we mention earlier in this chapter, the Channel Definition Format (CDF) is another XML vocabulary that was designed to describe the interrelation-ships between HTML pages and other Web resources. CDF can be used to create the following:

- ✔ CDF-aware clients, such as the next generation of Web browsers (check out HotMetal at www.softquad.com) that implement "smart-pull" techniques to download Web content automatically

- ✔ CDF-aware servers (such as the Web Automation Toolkit at www.webmethods.com) that use "true-push" mechanisms for automatic distribution of content from client to server

So, CDF provides a language for content push — sending Web pages in HTML format, such as what is done in e-mail programs and via the new Web browsers and PointCast software (see www.pointcast.com). It also furnishes a perfect leverage point that allows software push — sending instructions to open predetermined software programs — or automatic distribution of software. If CDF is going to activate a software push, it must reference an OSD-described software package using the <SOFTPKG> tag that is part of the CDF specification, as shown in this code snippet:

```
<CHANNEL HREF="http://www.acme.com.intropage.htm">
<SELF="http://www.acme.com/software.cdf" />
            <TITLE>A Software Distribution Channel</TITLE>
<SOFTPKG HREF="http://www.acme.com/aboutsoftware.htm"
            NAME="{D27CDB6E-AE6D-11CF-96B8-444553540000}"
            VERSION="1,0,0,0">
<IMPLEMENTATION>
        <OS VALUE="WinNT">
            <OSVERSION VALUE="4,0,0,0"/>
            </OS>
        <OS VALUE="Win95"/>
<PROCESSOR VALUE="x86" />
<CODEBASE HREF="http://www.acme.com/test.cab" />
</IMPLEMENTATION>
</SOFTPKG>
</CHANNEL>
```

The OSD Reference

The following sections provide short descriptions of the major elements in the OSD vocabulary. In the bulleted list at the end of this chapter, we include information about the relationship between major elements and the minor elements that they contain, as well as the attributes of all OSD elements.

OSD is not technically divided into major and minor elements, but the Note (online) and our own section have been organized this way to help describe the role each tag plays in OSD in general.

Major elements

- SOFTPKG: Defines a general software package. The document element of any OSD document is always SOFTPKG.

- IMPLEMENTATION: A tag nested within SOFTPKG that is used to describe a client-specific software package.

- DEPENDENCY: A tag nested within SOFTPKG or IMPLEMENTATION that describes a dependency between software distributions or components.

Minor elements

- TITLE: A tag nested within SOFTPKG that gives the name or friendly description of the software package.

- ABSTRACT: A tag nested within SOFTPKG that provides a short description of the package's functionality and intent.

- LICENSE: A tag nested within SOFTPKG that points to a file containing licensing information.

- CODEBASE: A tag nested within IMPLEMENTATION that points to a location — usually somewhere on the network — where an archive of the software distribution exists. One or more URLs may be specified to show that the software can be downloaded from several different places. CODEBASE is crucial to the function of the OSD document and cannot be omitted.

- OS: A tag nested within IMPLEMENTATION that defines the operating system the package requires. No OS must be specified, or multiple OSs may be defined. If an OS is not named, the software is presumed to run on all systems.

- OSVERSION: A tag nested within OS that defines which version of the operating system the package requires. No version must be specified, or multiple versions my be defined. If a version is not named, the software is presumed to run on all system versions.

- PROCESSOR: A tag nested within IMPLEMENTATION that defines which processor the software package requires. No processor must be specified, or multiple processors may be defined. If a processor is not named, the software is presumed to run on all processors.

- LANGUAGE: A tag nested within IMPLEMENTATION that defines which natural language is required in the user interface by the software package. No language must be specified, or multiple languages may be defined. If a language is not named, the software is presumed to run under all languages.

- VM: A tag nested within IMPLEMENTATION that defines the virtual machine required by the software.

- MEMSIZE: A tag nested within IMPLEMENTATION that specifies how much run-time memory is required by the software.

✔ DISKSIZE: A tag nested within IMPLEMENTATION that specifies how much disk space is required by the software.

✔ IMPLTYPE: A tag nested within IMPLEMENTATION that describes the type of implementation.

The following list provides OSD element definitions, their relationships, and attributes. Included in each description are the element's name, legal content, context information, and a list of attributes.

✔ ABSTRACT
   Content: <string>
   Child of: SOFTPKG
   Parent of: none
   Attributes: none

✔ CODEBASE
   Content: none
   Child of: IMPLEMENTATION
   Parent of: none
   Attributes: SIZE=<maxKB> — the maximum allowable size for the archive; HREF=<URL> — the location of the archive to be downloaded; FILENAME=<string> — specifies the software's filename if contained in an archive with an OSD document.

✔ DEPENDENCY
   Content: none
   Child of: SOFTPKG, IMPLEMENTATION
   Parent of: SOFTPKG
   Attributes: ACTION= (Assert | Install) — Assert causes the software to be ignored if the dependency is not already present on the client machine; Install causes the software to be installed as well as find and install all required dependencies.

✔ DISKSIZE
   Content: none
   Child of: IMPLEMENTATION
   Parent of: none
   Attributes: VALUE=<KB-number> — defines the amount of disk space required by the software package.

✔ IMPLEMENTATION
   Content: none
   Child of: SOFTPKG
   Parent of: CODEBASE, DEPENDENCY, DISKSIZE, IMPLTYPE, LANGUAGE, OS, PROCESSOR, VM
   Attributes: none

- IMPLTYPE
  Content: none
  Child of: IMPLEMENTATION
  Parent of: none
  Attributes: VALUE=<string> — describes the implementation's type.

- LANGUAGE
  Content: none
  Child of: IMPLEMENTATION
  Parent of: none
  Attributes: VALUE=<string> — defines the language of the software package as specified in ISO 639.

- LICENSE
  Content: none
  Child of: SOFTPKG
  Parent of: none
  Attributes: HREF=<URL> — the location of the licensing information.

- MEMSIZE
  Content: none
  Child of: IMPLEMENTATION
  Parent of: none
  Attributes: VALUE=<KB-number> — defines the amount of run-time memory required by the software package.

- OS
  Content: none
  Child of: IMPLEMENTATION
  Parent of: none
  Attributes: VALUE=<string> — specifies the operating system(s) required by the software package.

- OSVERSION
  Content: none
  Child of: IMPLEMENTATION
  Parent of: none
  Attributes: VALUE=<string> — specifies the operating system version(s) required by the software package.

- PROCESSOR
  Content: none
  Child of: IMPLEMENTATION
  Parent of: none
  Attributes: VALUE=<string> — specifies the processor(s) required by the software package.

✔ SOFTPKG
Content: none
Child of: DEPENDENCY
Parent of: ABSTRACT, CODEBASE, IMPLEMENTATION, DEPENDENCY, TITLE
Attributes: HREF=<URL> — the location of a Web page associated with the package; NAME=<string> — a unique identifier for the software package; Version=<string> — provides version information.

✔ TITLE
Content: <string>
Child of: SOFTPKG
Parent of: none
Attributes: none

✔ VM
Content: none
Child of: IMPLEMENTATION
Parent of: none
Attributes: VALUE=<string> — specifies the virtual machines(s) required by the software package.

The notion of using the network as a software distribution medium is not a new one, but the current solution offerings are all based on proprietary applications and format. OSD brings network-based software distribution into the public realm, and with two heavy hitters like Marimba and Microsoft (M&M as it were) behind it, OSD has a solid chance of going far.

Part IV
The Part of Tens

In this part . . .

The Part of Tens is the traditional capstone to all ...*For Dummies* books, wherein the authors sum up and distill the very essence of what you've discovered in each book's other pieces and parts. Thus, this part gives you the chance to review the important but often covert role that SGML plays with XML. In addition, you find a golden opportunity to observe some of the best and brightest uses of XML. We also select the "best of the best" XML resources online so that you, our gentle reader, may efficiently navigate to the most useful XML documents found on the Internet. From there, we tackle that most traditional of all sources of Internet-based help — the FAQ, or list of "Frequently Asked Questions," to let you ponder answers to some of the most common questions about XML. Finally, we end our XML odyssey by delivering information regarding the most compelling of all XML tools and software — programs that you can then investigate further online, or from the CD-ROM included with this book. After that, the rest is up to you!

Chapter 18

Nearly Ten Secrets to SGML Satisfaction

....

....

*O*kay, so this is The Part of Tens, but not every chapter in this section adds up to exactly that number. Although we came up a little short in terms of the number of avenues for exploring the vast and imponderable universe that is SGML, you'll find no shortage of materials, information, and assistance to help you get up to speed on this all-important technology. Because SGML lays the foundation for XML, knowledge of SGML is essential if you want to become a real XML expert. This chapter lays out some of the paths that you can use to pursue SGML wisdom and documents some of the many resources that can help you attain your goal of XML excellence. For the glorious details and more sources of information than you can shake a stick at, read on!

Specifications Form a Firm SGML Foundation

Getting started with SGML can sometimes seem a bit daunting, given that so much information is available. Our favorite SGML starting point resides at the W3C Web site, which is home to a lot of relevant material for XML and other Web-related markup languages and technologies.

Among its many other treasures, the W3C Web site includes a page called "Overview of SGML Resources." This gem contains pointers to all kinds of SGML information that you can use to cover most of the topics in this chapter, including pointers to relevant specifications. Find this treasure at `www.w3.org/MarkUp/SGML/`.

We can't think of a better place to begin a quest for SGML information than the W3C site. But if you're bound and determined to read the original version of the ISO 8879 spec that governs SGML, you can order a hard copy through the ISO itself, at this URL: `www.iso.ch/cate/d16387.html#0`.

In addition, take a look at Steve Pepper's Whirlwind Guide at `www.infotek.no/sgmltool/guide.htm`.

Personally, we think Charles Goldfarb's book titled *The SGML Handbook* (Clarendon Press, Oxford, UK, 1993), which contains the SGML specification in its entirety, is both more readable and more informative than the ISO documentation, and we highly recommend it.

Pursuing SGML in the Classroom

A surprising number of vendors offer SGML classroom training, which you can prove for yourself by visiting the search engine of your choice, and entering a search string such as "SGML AND training." Our identical search string at `www.excite.com` produced more than 100 responses, many of which looked quite interesting. But the following organizations or conferences are acknowledged as providing the best-known and best-revered SGML training classes. Note that most organizations with SGML expertise are jumping full-force onto the XML bandwagon because of the large degree of overlap in expertise involved.

✔ Isogen International has been known under a variety of names since its founding in the early 1990s (Insight Data Systems and Highland Consulting) but has always had a rich and varied set of SGML training offerings, some in conjunction with the SGML World trade show. Not coincidentally, this company is also a highly regarded source of SGML-related consulting. For more information, visit the company's Web site at `www.isogen.com/index.html`.

✔ The SGML Resource Center represents a consortium of training and consulting firms gathered under the SGML Open banner. SGML Open is an industry organization of SGML professionals of many stripes and acts as a gathering place for those in need of SGML expertise to meet with those who have such expertise to offer. To read more about this group's training and consulting offerings, visit this Web site: `www.mcs.net/~dken/`.

✔ The Graphic Communications Association (GCA) is another outstanding clearinghouse for SGML expertise, including some of the best training offerings around. GCA offers its training primarily at its SGML- and XML-related conferences, which provide the opportunity to encounter and examine vendors, consultants, and products as well as to take classes in this subject area. To find out more about GCA's shows and training classes, visit their Web site at `www.gca.org/`.

Although these outfits represent the cream of the crop, they are only the tip of a large iceberg of potential training providers. If SGML training is in your future, be sure to shop around for the best deals and the most convenient locations before spending any money. Expect to spend between $400 and $600 per classroom day of training in this area.

SGML Information Online

Plenty of useful Web sites and other compendia of SGML-related information are available online. Over the past few years, we've found the following sites to be among the most informative and useful:

✔ A Gentle Introduction to SGML from the Text Encoding Initiative (a group dedicated to the promulgation of SGML and related technologies) guidelines. This excellent starting point is for folks new to SGML terms and technologies who wish to get up to speed quickly — and painlessly. Find it at `www-tei.uic.edu/orgs/tei/sgml/teip3sg/SG.htm`.

✔ With more than 700 items, Robin Cover's SGML Bibliography represents the most extensive bibliography on SGML that we know of. If it ain't here, it ain't anywhere. This page also ties into his other resource pages, which cover both XML and SGML information online. The SGML bibliography entries are in the table of contents of this behemoth bibliography at `www.sil.org/sgml/sgml.html`.

✔ Erik Naggum's SGML archive contains a variety of SGML-related resources in downloadable file format. This provides a great jumping-off point for SGML exploration on the Web, because many of the entries point to other vendors, organizations, and SGML-related efforts. Find this archive at `ftp.ifi.uio.no/pub/SGML`.

Again, we can't begin to claim that this represents the majority of SGML resources online, but among these resources you'll find a great introduction to the subject matter, and pointers to most of the resources and sites about SGML that may conceivably be of interest in your further investigations into this topic.

Finding SGML Tools and Technologies

As with training, a quick hop to your favorite search engine with a string such as "SGML AND consulting" or "SGML AND consultant" will produce many hundreds of potential candidates. But, in the same vein as training, we found the large industry consortia like SGML Open (www.sgmlopen.org) — especially through the SGML Resource Center mentioned in the training section earlier in this chapter, the Graphic Communication Association (www.gca.org), and the International SGML Users Group (www.sil.org/sgml/isgmlug/isgmlug.htm) all to be valuable SGML resources. Finally, Steve Pepper offers a reasonably comprehensive listing of SGML software at his Web site, "The Whirlwind Guide to SGML & XML Tools and Vendors," at www.infotek.no/sgmltool/guide.htm.

But this is also an area where vendors ply their wares, so we would be remiss if we didn't mention the following players in the SGML software trade. Among a cast of many others, we picked the ones we think are most important.

- ✔ SoftQuad offers a wide variety of tools for SGML, XML, and HTML, including full-blown authoring tools, plus validation tools and a variety of productivity aids. Visit its Web site at www.softquad.com.

- ✔ Inso Corporation, formerly known as Electronic Book Technologies, offers sophisticated document design and management systems built around SGML technologies, including all kinds of electronic publishing tools for high-volume data. Visit its Web site at www.inso.com/.

- ✔ James Clark is a deity in the pantheon of SGML software developers. James continues to build some of the best SGML parsers and validation tools around, including the highly regarded SP SGML parser, and the SGML composer known as JADE. Visit his home page at www.jclark.com/.

- ✔ Arbortext offers an extremely broad range of SGML and XML tools and technologies, not to mention training and consulting services as well. Arbortext is one of the oldest names in the SGML game; visit its Web site for more information at www.arbortext.com/.

- ✔ DataChannel is a relatively new entrant into the marketplace but offers a strong background in XML and SGML technology. One of our authors works for this company, so his participation merits mention of this company, which offers composition and editing tools for XML and SGML. Visit its Web site at www.datachannel.com.

SGML Print Resources

You find no shortage of resource materials on SGML in print. A quick hop to Amazon (www.amazon.com) to search for books with SGML in their titles produced a list of 46 books in this area. Although we can't say we've read all 46 of them, we have found these to be particularly useful, and we've included a few titles on XML for good measure:

- ✔ Dan Connolly, editor: "XML: Principles, Tools, and Techniques." *The World Wide Web Journal*, Volume 2, Number 4, Winter 1997. O'Reilly & Associates, Sebastopol, CA, 1997. ISBN 1-56592-349-9. Reports from a wide range of XML experts and W3C XML Working Group participants on the state of XML, developing XML dialects, implementing XML software, and more. A must-read for those truly interested in XML.

- ✔ Charles F. Goldfarb: *The SGML Handbook*. Oxford University Press, Oxford, UK, 1990. ISBN 0-19-853737-9. The definitive reference on SGML, written by one of its co-inventors, and the most often cited reference on the subject. A much cheaper paperback version is due to appear some time in 1998, so keep your eyes peeled!

- ✔ Eric van Herwijnen: *Practical SGML*, 2nd Edition. Kluwer Academic Publishers, Boston, 1994. ISBN 0-7923-9434-8. An outstanding guide to understanding and using SGML in a working environment; short on theory and rumination, long on practical advice and insight.

- ✔ Richard Light: *Presenting XML*, Sams.Net, Indianapolis, IN, 1997. ISBN 1-57521-334-6. Currently the only overview book on XML available; Light and his colleagues do a good job of covering the state of XML notation and technology as of mid-1997. In the wake of the latest standard (December 1997), this work is a bit dated but nevertheless quite informative and a great place to start gaining knowledge about this technology.

- ✔ Eve Maler and Jeanne El Andaloussi: *Developing SGML DTDs: From Text to Model to Markup*. Prentice Hall, Upper Saddle River, NJ, 1996. ISBN 0-13-309881-8. Even though this book predates XML and is focused entirely on SGML DTDs, no designer who's serious about developing an XML dialect or tweaking an existing DTD will want to be without this book. This book provides the best nuts-and-bolts coverage of this troublesome topic that we've ever seen anywhere.

- ✔ Bill Von Hagen: *SGML For Dummies*. IDG Books Worldwide, Indianapolis, IN, 1997. ISBN 0-7645-0175-5. The best and most gentle introduction to this awe-inspiring topic, and certainly the one that takes itself the least seriously (we enjoy an opportunity to laugh when studying such weighty matters).

Practice Makes Perfect

No matter where your expertise in SGML originates — be it in the classroom, from the specification itself, from books, from tutorials, or from tools — no amount of learning and exposure by itself can help you develop proficiency in using SGML. Only practice and review of your efforts will help you become sufficiently fluent to understand and use this challenging standard document description technology.

We especially recommend that you work on your proficiency at designing and deploying Document Type Definitions (DTDs), because they define the essence of all existing XML dialects, and they give you the ability to customize existing XML or to develop your own markup and notation. In fact, this explains why no discussion of XML is complete without some coverage of SGML and why this chapter appears in this book!

Chapter 19
Ten Best Uses for XML

*A*lthough much can be said for XML and what it can do for its users, its biggest benefits fall into two major areas, which we explore in this chapter. The first great benefit is XML's innate capabilities as a representational mechanism, giving XML the ability to

✔ Create shortcuts through character entities

✔ Use single links to perform multiple actions simultaneously

✔ Apply built-in "document quality control" through syntax checking and automated validation

The second great benefit results from XML's abilities to represent all kinds of arbitrary and complex data, making it suitable for everything from abstruse mathematical notation to defining graphical interfaces. Both areas combine to make XML pretty powerful stuff, indeed!

ENTITY *Can Be a Labor-Saving Device*

Among its many capabilities, the XML/SGML ENTITY DTD declaration makes it possible to substitute properly formatted strings of arbitrary length with named symbols that take the form &*name*;, where *name* is easy to make much shorter than what it replaces. Thus "The AA ACME Merchandising Company" can be replaced with &acme; in the text of any document where the proper ENTITY declaration occurs, namely:

```
<!ENTITY acme "The AA ACME Merchandising Company">
```

Remember that case counts with XML, so all references to the entity must take the form &acme; in the document body. Just think how much easier this might make placing orders for a certain coyote!

Rich Links Enrich Functionality

XML supports extended link types, in addition to the simple one-way links that are the only kind supported by HTML. The Text Encoding Initiative (TEI) defines a compact syntax for creating complex links, and HyTime is an ISO standard that develops its own set of useful linking concepts and mechanisms. Both of these help to inform the XPointer mechanism that is at the core of XML's extended linking capabilities — for more information on XPointer, see Chapter 7. Suffice it to say here that such links can be bi-directional and that a single link can connect from one point in a single document to multiple documents (or to multiple points in a single document, and so forth).

For more information about this topic and the underlying technologies, visit the W3C Web site and look for link information under the XML home page; also check out these pages:

- ✔ Lloyd Rutledge wrote a short overview of HyTime, with good entry pointers, located at www.sil.org/SGML/hytimeWhatRutledge.html.

- ✔ Robin Cover provides an excellent set of pointers, including discussion of an emerging XML Linking Language (XLL) at www.sil.org/sgml/xll.html.

- ✔ The University of Virginia has put together a set of documents and overviews on TEI located at etext.lib.virginia.edu/tei/uvatei.html.

Well-Formed or Valid XML Guarantees Readability

Part of the mechanism inherent in parsing any XML document for rendering involves checking that the related DTD — whether that DTD is implied, as in the case of a well-formed XML document, or whether it's present by inclusion or by references, as in the case of a valid XML document — is in agreement with the document contents that follow the DTD. Unlike HTML, every XML document that does not exhibit such agreement between DTD and content is flagged with error messages and may not be displayed by some viewers.

This conflict puts considerable pressure on content developers to publish XML documents that do not provoke such error messages and helps to guarantee viewing experiences for document readers that are substantially the same, no matter what platform or software they may employ to view documents. The requirements of XML should help to overcome the Tower of Babel effect that plagues so many complex HTML-based sites nowadays, where Webmasters must create multiple versions of the same pages to ensure that their content can reach the broadest possible audience. XML should help consolidate this fragmented audience and bring them all together under a single standard and software umbrella.

MathML Captures Mathematical Requirements

Of course, MathML (discussed in Chapter 14) is unlikely to be of interest to those whose document content does not require representing things mathematical. But for those with complex notation or formulae to dispense, nothing else will quite do the trick. That's why MathML is perceived as a boon to mathematicians everywhere and offers long-sought closure to early proponents of HTML 3.0, who tried to introduce mathematical support in that version of the language.

Ultimately, XML has proved to be a friendlier environment for this special notation, because it permits those communities interested in such esoteric matters to solve them to their own satisfaction. Those who are disinterested are safe to pursue their interests elsewhere.

For more information on MathML, start your research with this URL for the current W3C Working Draft on the topic: `www.w3.org/TR/WD-math-980106/`.

CML Has Good Chemistry

The Chemical Markup Language, detailed in Chapter 10, represents one of the earliest efforts to define a specialized XML dialect and arises mainly from the efforts of Peter Murray-Rust, who has created a language that can

- Represent complex atomic and molecular arrangements
- Handle the appurtenances of academic papers — footnotes, citations, exhibits, and so forth

Those outside the obvious communities of chemical interest are unlikely to find this work compelling (except, perhaps, as a case in point to demonstrate what's possible with XML and how to do the job quite nicely).

But for those with a chemical itch to scratch, please visit Robin Cover's excellent overview page on CML at `www.sil.org/sgml/gen-apps.html#cml`.

CDF Brings Beaucoup Channels to the Web

The Channel Definition Format, covered in Chapter 11, has been endorsed by all kinds of Internet industry players, including DataChannel and Microsoft. CDF defines a mechanism whereby collections of data called channels may be defined and delivered from a "push" server to lists of subscribing clients. This permits a single server to deliver an almost arbitrary number of different information feeds, software updates, and other regularly changing types of data. This technology supports, among other applications, the channels that Internet Explorer can now open on any desktop.

Robin Cover's overview page provides a great starting point for finding out more about CDF. Look for that page at `www.sil.org/sgml/gen-apps.html#cdf`.

DRP Makes Mirrors on the Web

The HTTP Distribution and Replication Protocol (DRP) — discussed in Chapter 13 — represents the joint efforts of Marimba, Inc., Netscape Communications, Sun Microsystems, @Home, Inc., and Novell to define a way to "significantly improve the efficiency and reliability of data distribution over HTTP" (to quote from the group's press release on the subject). This mechanism is primarily aimed at using the Internet as a vehicle to distribute software and regular software updates to subscribers and will probably be supplanted by the Resource Definition Framework (RDF) mentioned later in this chapter's section, "RDF Frames All Kinds of Resources," and in Chapter 12 of this book. In the meantime, DRP represents an interesting effort by members of the "anybody but Microsoft" camp and is probably worth watching.

Robin Cover has an exceptional overview on DRP, available at www.sil.org/sgml/xml.html#xml-drp.

SMIL Synchronizes Multimedia Elements

In late 1997, the W3C announced its first draft of the Synchronized Multimedia Integration Language, which we discuss in Chapter 16. This XML-based effort represents a serious attempt to define data delivery mechanisms that can handle the need for timely delivery of sound, video, graphics, and text to permit simultaneous display of many different kinds and streams of data in synchronized fashion on users' displays. Although this may remind you of the hilarious effects pioneered by Woody Allen in *What's Up, Tiger Lily?* where he deliberately timed the voice-overs to conflict with the on-screen action, it promises to make the jobs of those who seek to use the Web as a vehicle for delivering multimedia content much easier.

For more information on this emerging XML initiative, Robin Cover's overview and pointers are a good place to start; visit www.sil.org/sgml/xml.html#xml-smil.

RDF Frames All Kinds of Resources

The Resource Definition Framework represents a massive effort from the W3C to consolidate and coordinate many related efforts to define metadata that can describe what documents contain (or what they can deliver) using consistent, coherent markup and notation. The W3C October 1997 press release provides the most succinct definition available for such an all-encompassing initiative, when it explicitly identifies these six potential uses for RDF metadata:

As stated in the W3C press release on this topic, RDF metadata can be used in a variety of application areas such as:

(1) in resource discovery to provide better search engine capabilities;

(2) in cataloging for describing the content and content relationships available at a particular Web site, page, or digital library;

(3) by intelligent software agents to facilitate knowledge sharing and exchange;

(4) in content rating for child protection and privacy protection;

(5) in describing collections of pages that represent a single logical document;

(6) for describing intellectual property rights of Web pages.

Because RDF covers so much ground and encompasses so much existing work, getting your arms around it can be a real stretch. But Robin Cover's overview and pointers offer an excellent place to start reaching for these stars: www.sil.org/sgml/xml.html#xml-rdf.

In addition, you can visit the W3C site for information on the RDF tags and their attributes; visit www.w3.org/TR/WD-rdf-syntax/.

WIDL Makes Web Interfaces Easy

The Web Interface Definition Language (WIDL) — covered in Chapter 15 — seeks to bring HTML and XML closer together by defining a set of XML-based HTML extensions that may be used to define user interfaces for Web sites. This approach permits the work on the Document Object Model (DOM) at the W3C to drive the structure and behavior of underlying documents and creates a common, consistent framework to support dynamic display behavior (à la Dynamic HTML) and to support queries into page contents and structures. In turn, this makes it much easier for Web site designers to create consistent navigation tools, tables of contents, on-screen menus, and so forth. Thus, this effort is also aimed at reducing some of the complexity that supporting multiple browser types has imposed on Webmasters everywhere.

To find out more about this initiative, start with Robin Cover's overview at www.sil.org/sgml/xml.html#widl.

Keep in mind that WIDL is still a proposed standard. The best source for this information until it becomes official is the WebMethods site at www.webmethods.com.

But Wait, There's More . . .

Unlike the old Ronco ads, you won't get a free set of Ginsu knives with each XML purchase, but this list of potential benefits by no means exhausts all the capabilities in the works for XML. And although we don't plan to slice a beer can in half and then do the same to some poor tomato, we would like to point out that lots of new functionality and new markup dialects may be coming soon to a "Web site near you!" These include the eXtensible Style Language (XSL — covered in Chapter 8), an attempt to bring dynamic behavior to style data for XML; all kinds of electronic commerce initiatives based on XML; and further developments to enrich XML's multi-talented linking mechanisms, among many other XML-related activities.

A good way to keep up with the latest XML developments is to visit the resource sites recommended in Chapter 20 of this book and Extra 24 on the CD regularly and attentively.

You can also track what's new with XML at the W3C's XML home page, which you may call "the mother of all XML resources." It's located at www.w3.org/XML/.

Hopefully, we've shown you that XML makes custom markup easy, but also that the markup it can make has nearly limitless representational capabilities. Although you may never need to use all these capabilities in a single document or draw on multiple XML dialects at the same time, it's nice to know they're there. In Extra 24, we show you where to look for enlightenment about XML in general, as we survey the top XML-related resources online.

Chapter 20

Ten Terrific XML Sites

*B*ecause of the ever-changing nature of cutting-edge technologies such as XML, you probably aren't surprised that the best resources for up-to-the-minute information reside online. In this member of The Part of Tens, we take you on a lightning tour of the electronic landscape for XML, stopping only at those watering holes of sufficient depth or breadth to tempt even the most hardened information miner to dig for a nugget or two while passing through.

It All Starts at the W3C

You probably know that the ultimate source of Web wisdom resides at the World Wide Web Consortium's Web site. Where XML is concerned, the site is no exception to the rule. One excellent set of pointers to XML stuff, including the XML specification itself, exists at the W3C's XML home page.

You find this nonpareil of XML resources at www.w3.org/XML/.

Read the FAQ!

On the Internet, creating and maintaining a list of frequently asked questions — and more important, the answers that go with them — is part of the "standard method" for helping newcomers find their way into any subject area. Here again, XML is no exception.

You can find and read the FAQ, which is lovingly compiled and maintained by a variety of members of the W3C's XML Working Group (most notably, Peter Flynn) at www.ucc.ie/xml/.

Remember that the ultimate adage when considering asking for help on any topic in the Internet world is to "read the FAQ" before asking. Follow this advice and you'll never get embarrassed by rehashing old, timeworn topics.

Robin's Got Everything Covered

Robin Cover is a well-known expert on matters related to SGML and XML. His Web sites are widely renowned and heavily used. Visit his SGML/XML Web page at www.sil.org/sgml/ and you can find pointers to all kinds of interesting — and sometimes highly relevant — information about SGML and XML.

By far the most outstanding resource in this collection of goodies is Cover's exhaustive (if not exhausting) compendium of XML resources, which you can find at www.sil.org/sgml/xml.html.

SGML University Adds XML to Its Curriculum

When it comes to things SGML, SGML University is a purveyor of training on SGML and related topics. Given the natural synergy that exists between SGML and XML, the fact that they now offer XML training comes as no surprise.

SGML University's offerings now include a class titled "Making XML Work," along with numerous SGML and XML Tools surveys. For more information about their classes, visit their tutorials listing at www.sgmlu.com/tut.htm.

Microsoft Makes XML Part of Its Game

Despite its reputation as a "dog in the manger" when it comes to standards versus proprietary technologies, Microsoft offers plenty of information about XML to go along with its software offerings that support this technology. For more information on XML than you may believe possible from the Redmondians, visit the company's XML home page at `www.microsoft.com/xml/`.

The SGML Resource Center Does XML, Too

Because of the deep and fundamental linkage between XML and SGML, most sources of SGML enlightenment can also shed light on XML topics as well. One of the better SGML resources on the Web is Dianne Kennedy's SGML Resource Center, located at `www.mcs.net/~dken/`.

You can find the resource center's list of XML resources at `www.mcs.net/~dken/xml.htm`.

The GCA Offers XML Goodies Galore

The Graphics Communication Association, despite its somewhat nondescript name, has long been active as a purveyor of conferences, training, and publications for the SGML community. Now they've taken their expertise into the XML world, with predictably excellent results. Whether you're looking to mingle with other XML-ites, to take a class, or to survey a list of available publications, you can find XML-related information on the XML pages at the GCA.

To jump straight to the GCA's XML stuff, visit their "What is XML?" Web page at `www.gca.org/conf/xml/xml_what.htm`.

To check out the Graphics Communication Association itself, simply lop off everything to the right of `.org` in the URL in the preceding paragraph.

Expert Is as Expert Does

James K. Tauber is one member of the W3C's XML Working Group who has put his knowledge and commitment on display through a well-executed set of XML-related Web pages. At his site, you can find everything from pointers to standards and discussions, to mailing lists and newsgroups, bibliographies, and other collections of XML information. Along with Robin Cover's work, Tauber's XML pages are among the most frequently cited starting points for XML investigations.

Check out Tauber & Associates' list of XML resources at www.jtauber.com/xml/.

ArborText Offers More Than XML Software

Although we mention ArborText's outstanding ADEPT XML/SGML authoring tools in Chapter 22, the company also offers a great clearinghouse of XML pointers and information to boot.

You can find ArborText's collection of XML pointers and information at www.arbortext.com/xml.html.

DataChannel Does XML, Too!

Norbert Mikula is a co-author for this book. His employer, DataChannel, just happens to offer a creditable collection of XML resources. Despite our close affiliation with this company, we think this list is worth visiting anyway!

Check our sincerity and veracity at www.datachannel.com/channelworld/XML/XMLIndex.htm.

Although we can't claim to have covered everything that matters about XML in this short chapter, if you checked out every pointer in every site mentioned herein, you'd probably notice that the information was changing faster than you could read it. Nevertheless, we think you'll find this collection of starting points as good as or better than any you could find on your own.

Chapter 21

Ten Burning XML Questions (And Answers)

Upon first studying XML, would-be users have lots of questions. One good source for answers is the XML FAQ, which you can find at www.ucc.ie/xml/. FAQ stands for *frequently asked questions,* so you won't be surprised that the complete title of the document is "Frequently Asked Questions about the Extensible Markup Language," subtitled "The XML FAQ." This FAQ is maintained on behalf of the World Wide Web Consortium's XML Special Interest Group by Peter Flynn.

In the Internet world, FAQs represent collective wisdom in response to questions that newcomers to a field ask. A common reply on newsgroups and mailing lists, when newbie questions pop up — as they inevitably do from time to time — is "Read the FAQ!" In general, good manners suggest that you read the FAQ document before asking any questions. The idea is to keep dialog focused on interesting questions, instead of repeating and answering common ones all the time.

Theory and practice sometimes diverge, which is why "Read the FAQ!" remains a standard e-mail and newsgroup message staple. We suggest that you, too, read the XML FAQ, but we present the most popular of these most commonly asked questions in this chapter, so you should read this first. Think of this as the FAQ for *XML For Dummies!*

Why Is XML Important?

The first letter in the acronym for XML stands for "extensible" (or perhaps "eXtensible," if you're more literally minded), and this word explains why XML matters to the future of the Web. XML extends the markup that browsers can read and permits well-informed document designers to add functionality and controls to the documents that they build. In other words, XML opens up the closed world of HTML and lets designers create the markup they need when they need it, without forcing them to wait for the browser vendors to add new functionality or for the standards-makers to incorporate such new capability in the closed (but ever-changing) definition of HTML.

On the other hand, XML provides most of the functionality and power of SGML, but without imposing the complexity and "everything including the kitchen sink" mentality that SGML embodies. XML's functionality makes work easier for software developers who write compact parsers, interpreters, and rendering tools, which in turn makes using XML in everyday environments easier, even on low-powered computers. In other words, XML is designed as a workable compromise between HTML (which is simple but closed and constrained in what it can do) and SGML (which is unbelievably rich and powerful in what it can do but a real bear to implement and maintain). XML does a creditable job of offering the best of both worlds and promises to enhance tremendously the kinds of information that the Web can deliver and the ways that users can interact with that information.

Why Use XML Rather Than HTML?

Because XML is extensible, XML allows document designers to handle multiple sources of data and to create their own customized environments for special kinds of data, where necessary. This means that the content and the way it appears can stay within the confines of a standard document environment, as long as the right kind of Document Type Definition (DTD) is defined for the XML document in use.

To achieve the same results with HTML, designers must resort to Java applets, ActiveX components, or other contortions. Because these approaches split the content of the resulting HTML documents between the documents themselves and the programs they call, this creates a potential maintenance nightmare because the content that has to be maintained for such materials can be spread across multiple HTML pages and embedded within numerous Java applets, ActiveX components, or CGI programs. In other words, XML allows designers to more easily keep the content and the presentation instructions together, which in turn makes such documents easier to build and maintain.

XML has two additional advantages:

✔ Valid XML markup can be reused wherever it's needed, and any XML parser can grab it and use it. Today, HTML has fragmented into numerous "dialects," primarily to reflect the capabilities of certain browsers or browser plug-ins. XML is XML, no matter where it runs. This capability helps eliminate platform and browser dependencies in HTML pages that cause intense design and maintenance headaches for Webmasters today.

✔ Any valid XML document conforms to a strict subset of SGML; in English, this means that XML documents aren't restricted to use within Web browsers and that XML documents are readable in any SGML environment. This capability may not sound like much until you recognize that most document management systems use SGML. So XML lends itself more readily to a "write once, publish many ways" approach that many organizations would like to use with the content they develop. XML makes this approach more natural and easier to achieve.

As long as an organization is willing to absorb the costs of training its people, buying new tools, and creating the necessary DTDs (which is by no means trivial), XML offers significant benefits over HTML.

Must All Web Sites Convert to XML?

More than 99 percent of Web content is written in HTML right now. Much of this content will remain unchanged, even as XML becomes more pervasive and widespread. Unless you need to take advantage of XML's richer representational capabilities, its more powerful hyperlinks, or its ability to handle multiple data sources and special forms of notation, you may find no need to convert anything from HTML to XML. Today, Internet Explorer 4.0 can already handle XML content; in the near future, most Web browsers will also be able to render XML and HTML. XML-capable browsers make it possible to mix content at will and to use XML where it's useful or necessary.

Thus, the answer to the question stated in the heading is a resounding "No!"

Moving from HTML to XML

Because we can find no absolute requirement to use XML instead of HTML, Web sites can use XML as they see fit. Many organizations are adopting a "wait and see" approach — that is, many are investigating and learning the underlying XML technologies and working on experimental or pilot implementations. As the marketplace moves toward XML and the software that understands such markup becomes more available, more content will appear in XML.

But where XML provides significant advantages — for example, for complex mathematics, chemical formulae, or delivery of binary information — the market will push to exploit XML's richer capabilities and open-ended markup. As XML's abilities become better understood and exploited, more users will find the content compelling, and early adopters who offer XML content with real value to users will be at the forefront of a new way to deliver Web content.

Moving from HTML to XML will be gradual and incremental, and shall proceed most quickly where it adds the most value. In many ways, this strongly resembles the original proliferation of HTML itself: HTML started in a cloistered, research and academic setting where professionals had compelling reasons to share information, but it spread to an ever-broader audience as more and more people were convinced of its usefulness and began to exploit its capabilities. We believe the same pattern will ultimately describe XML's proliferation and adoption as well.

Discovering — and Using — XML DTDs

The heart and soul of any XML document lies in the DTD or DTDs that govern its forms of expression and markup. Becoming familiar with and using DTDs is absolutely essential to becoming proficient in XML and in making the most of XML's capabilities. Becoming educated on DTDs is no simple task and may require some classroom time, in addition to lots of learning through trial and error.

Of all the resources on writing DTDs we've found — and you can use a search engine to find tutorials and overviews galore on the Web — the best resource we've located to date is Eve Maler and Jeanne El Andaloussi's book, *Developing SGML DTDs from Text to Model to Markup* (Prentice-Hall, Upper Saddle River, NJ, 1996. ISBN 0-13-309881-8). Even though the book is not oriented toward XML explicitly and must, therefore, be interpreted with care, it is an excellent place to start learning about writing and using DTDs correctly.

XML Links Offer Numerous Advantages over HTML

XML offers more powerful and flexible links than HTML. Although you can still use simple, one-way, one-target links like those in an image (IMG) or anchor (A) tag in HTML, XML supports bi-directional links, so that an anchor on one end of a link can be a target on the other end of the same link. XML also supports multiway links so that selecting a single link can lead to multiple targets or can cause multiple reactions to occur more or less simultaneously. If you're familiar with HTML frames, think of this ability as a way to cause the content that appears in multiple frames to be updated at the same time by selecting a single link in a document. XML will support more complex kinds of user interactions and permit more flexible kinds of screen updates to occur when users follow enriched links in XML documents.

XML and Matters of Style

Because XSL is still the subject of intense discussion and experimental development, the best take on style for XML right now is to familiarize yourself with the stylesheet languages that also work with HTML and Dynamic HTML — namely, the Cascading Style Sheets languages, versions 1 and 2 (CSS1 and CSS2). These provide the ability to control most aspects of a document's layout, positioning, text color, and so forth and offer powerful (but not dynamic) capability that XSL will ultimately provide. As workarounds go, however, CSS1 and CSS2 are not at all shabby. Check them out at the W3C site, along with other alternatives and style-conscious publishing systems, at www.w3.org/Style/.

Integrating Code with XML

When it comes to calling code inside XML, the viewer or browser software that's used to access the document in question comes into play. In other words, although XML includes markup needed to implement scripting languages or calls to external programs, it does not endorse any one scripting or programming language over another and leaves the software implementers to figure out how to bring XML document-rendering capabilities together with access to client-side software interpretation or execution abilities. Discussion and development remain active in this area, so check the XML pages at the W3C site (www.w3.org) for the latest information on this topic. Also, the eXtensible Style Language (XSL) covers the use of scripting languages, so be sure to check the XSL-related pages at the W3C site, too. As we wrote this book, however, this information was still too much in flux to cover with any degree of finality or confidence. At present, the best place to start researching XSL is at www.w3.org/TR/NOTE-XSL-970910.

Using Metadata in XML Documents

Because XML has no predefined elements — unlike HTML, where all elements are predefined — metadata in the DTD is *required* to make XML markup possible. This requirement makes for more work up front, both literally and figuratively (because internal DTDs and invocations to external DTDs must occur at the head of XML documents), but it also makes XML able to incorporate all kinds of metadata as part and parcel of any document. You can use any of several predefined metadata schemes (see the following list) or even invent your own if you like. Thus, XML documents can be as self-descriptive as you want to make them.

The following formats for metadata can be explicitly invoked in any suitably constructed XML document:

✔ **Dublin Core:** A joint project undertaken by librarians and computer specialists to devise a powerful, searchable document description language; visit their site at purl.oclc.org/metadata/dublin_core/.

✔ **Warwick Framework:** Another container architecture, this one from the metadata workshop at Warwick University, England; for an overview document, visit www.dlib.org/dlib/july96/lagoze/07lagoze.html.

✔ **Resource Description Format (RDF):** An XML dialect described in Chapter 12 of this book.

✔ **Platform for Internet Content Selection (PICS):** Another form of metadata, PICS is not covered in this book; PICS describes what kind of content appears on Web sites to allow control over who gets access to what. For more information about PICS, visit the W3C's pages on the subject at www.w3.org/PICS/.

Converting HTML to XML

For one thing, converting HTML to XML requires that the proper DTD that governs the HTML code be included with the document. In addition, HTML code must be converted to a well-formed alternative because XML does not permit the absence of end-tags. (For example, HTML will happily support paragraphs that open with <P> but don't close with a matching </P>; however, XML insists that both tags be supplied.) Other such cases must also be corrected when converting HTML to XML.

The first step to such a conversion requires that you validate your HTML using a tool like DataChannel's validating DXP parser (see the "About the CD" Appendix for more information on DXP). Get the tool and then follow this conversion recipe:

1. **Replace the** DOCTYPE **declaration at the head of the document that begins** <!DOCTYPE HTML ...> **with an XML declaration such as** <?XML version = "1.0" standalone="yes"?>

2. **Change any empty elements to end with the notation** /> **rather than** >.

   Empty elements are those that do not have matching end tags (optional or otherwise). This step makes the HTML document conform to the requirement that singleton tags in XML be properly indicated. Thus, for example, the IMG tag would read <IMG SRC="img.gif"/>.

3. **Verify that the content associated with all non-empty start tags is bracketed by an end tag.**

   For example, make sure that each <P> is matched by a </P> at the end of the paragraph. XML is also case-sensitive to tag names and attributes, so start tags and end tags must use the same case throughout, as defined in the DTD. All attribute invocations must follow this rule.

4. **Verify that any reserved characters used as literals are denoted using character entities.**

   This requirement is especially significant for the left angle bracket (<) and the ampersand (&). To verify that these literals are denoted using character entities, you use & for ampersand and < for left bracket.

5. **Verify that all attribute values are enclosed in double quotation marks.**

   Although HTML is forgiving about quotes for attribute values, *all* attribute values in XML must be enclosed within double quotation marks; thus, although HTML will accept the attribute string HEIGHT=120 quite happily for the IMG tag, XML would require this to read HEIGHT="120".

The main thing to watch out for is that HTML-only browsers will not be able to recognize this converted markup, which means that such "converted HTML" will not render properly, except in a viewer that knows how to deal with XML!

Chapter 22
Top Ten XML Tools

*A*s we say repeatedly throughout this book, nobody, but nobody tackles too much XML authoring without the help of some authoring tool. And no one should try to manage a collection of XML documents without some software tools to assist them along the way. For that reason, we've collected a list of the "the best of the best" tools for authoring, checking, and managing XML documents and document collections. If you have only a limited amount of time or your resources are limited, you absolutely *must* check out these tools!

Only Valid XML Is Worth Publishing

By now, you should recognize that a valid XML document is any well-formed XML document that includes all the necessary internal DTD structures and external DTD references to fully define every markup element and entity that occurs within that document. Although tools abound to check your work in this regard, we're familiar with — and fond of — DataChannel's DXP (which is an acronym for DataChannel XML Parser). Because Norbert (the original developer of this tool) is one of this book's authors, we can't completely deny being a little biased on his behalf, but it was this very tool that led us to ask him to join our band of authors.

You can find DXP on the CD that accompanies this book or on the Web at this URL: www.datachannel.com/products/xml/index.

The Ultimate SGML Tool Works for XML, Too!

James Clark is a legend in the SGML community for his amazing collection of tools that support all kinds of cool functionality, most of it in the form of freeware that works like the dickens despite its affordability. His state-of-the-art SP parser can be configured to parse and validate XML as well as SGML, and it makes a dandy tool for that very reason. Likewise, Clark's Jade tool implements support for the SGML view of document style as defined in the Document Style Semantics and Specification Language (DSSSL, pronounced "distle" to rhyme with "whistle").

Pick up either or both of these fine tools on the CD that accompanies this book or on the Web at www.jclark.com/.

The Ultimate XML Grab Bag and Goodie Box

Poet Software offers all kinds of XML resources: white papers, an XML Repository, and an XML Resource Library. This company makes a powerful object-oriented database that embodies the Common Object Request Broker Association (CORBA) model for providing shared access to data across many database engines and applications. Apparently, the folks at Poet Software have also taken the cross-platform, open-ended capabilities of XML equally seriously and are promoting this technology relentlessly and enthusiastically.

For access to their treasure trove of goodies, which includes an ever-changing set of pointers to interesting XML software, visit the Web site at www.poet.com/xml/.

Microsoft Does XML, as Well

In its search to extend the reach and capability of its Internet software, particularly the Internet Explorer Web browser, Microsoft has proved an unexpected and ardent supporter of XML, particularly the Channel Definition Format (CDF) and the Resource Description Framework (RDF), among other XML dialects.

Microsoft also offers an XML parser for download from the Web; to obtain a copy of their XML parser, visit the Web site at `www.microsoft.com/xml/parser/`.

Tim Bray's Work Is a Real Lark!

Tim Bray has been a member of the W3C's XML Working Group since long before it operated under that name (it all started as a special interest group within the SGML cadre at the W3C, in fact). His work on XML is widely recognized and deservedly renowned. Among other things, Tim was the co-editor of the XML specification. He has also written a Java-based XML processor called Lark that he built as a way to sanity-check the XML design requirement, declaring that "it shall be easy to write programs that process XML documents." It could be a useful example for other programmers who seek to follow in his footsteps. The fruits of this labor are available at `www.textuality.com/Lark/`.

Copernican Puts XML at the Center of the Web

Copernican Solutions, Inc., is a self-professed document technology company. The company offers a series of software developer kits (SDKs), including a DSSSL Application Environment that supports both SGML and XML. This tool will be particularly useful for those already working in (or considering) SGML-based authoring or document management systems and who also seek to publish their content in XML form. The company has been heavily involved in defining and refining XML standards and specifications since the XML Working Group was formed at the W3C, and their expertise and investment in this technology are worth weighing carefully.

For more information about the company's DSSSL Application Environment (DAE), visit its Web site at `www.copsol.com/products/dae/index.html`.

Automating XML Excellence

webMethods has constructed the core of its Web Automation Toolkit around XML and Java technology, and the company is marketing it heavily for use in electronic commerce and related applications and for automating access to a variety of Web-based data and services, both in HTML and XML formats. The toolkit has been very well received in the marketplace and is worth investigating for those who seek to improve data access, data handling, and data security in their Web sites.

To obtain an evaluation copy of the toolkit or for more information about the company and its products, visit them on the Web at `www.webmethods.com/`.

Channeling Content with ChannelManager

Push technology refers to the technique of initiating delivery of material from a server to a properly equipped client and has become something of a rage on the Web, particularly for distribution of software updates, regular newsfeeds, ongoing data streams (such as stock quotes), and other forms of data that come regularly and predictably. DataChannel brings an XML slant to this technology with its XML-based ChannelManager product; ChannelManager has been recognized as a leader in its field, not just by the trade press, but through a joint marketing agreement with the software moguls at Microsoft.

To download a version of the software, visit the DataChannel Web site at `www.datachannel.com/`. To read a review about this interesting software technology, check out Wes Thomas's review at `www.webreview.com/97/12/05/addict/index.html`.

Experience Pays Dividends with ArborText's ADEPT

ArborText helped pioneer "write once, publish many ways" technologies and has built such technologies for years around SGML. With their ADEPT editor, they add XML to this mix in a product that can create output destined for use on the printed page, a Web site, or a CD-ROM (or all three). ADEPT is designed especially for handling high-volume document collections, where large teams of authors and maintainers must collaborate on a repository of new and constantly updated materials.

For more information about ADEPT and its capabilities, visit the company's Web site at www.arbortext.com/editor.html.

This ends our tour of the top ten XML tools and the regular text portion of the book. Don't forget to consult the Appendix, "About the CD," to help you explore the CD's contents, and don't overlook the Glossary when it comes to decoding the sometimes mysterious terminology you're likely to encounter when canvassing the wild and woolly intellectual landscape of XML!

Appendix

About the CD

● ●

*T*he *XML For Dummies* CD is loaded with stuff to help you use XML and this book more effectively and easily; you'll find these goodies:

- ✔ Extra information about online XML and SGML resources and links to information about XML software packages

- ✔ Freeware and evaluation (trial) versions of various XML software packages

- ✔ A click-and-go hotlist of all the URLs mentioned in the book

- ✔ The *XML For Dummies* glossary in electronic form for fast searching

- ✔ All the book's XML examples, sorted by chapter

- ✔ A list of what you can find in each of this book's chapters, for your easy reference in electronic form

This appendix assumes a basic knowledge of computer systems. If you need further information (especially regarding how to check whether your system meets the minimum system requirements), see one of the following books from IDG Books Worldwide, Inc.: *PCs For Dummies,* 4th Edition, by Dan Gookin; *Macs For Dummies,* 4th Edition, by David Pogue; *Windows 95 For Dummies* by Andy Rathbone; or *Windows NT For Dummies* by Andy Rathbone and Sharon Crawford.

Making Sure Your Computer Meets the System Requirements

You may have problems using the *XML For Dummies* CD if your computer doesn't meet these minimum system requirements:

- ✔ A PC with a 486 or faster processor, or a Mac OS computer with a PowerPC or faster processor

- ✔ Microsoft Windows NT 4.0 or 95 or later, or Mac OS system software 7.5 or later

✔ At least 16MB of total RAM installed on your computer; for best performance on Windows 95–equipped PCs and Mac OS computers with PowerPC processors, at least 24MB of RAM installed

✔ At least 30MB of hard drive space available to install all the software from this CD (less space is required if you don't install every program)

✔ A CD-ROM drive — quad-speed (4x) or faster

✔ A monitor capable of displaying at least 256 colors or grayscale

✔ A modem with a speed of at least 14,400 bps (preferably 33,600 bps)

Getting Started with the CD

The *XML For Dummies* CD works equally well in Windows and on the Macintosh, though you need to follow different steps to use the CD on these two types of systems.

Windows 95, Windows 98, and Windows NT

If you're running Windows, follow these steps to access the CD's contents:

1. **Insert the CD into your computer's CD-ROM drive.**

2. **After the light on your CD-ROM drive goes out, double-click the My Computer icon on your desktop.**

3. **In the My Computer window that appears, double-click the icon for your CD-ROM drive.**

   Another window opens, showing you all the folders and files on the CD.

4. **Double-click the** License.txt **file, read it, and close the program that opened it (most likely Windows Notepad).**

   You need to read this file, which is the end-user license agreement, because when you start using the CD's contents, you're saying that you agree to all the requirements of this agreement.

5. **Double-click the** Readme.txt **file.**

   This text file contains instructions about installing the software from this CD, as well as information about the contents of the CD. If you want, you can leave this file open while you're using the CD so that you can refer to this information later.

6. **To access a particular program or file, double-click on one of the software folders.**

Later in this appendix, "Making Use of the CD's Contents" describes what you can find on the CD (you can also find much information in the Readme.txt file).

7. **Double-click the installation file (usually called** Setup.exe **or** Install.exe**).**

The program's installer walks you through the process of setting up your new software.

Macintosh

If you're using a Macintosh, install the items from the CD to your hard drive as follows:

1. **Insert the CD into your computer's CD-ROM drive.**

   In a moment, an icon representing the CD (the icon probably looks like a CD) appears on the desktop.

2. **Double-click the CD icon to show the CD's contents.**

3. **Double-click the Read Me First icon.**

   This text file contains information about the CD's programs and may contain setup instructions that don't appear in this appendix, so be sure to look it over carefully.

4. **To install most programs, drag the program's folder from the CD window and drop the folder on your hard drive icon.**

   For programs that come with installation routines, open the program's folder on the CD and double-click the icon that says *Install* **or** *Installer.*

   Later in this appendix, "Making Use of the CD's Contents" describes what you can find on the CD.

   After you install the programs that you want, you can eject the CD (you may want to put it back in its sleeve on the book's back cover so that you can use it again later if you need to).

Making Use of the CD's Contents

Here are the major categories of what you can find on the CD:

✔ xml4dum: This folder contains all the *XML For Dummies* HTML files (the book-related files).

✔ **Folders for freeware and evaluation (trial) programs:** Some of the best XML applications available are represented here.

✔ **License agreement:** This text file tells you what you agree to when you use this CD's contents.

✔ **Read Me:** This text file contains all the text of this appendix and any last-minute changes for easy electronic reference.

Book-related Web pages

The xml4dum folder contains the majority of the *XML For Dummies* files, most of which are HTML documents. Here's what this folder contains:

✔ `default.htm`: The home page for the whole collection (start off your exploration of this folder here). *Note:* The CD contains several files called `default.htm`; this home-page file is at the root of the xml4dum folder, at the same level as all the subfolders.

✔ `menu.htm`: List of all the files in this xml4dum folder, with hyperlinks and graphics.

✔ `contact.htm`: List of e-mail links for the authors and the CD's Webmaster.

✔ `copy.htm`: Important copyright information.

✔ `xml4dum/contents`: Listing of the book contents by chapter. Open the `default.htm` file in this subfolder to see a hyperlinked listing of all the chapter titles; then just click on a chapter title to see a list of what that chapter of the book covers. To return to the list of chapter titles, click on Chapter Contents from the bottom image map or text navigation.

Or you can go straight to a chapter by clicking on the appropriate filename (the files are named `ch`*nn*`cont.htm`, where *nn* is the chapter number).

✔ `xml4dum/examples`: Examples used in the book, sorted by chapter. Open the `default.htm` file in this subfolder to see a hyperlinked listing of all the chapter titles; then just click on a chapter title to see that chapter's examples. To return to the list of chapter titles, click on Chapter Examples from the bottom image map or text navigation.

Or you can go straight to a chapter by clicking on the appropriate filename (the files are named `ch`*nn*`exmp.htm`, where *nn* is the chapter number, or `ch`*nn*`ex`*xx*, where *xx* is the example number) to see the examples from that chapter.

✔ `xml4dum/extras`: Two bonus chapters, a glossary of terms, and five bonus character sets; you can find information about XML and SGML online resources and about XML applications here. Open the `default.htm` file in this subfolder to see a hyperlinked table of contents for this folder; then just click on an item's name to view that item. Use the text links at the bottom of each page to move back and forth. To return to the list of titles, click on Extras from the bottom image map or text navigation.

✔ graphics: All the graphics used in the *XML For Dummies* Web pages.

✔ xml4dum/urls: URLs mentioned in the book. Open the default.htm file in this subfolder to see a hyperlinked listing of all the chapter titles; then just click on a chapter title to see the URLs cited in that chapter. To return to the list of chapter titles, click on Chapter URLs from the bottom image map or text navigation.

Or you can go straight to a chapter by clicking on the appropriate filename (the files are named chnncont.urls, where *nn* is the chapter number) to see that chapter's URLs.

Software

You can construct your own customized set of XML tools by sampling the evaluation and freeware versions of products on the *XML For Dummies* CD. Table A-1 gives you details about the packages on the CD. For specific information about a tool, read the Readme.txt file included for that tool on the CD.

Note: You can access only the packages that run on the platform you're using. That is, Windows users can't access Macintosh products, and vice versa. To see the tools for the system you're not using, you need to load the CD on a computer that uses the other system.

Table A-1		CD Software List	
Package	***Platform***	***Type***	***Windows Installation Path***
Interaction 2.0	Mac	Evaluation version	
Balise r4.0	Windows	Evaluation version	D:\BALISE\Setup.exe
Lark	UNIX	Freeware	
MSXML	Windows	Freeware	D:\MSXML\xmlinst.exe
DataChannel XML Parser; DXP	Windows, UNIX	Freeware	D:\DXP\README.html
DataChannel XML Viewer (DXDE)	Windows, UNIX	Freeware	D:\XMLVIEW\readme.htm
Channel Manager 2.0	Windows, UNIX	Freeware	D:\CHANMANG\ cm20beta1.exe
LT XML Toolkit v.1b	UNIX	Evaluation version	
Internet Explorer 4.0	Windows, Mac	Commercial product	D:\MSIE401 \ie4setup.exe
Jade	Windows, UNIX	Freeware	D:\JADE\jade.htm

(continued)

Table A-1 *(continued)*			
Package	*Platform*	*Type*	*Windows Installation Path*
SP SGML 1.2 parser	Windows	Freeware	D:\SPSGML\readme.txt
ArborText XML Styler	Windows	Freeware	D:\ARBORSTY\ Xinstall.exe

Troubleshooting: Getting Things to Work

If your computer meets the minimum system requirements outlined at the beginning of this appendix and you can't get the programs on the CD to work, you probably have one of two problems: You don't have enough memory (RAM) for the programs you want to use, or you have other programs running that are affecting the installation or running of a program. In those two cases, you get error messages such as Not enough memory or Setup cannot continue. If you do, try one or more of these methods and then try using the software again:

✔ Turn off any anti-virus software that you have on your computer. Installers sometimes mimic virus activity and may make your computer incorrectly believe that it's being infected by a virus.

✔ Close all running programs. The more programs you're running, the less memory is available to other programs. Installers also typically update files and programs. So if you keep other programs running, installation may not work properly.

✔ Have your local computer store add more RAM to your computer. This step is drastic and somewhat expensive. However, if you have a Windows 95 PC or a Mac OS computer with a PowerPC chip, adding more memory can really increase the speed of your computer and allow more programs to run at the same time.

✔ Check out the folder D:\Short (where D is the letter for your CD-ROM drive) if you have trouble accessing certain folders on the CD, or if you can't seem to read the xml4dum HTML pages. If you experience these problems, your CD-ROM driver may be a 16-bit driver. Such drivers may make it impossible for you to read files with long filenames (names more than 8 characters long) from the CD, or access folders that contain files with long filenames. The CD folder called D:\Short contains self-extractors of each folder that holds files with long filenames. Run these self-extractors to copy the folders and contents to your hard drive; then you can install or access the files from your hard drive just as you would from the CD.

If you still have trouble installing the items from the CD, please call IDG Books Worldwide Customer Service at 800-762-2974 (outside the U.S.: 317-596-5430).

Index

(continued)

Notes

Notes

OPERATING SYSTEMS...

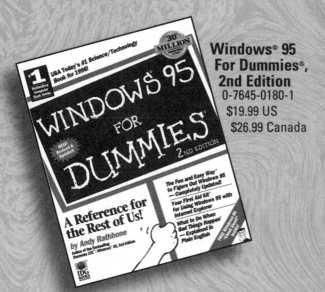

**Windows® 95
For Dummies®,
2nd Edition**
0-7645-0180-1
$19.99 US
$26.99 Canada

**Windows® CE
For Dummies®**
0-7645-0260-3
$19.99 US
$26.99 Canada

**Dummies 101®:
Windows NT®**
0-7645-0167-4
Includes one CD-ROM
$24.99 US
$34.99 Canada

**DOS For
Dummies®,
Windows® 95
Edition**
1-56884-646-0
$19.99 US
$26.99 Canada

**Windows® 3.11
For Dummies®,
3rd Edition**
1-56884-370-4
$16.95 US
$22.95 Canada

PC GENERAL COMPUTING...

**PCs For
Teachers™,
2nd Edition**
0-7645-0240-9
Includes one
CD-ROM
$24.99 US
$34.99 Canada

**Upgrading &
Fixing PCs
For Dummies®,
3rd Edition**
0-7645-0129-1
$19.99 US
$26.99 Canada

**PCs For Dummies®,
5th Edition**
0-7645-0269-7
$19.99 US
$26.99 Canada

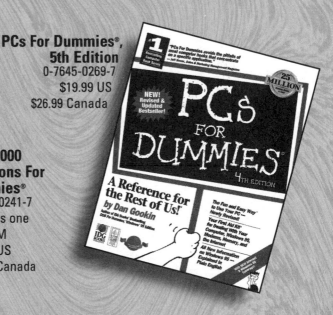

**PCs For Kids &
Parents™**
0-7645-0158-5
Includes one
CD-ROM
$24.99 US
$34.99 Canada

**Modems For
Dummies®,
3rd Edition**
0-7645-0069-4
$19.99 US
$26.99 Canada

**Year 2000
Solutions For
Dummies®**
0-7645-0241-7
Includes one
CD-ROM
$24.99 US
$34.99 Canada

**Great Software
For Kids &
Parents™**
0-7645-0099-6
Includes one
CD-ROM
$24.99 US
$34.99 Canada

**Mobile
Computing For
Dummies®**
0-7645-0151-8
$19.99 US
$26.99 Canada

DATABASE...

**Approach® 97
For Windows®
For Dummies®**
0-7645-0001-5
$19.99 US
$26.99 Canada

**Access 97
For Windows®
For Dummies®**
0-7645-0048-1
$19.99 US
$26.99 Canada

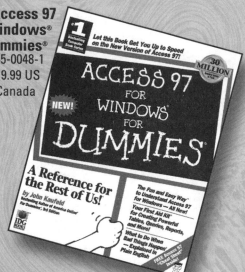

**Access 2 For
Dummies®**
1-56884-090-X
$19.95 US
$26.95 Canada

**Filemaker® Pro
3 For Macs® For
Dummies®**
1-56884-906-0
$19.99 US
$26.99 Canada

SPREADSHEETS/FINANCE/ PROJECT MANAGEMENT...

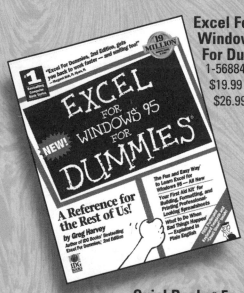

**Excel For
Windows® 95
For Dummies®**
1-56884-930-3
$19.99 US
$26.99 Canada

**Excel 97
For Windows®
For Dummies®**
0-7645-0049-X
$19.99 US
$26.99 Canada

**Quicken® 6
For Windows®
For Dummies®,
4th Edition**
0-7645-0036-8
$19.99 US
$26.99 Canada

**Microsoft®
Money 98
For Dummies®**
0-7645-0295-6
Includes one
CD-ROM
$24.99 US
$34.99 Canada

**QuickBooks® 5
For Dummies®,
3rd Edition**
0-7645-0043-0
$19.99 US
$26.99 Canada

**Microsoft®
Project 98
For Dummies®**
0-7645-0321-9
Includes one
CD-ROM
$24.99 US
$34.99 Canada

**Microsoft®
Project For
Windows® 95
For Dummies®**
0-7645-0084-8
Includes one
CD-ROM
$24.99 US
$34.99 Canada

**Quicken® 98
For Windows®
For Dummies®**
0-7645-0243-3
$19.99 US
$26.99 Canada

OFFICE SUITES...

**Microsoft®
Office For
Windows® 95
For Dummies®**
1-56884-917-6
$19.99 US
$26.99 Canada

**Microsoft® Office 97
For Windows®
For Dummies®**
0-7645-0050-3
$19.99 US
$26.99 Canada

**Microsoft®
Works For
Windows® 95
For Dummies®**
1-56884-944-3
$19.99 US
$26.99 Canada

**ClarisWorks®
Office For
Dummies®**
0-7645-0113-5
$19.99 US
$26.99 Canada

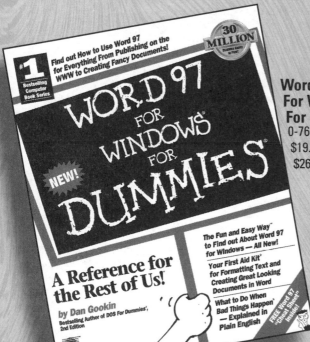

WORD PROCESSING...

**Word 97
For Windows®
For Dummies®**
0-7645-0052-X
$19.99 US
$26.99 Canada

**Corel® WordPerfect® 8
For Windows®
For Dummies®**
0-7645-0186-0
$19.99 US
$26.99 Canada

**Word For
Windows® 95
For Dummies®**
1-56884-932-X
$19.99 US
$26.99 Canada

DESKTOP PUBLISHING GRAPHICS MULTIMEDIA...

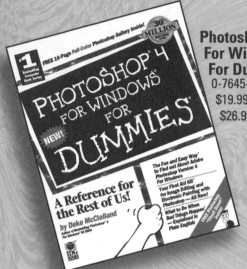

**Photoshop® 4
For Windows®
For Dummies®**
0-7645-0102-X
$19.99 US
$26.99 Canada

**Digital
Photography
For Dummies®**
0-7645-0294-8
Includes one
CD-ROM
16 page
color insert.
$24.99 US
$34.99 Canada

**CorelDRAW™ 7
For Dummies®**
0-7645-0124-0
$19.99 US
$26.99 Canada

**AutoCAD®
Release 14 For
Dummies®**
0-7645-0104-6
Includes one
CD-ROM
$24.99 US
$34.99 Canada

**PowerPoint® 97
For Windows®
For Dummies®**
0-7645-0051-1
$19.99 US
$26.99 Canada

MACINTOSH GENERAL COMPUTING...

**Macs®
For Teachers™,
3rd Edition**
0-7645-0226-3
Includes one
CD-ROM
$24.99 US
$34.99 Canada

**Macs®
For Kids & Parents™**
0-7645-0157-7
Includes one CD-ROM
$24.99 US
$34.99 Canada

**Macs®
For Dummies®,
5th Edition**
0-7645-0225-5
$19.99 US
$26.99 Canada

PLUS - References For The Rest of US!® on Networking, Programming, Web Design, and Web Publishing. For a complete list of Dummies Books® and cool DummiesWear® (t-shirts, hats, etc.), check out our Website at www.dummies.com

FOR A COMPLETE LISTING OF ALL OUR DUMMIES BOOKS™, VISIT OUR WEB SITE AT,
www.dummies.com

There are 4 easy ways to order

1) **CALL: 800-762-2974**
   (24 hours a day, 7 days a week)

2) **FAX: 317-596-5295**

3) **VISIT our Web Site**

4) **MAIL THIS ORDER FORM TO:**
   IDG Books Worldwide, Inc.
   attn: Order Entry
   7260 Shadeland Station, Ste 100
   Indianapolis, IN 46256

QUANTITY	ISBN	TITLE	RETAIL PRICE	TOTAL

SHIP TO:

Name_____

Company_____

Address_____

City/State/Zip_____

Daytime Phone_____

Payment ❑ Check to IDG Books (US Funds Only)

❑ Visa ❑ Mastercard ❑ American Express

Card #_____ Exp._____ Signature_____

Price subject to change without notice.

Promo Code: BOB

Shipping & Handling Charges	Description	First Book	Each Additional Book	Total
Domestic	Normal	4.50	1.50	$
	Two Day Air	8.50	2.50	$
	Overnight	18.00	3.00	$
International	Surface	8.00	8.00	$
	Airmail	16.00	16.00	$
	Overnight	17.00	17.00	$
CA residents add applicable sales tax				
IN, MA, and MD residents add 5% sales tax				
IL residents add 6.25% sales tax				
RI residents add 7% sales tax				
TX residents add 8.25% sales tax				
Shipping				
TOTAL				

IDG BOOKS WORLDWIDE™

IDG Books Worldwide, Inc., End-User License Agreement

READ THIS. You should carefully read these terms and conditions before opening the software packet(s) included with this book ("Book"). This is a license agreement ("Agreement") between you and IDG Books Worldwide, Inc. ("IDGB"). By opening the accompanying software packet(s), you acknowledge that you have read and accept the following terms and conditions. If you do not agree and do not want to be bound by such terms and conditions, promptly return the Book and the unopened software packet(s) to the place you obtained them for a full refund.

1. **License Grant.** IDGB grants to you (either an individual or entity) a nonexclusive license to use one copy of the enclosed software program(s) (collectively, the "Software") solely for your own personal or business purposes on a single computer (whether a standard computer or a workstation component of a multiuser network). The Software is in use on a computer when it is loaded into temporary memory (RAM) or installed into permanent memory (hard disk, CD-ROM, or other storage device). IDGB reserves all rights not expressly granted herein.

2. **Ownership.** IDGB is the owner of all right, title, and interest, including copyright, in and to the compilation of the Software recorded on the CD-ROM ("Software Media"). Copyright to the individual programs recorded on the Software Media is owned by the author or other authorized copyright owner of each program. Ownership of the Software and all proprietary rights relating thereto remain with IDGB and its licensers.

3. **Restrictions on Use and Transfer.**

   (a) You may only (i) make one copy of the Software for backup or archival purposes, or (ii) transfer the Software to a single hard disk, provided that you keep the original for backup or archival purposes. You may not (i) rent or lease the Software, (ii) copy or reproduce the Software through a LAN or other network system or through any computer subscriber system or bulletin-board system, or (iii) modify, adapt, or create derivative works based on the Software.

   (b) You may not reverse engineer, decompile, or disassemble the Software. You may transfer the Software and user documentation on a permanent basis, provided that the transferee agrees to accept the terms and conditions of this Agreement and you retain no copies. If the Software is an update or has been updated, any transfer must include the most recent update and all prior versions.

4. **Restrictions on Use of Individual Programs.** You must follow the individual requirements and restrictions detailed for each individual program in the Appendix of this Book. These limitations are also contained in the individual license agreements recorded on the Software Media. These limitations may include a requirement that after using the program for a specified period of time, the user must pay a registration fee or discontinue use. By opening the Software packet(s), you will be agreeing to abide by the licenses and restrictions for these individual programs that are detailed in the Appendix and on the Software Media. None of the material on this Software Media or listed in this Book may ever be redistributed, in original or modified form, for commercial purposes.

5. Limited Warranty.

   (a) IDGB warrants that the Software and Software Media are free from defects in materials and workmanship under normal use for a period of sixty (60) days from the date of purchase of this Book. If IDGB receives notification within the warranty period of defects in materials or workmanship, IDGB will replace the defective Software Media.

   (b) IDGB AND THE AUTHOR OF THE BOOK DISCLAIM ALL OTHER WARRANTIES, EXPRESS OR IMPLIED, INCLUDING WITHOUT LIMITATION IMPLIED WARRANTIES OF MERCHANTABILITY AND FITNESS FOR A PARTICULAR PURPOSE, WITH RESPECT TO THE SOFTWARE, THE PROGRAMS, THE SOURCE CODE CONTAINED THEREIN, AND/OR THE TECHNIQUES DESCRIBED IN THIS BOOK. IDGB DOES NOT WARRANT THAT THE FUNCTIONS CONTAINED IN THE SOFTWARE WILL MEET YOUR REQUIREMENTS OR THAT THE OPERATION OF THE SOFTWARE WILL BE ERROR FREE.

   (c) This limited warranty gives you specific legal rights, and you may have other rights that vary from jurisdiction to jurisdiction.

6. Remedies.

   (a) IDGB's entire liability and your exclusive remedy for defects in materials and workmanship shall be limited to replacement of the Software Media, which may be returned to IDGB with a copy of your receipt at the following address: Software Media Fulfillment Department, Attn.: *XML For Dummies,* IDG Books Worldwide, Inc., 7260 Shadeland Station, Ste. 100, Indianapolis, IN 46256, or call 800-762-2974. Please allow three to four weeks for delivery. This Limited Warranty is void if failure of the Software Media has resulted from accident, abuse, or misapplication. Any replacement Software Media will be warranted for the remainder of the original warranty period or thirty (30) days, whichever is longer.

   (b) In no event shall IDGB or the author be liable for any damages whatsoever (including without limitation damages for loss of business profits, business interruption, loss of business information, or any other pecuniary loss) arising from the use of or inability to use the Book or the Software, even if IDGB has been advised of the possibility of such damages.

   (c) Because some jurisdictions do not allow the exclusion or limitation of liability for consequential or incidental damages, the above limitation or exclusion may not apply to you.

7. U.S. Government Restricted Rights. Use, duplication, or disclosure of the Software by the U.S. Government is subject to restrictions stated in paragraph (c)(1)(ii) of the Rights in Technical Data and Computer Software clause of DFARS 252.227-7013, and in subparagraphs (a) through (d) of the Commercial Computer–Restricted Rights clause at FAR 52.227-19, and in similar clauses in the NASA FAR supplement, when applicable.

8. General. This Agreement constitutes the entire understanding of the parties and revokes and supersedes all prior agreements, oral or written, between them and may not be modified or amended except in a writing signed by both parties hereto that specifically refers to this Agreement. This Agreement shall take precedence over any other documents that may be in conflict herewith. If any one or more provisions contained in this Agreement are held by any court or tribunal to be invalid, illegal, or otherwise unenforceable, each and every other provision shall remain in full force and effect.

Installation Instructions

For Windows 95, Windows 98, and Windows NT users

1. **Place the CD in your CD-ROM drive.**

   Your CD-ROM drive takes a few seconds to read the CD.

2. **Choose the Windows Explorer from the Start menu and double-click on the CD-ROM drive.**

   The contents of the CD-ROM will be displayed in the right-hand frame of the Windows Explorer window.

3. **Read both the** `readme.txt` **(CD-ROM ReadMe) and** `license.txt` **(End-User License) files by double-clicking their names.**

To view the *XML For Dummies* Web pages — including the contents, extras, URLs, and code described in the "About the CD" Appendix — launch your Web browser and open the file `xml4dum.htm` in the `xml4dum` folder by using the Open or Open File command in your Web browser's File menu.

To install any of the applications included on the CD, double-click the folder for the desired application and run the program's setup or installation file. These files usually end with the `.exe` extension.

For Mac OS users

1. **Place the CD in your CD-ROM drive.**

   After a few seconds, the *XML For Dummies* CD icon will appear on your desktop.

2. **To view the contents of the CD, double-click the *XML For Dummies* CD icon.**

3. **Read both the** `readme.txt` **(CD-ROM ReadMe) and** `license.txt` **(End-User License) files by double-clicking their icons.**

To view the *XML For Dummies* Web pages, follow the instructions in the preceding section, "For Windows 95, Windows 98, and Windows NT users." To install any of the applications included on the CD, double-click the folder for the desired application and run the program's setup or installation file.

For more information about the CD and its contents, flip to the Appendix, "About the CD."

Discover Dummies Online!

The Dummies Web Site is your fun and friendly online resource for the latest information about ...*For Dummies*® books and your favorite topics. The Web site is the place to communicate with us, exchange ideas with other ...*For Dummies* readers, chat with authors, and have fun!

Ten Fun and Useful Things You Can Do at www.dummies.com

1. Win free ...*For Dummies* books and more!
2. Register your book and be entered in a prize drawing.
3. Meet your favorite authors through the IDG Books Author Chat Series.
4. Exchange helpful information with other ...*For Dummies* readers.
5. Discover other great ...*For Dummies* books you must have!
6. Purchase Dummieswear™ exclusively from our Web site.
7. Buy ...*For Dummies* books online.
8. Talk to us. Make comments, ask questions, get answers!
9. Download free software.
10. Find additional useful resources from authors.

Link directly to these ten fun and useful things at
http://www.dummies.com/10useful

For other technology titles from IDG Books Worldwide, go to
www.idgbooks.com

Not on the Web yet? It's easy to get started with *Dummies 101*®: *The Internet For Windows*® *95* or *The Internet For Dummies*®, 5th Edition, at local retailers everywhere.

Find other ...*For Dummies* books on these topics:
Business • Career • Databases • Food & Beverage • Games • Gardening • Graphics • Hardware
Health & Fitness • Internet and the World Wide Web • Networking • Office Suites
Operating Systems • Personal Finance • Pets • Programming • Recreation • Sports
Spreadsheets • Teacher Resources • Test Prep • Word Processing

IDG BOOKS WORLDWIDE
BOOK REGISTRATION

We want to hear from you!

Register This Book and Win!

Visit **http://my2cents.dummies.com** to register this book and tell us how you liked it!

- ✔ Get entered in our monthly prize giveaway.

- ✔ Give us feedback about this book — tell us what you like best, what you like least, or maybe what you'd like to ask the author and us to change!

- ✔ Let us know any other ...*For Dummies*® topics that interest you.

Your feedback helps us determine what books to publish, tells us what coverage to add as we revise our books, and lets us know whether we're meeting your needs as a ...*For Dummies* reader. You're our most valuable resource, and what you have to say is important to us!

Not on the Web yet? It's easy to get started with *Dummies 101*®: *The Internet For Windows*® *95* or *The Internet For Dummies*,® 5th Edition, at local retailers everywhere.

Or let us know what you think by sending us a letter at the following address:

...*For Dummies* Book Registration
Dummies Press
7260 Shadeland Station, Suite 100
Indianapolis, IN 46256-3945
Fax 317-596-5498

BUSINESS AND GENERAL REFERENCE BOOK SERIES FROM IDG

COMPUTER BOOK SERIES FROM IDG